EMPIRES, WARS, AND BATTLES

FORGE BOOKS BY T. C. F. HOPKINS

Confrontation at Lepanto
Empires, Wars, and Battles

Empires, Wars, and Battles

The Middle East
from Antiquity to the Rise of the New World

T. C. F. HOPKINS

A TOM DOHERTY ASSOCIATES BOOK
NEW YORK

EMPIRES, WARS, AND BATTLES:
THE MIDDLE EAST FROM ANTIQUITY
TO THE RISE OF THE NEW WORLD

A Forge Book
Published by Tom Doherty Associates, LLC
175 Fifth Avenue
New York, NY 10010

www.tor-forge.com

Forge® is a registered trademark of Tom Doherty Associates, LLC.

Library of Congress Cataloging-in-Publication Data

Hopkins, T. C. F.
    Empires, wars, and battles : the Middle East from antiquity to
the rise of the new world/T. C. F. Hopkins.—1st hardcover ed.
        p. cm.
    ISBN-13: 978-0-7653-0326-4
    ISBN-10: 0-7653-0326-4
    1. Middle East. I. Title.
    DS44.H75 2007
    956—dc22

                                            2007006517

First Edition: July 2007

Printed in the United States of America

0   9   8   7   6   5   4   3   2   1

For
BILL
of course

CONTENTS

8   CONTENTS

INTRODUCTION

For many people in the West, the Middle East is puzzling: how did it get like that? is a frequently asked question, especially in the Americas, where the ancient Middle Eastern clashes with the West have not been accessible to us. The answers are not easy, and many are caught up in traditions of conflict; understanding those traditions and the history that spawned them can be a first step to a better grasp of the evolution of the problems of the historical and present-day Middle East.

The Middle East has functioned as a cultural and political hinge for more than eight millennia, and, as such, its influence is very widespread, as is the case with geo-political hinges. Almost nothing in history exists in isolation, and that is all the more the case in the Middle East: from Afghanistan to Egypt to the Carpathians, the Middle East has long played a crucial role in world events. All events create their own kinds of ripples in the cultural and historical fabric, and none of them are without context and consequences. Until the arrival of complex technology in the nineteenth century, the most socially intrusive events were wars and plagues. In discussing the military events in this book, one of the factors included is the socio-cultural impact of the events, and the cultural interactions that are part of the experience of these campaigns.

Every epoch is significant in its own way, and in all instances, the shifts in the politico-cultural climate are as much a part of the regional evolution as the shifting weather patterns that have left their marks on all parts of the world. By dividing the history of the region into characteristic blocks, I have hoped to align the events with recognizable stages of cultural developments and the social changes that accompanied them, creating a discrete identity for each of the various periods covered. As with this book's companion volume, *Confrontation at Lepanto*, I have attempted to peel back the layers of traditions, ethnicity, religion, and cultures in order to make the past events more accessible for modern readers.

Some dates, particularly those in the distant past, are not easily authenticated. Where doubts exist, I have used the best information currently available. Rectification of historical dates is an ongoing process and one that will improve as the technology improves.

The maps, by Chelsea Quinn Yarbro, are intended to show not only the military movements but also the geological, cultural, national, tribal, and other environmental factors that were crucial to the outcomes of these clashes, and help to clarify the events described. Thanks are due to the many people who gave of their time and expertise to the preparation of this book, and this should be their acknowledgment, along with my appreciation for the information they have provided me. Special mention should go to Howard Wilson, Sayeed and Noura Malik, Salah Alim, and D. G. Everett, who gave of their expertise above and beyond. Any errors in the material ought not to be attributed to anyone but me.

T. C. F. HOPKINS
Berkeley, California

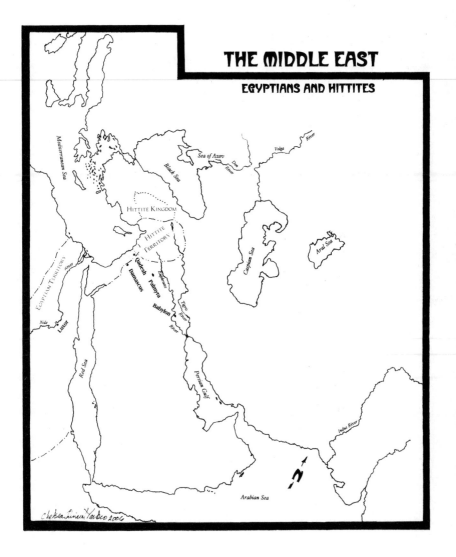

THE MIDDLE EAST

EGYPTIANS AND HITTITES

Mediterranean Sea

Black Sea

Sea of Azov

Volga River

Don River

HITTITE KINGDOM

HITTITE TERRITORY

Caspian Sea

Aral Sea

EGYPTIAN TERRITORY

Qadesh

Palmyra

Damascus

Euphrates River

Babylon

Tigris River

Nile

Luxor

Red Sea

Persian Gulf

Indus River

Arabian Sea

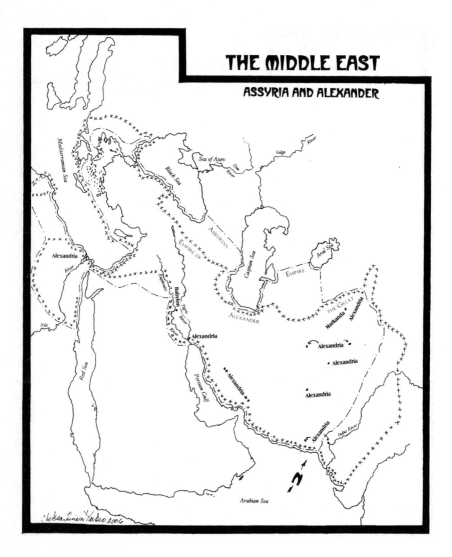

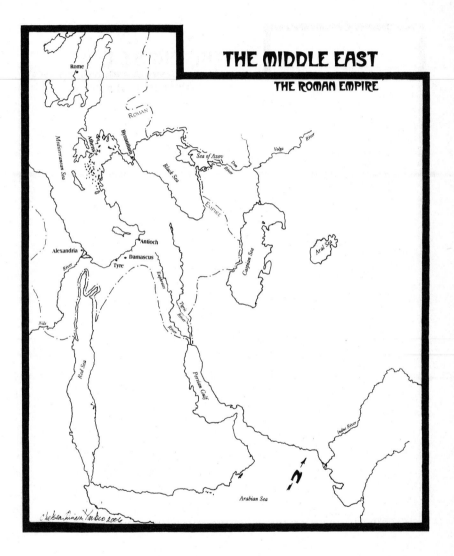

THE MIDDLE EAST

THE ROMAN EMPIRE

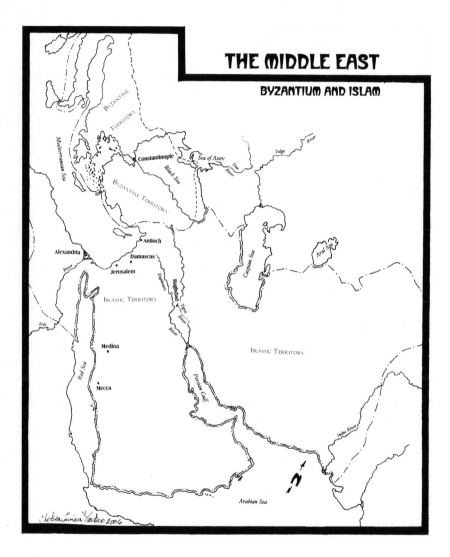

THE MIDDLE EAST

BYZANTIUM AND ISLAM

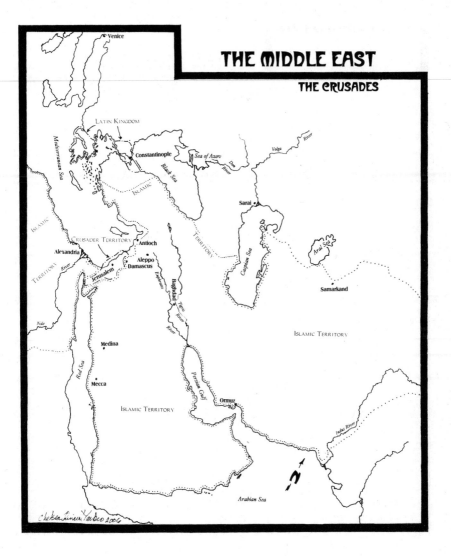

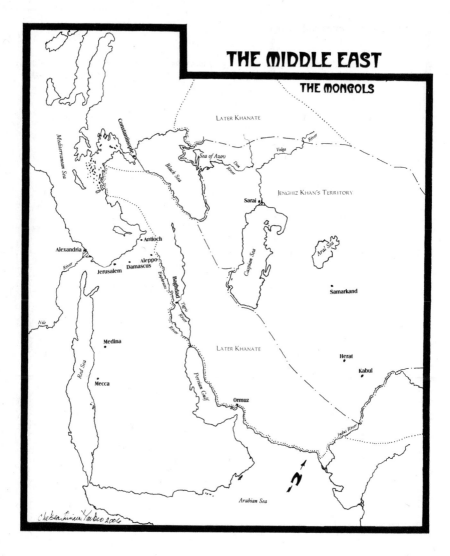

THE MIDDLE EAST

THE MONGOLS

LATER KHANATE

JENGHIZ KHAN'S TERRITORY

Mediterranean Sea

Constantinople

Black Sea

Sea of Azov

Don River

Volga River

Sarai

Caspian Sea

Aral Sea

Alexandria

Antioch

Aleppo
Damascus

Jerusalem

Euphrates River

Baghdad

Tigris River

Samarkand

Nile

Red Sea

Medina

Mecca

LATER KHANATE

Persian Gulf

Ormuz

Herat

Kabul

Indus River

Arabian Sea

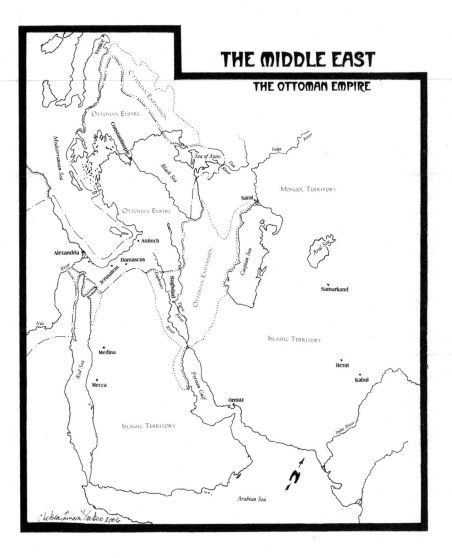

THE MIDDLE EAST

THE OTTOMAN EMPIRE

OTTOMAN EXPANSION

Venice

OTTOMAN EMPIRE

Constantinople

Mediterranean Sea

Sea of Azov

Black Sea

Don River

Volga River

OTTOMAN EMPIRE

MONGOL TERRITORY

Sarai

Aral Sea

Antioch

Alexandria

Caspian Sea

Damascus

Samarkand

River

Jerusalem

Baghdad

Euphrates River

Tigris River

OTTOMAN EXPANSION

Nile

ISLAMIC TERRITORY

Medina

Herat

Kabul

Red Sea

Persian Gulf

Mecca

Ormuz

Indus River

ISLAMIC TERRITORY

Arabian Sea

ChelseaWinsinTurbco 2006

EMPIRES, WARS, AND BATTLES

THE ANCIENT WORLD

Antiquity to Alexander the Great

ORIGINS of Western civilization are often deemed to have been in the Middle Eastern region called Mesopotamia, the then-fertile plain located, as the name implies, between the Tigris and the Euphrates Rivers, and beyond their confluence into the Persian Gulf. This region ten thousand years ago was markedly less arid than it is today—mostly savannah grasslands on the plains, groves of trees in protected areas, and upland forests—and lent itself to cultivation, fenced grazing, and the establishment of permanent communities. Villages made of mud-brick buildings sprang up in this part of the world, literally laying the foundations for cities to follow. From these simple villages came cottage industries, because in part there were now cottages for them to develop in rather than the tents of nomadic herders, and permanent markets from which the goods of cottage industries could be traded, making the Middle East the home of one of the first major centers of commerce. Subsistence farming and farm crafts as an economic base worked well enough for a time, but gradually the advantages of towns became apparent, and villages grew in size and social complexity, stratifying the population even as the cities reached beyond their limits for markets and goods. Mercantilism quickly led to the need to protect the merchandise, and that created a new kind of tension among the various cities, based on the perceived menace of commercial rivals.

That is not to say that commerce was the sole component of the burgeoning of civilization and military regularization: traditional regional warfare, local pillaging, and the slave trade were also crucial to the increasing importance of cities, which provided defense and shelter for more inhabitants than did the mud-brick walls of villages. Cities also provided places for the development of professions, where crafts could become something more than an adjunct to farming, and where skilled labor could be the means of earning a living. Still, the demands of agriculture were uppermost: all but the most ambitious wars were waged seasonally, so as not to interfere with producing crops, and resembled organized raiding skirmishes more than even so ancient a battle as the long campaign at Troy. Very few of the first cities could afford to have fighting men away for more than a few months at a time, and only the wealthiest could afford the considerable cost of supplying and maintaining a standing army.

Taking in the lands from the Caspian Sea to Libya, from the Mediterranean to the mountains of Afghanistan, and from Ukraine to Sudan, and occasionally including Greece, the Balkans, the Carpathians, and what is now Crimea, the Middle East has been a crucial link between East and West since the earliest days of established walled cities. The names of these cities still excite the imagination: Ashur, Eridu, Uruk, Sumer, Ur, and Babylon. Beyond Mesopotamia lay, eastward, Susa and Rhagae, to the west, Ebla, Petra, Jericho, and Egypt, as well as Hattushash and Troy in what is now Turkey, where the Hittites came to prominence. During this emergent period, in most places there were campaigns to establish and enforce hegemonies; over time this gave way to diplomacy and gradually alliances were made from which the early empires emerged.

One of the factors that gave the Middle East such a rapid start in the matter of establishing permanent settlements was that whereas most regions had just one or two, the Middle East had three major domestic animals to exploit: the camel, the ass, and the goat. Dogs had long since made their alliance with humans and were found ubiquitously; cats had yet to condescend to deal with people. Two of these major domestic animals—the camel and the ass—were hardy beasts of burden; all three were sources of milk, meat, hide, and hair, and their use in all aspects of settled life enlarged the range of trade and travel for the growing villages and made cities a viable proposition. Sheep and horses were soon brought into the region by trade with the steppes of Central Asia, cattle came along the earliest trade routes from northern India and eastern Persia, and pigs arrived from the Balkans. When these food sources were combined with the fowl and fish already in the area, a varied and dependable diet high in protein and grains was by the third millennium B.C. within reach of all but the poorest people; with these additional animals added to the three already established, confined agriculture was launched and permanent towns expanded into cities; for the first time, division of labor and nonagricultural or nonaquatic occupations became not only possible but also desirable. Secondary professions became primary ones, and a layered economy emerged.

These ancient beginnings created some startling new developments in human culture, from regularized weights and measures, to official legal codes, to writing and mathematics, to astronomy and calendars. These cultures were aware of the usefulness of record keeping, and of standardization of all sorts, and although they tended to view studies of what we now consider scientific or mathematical material as mysterious disciplines possessing mystical properties, they nonetheless encouraged their study and supported those who pursued such knowledge. Religions expanded from ancient fertility-weather-and-agriculture cults and embraced all secondary sorts of learning, so that most of what are now intellectual subjects were considered part of religion and were the province of priests, not professors or accountants or attorneys; in Egypt particularly, the recording of events reached truly epic proportions, as the huge friezes and walls of hieroglyphics show to this day. These various disciplines, as well as the more pragmatic matters of exchange and compensation, were recorded and retained by the various jurisdictions of the cities; as a result, now, as we unearth the past, we can have a glimpse into those long-vanished times. That the Middle East provided fertile soil in which to plant human ingenuity is obvious; what is less apparent is the means by which they kept and enlarged their holdings.

Another development of these very early city-based societies was raiding warfare: as neighbors' fortunes waxed and waned, the inclination to fight for what was available became intrinsic to the social organization of the period; tribal and clan alliances became formalized, and kinship bonding soon developed into the cultural mainstay it is in most Middle Eastern societies to this day, identifying the clan and tribe members within the kinship bonds above individual personalities for any but those in positions of leadership. Beginning with volunteers willing to makes forays into neighboring territories for goods, food, slaves, and animals, over time these parties became more organized and selective, trained in the use of arms and paid for their work, and professional armies arose.

Some fifty-four hundred years ago, Pharaonic Egypt began at the city that became Memphis, named for the Pharaoh who brought Upper (in the south) and Lower (in the north) Egypt together: Menes. Egypt had had permanent settlements for well over a thousand years before Menes, spurred on by the need to irrigate fields as the post-ice-age climate-shift continued to dry out the savannah, took on the unification of the country and the regulation of its economy and the centralization of religious institutions, which were also the distribution mechanism for the general provision of the inhabitants. Although predynastic Egypt did have a fair number of these permanent settlements, it is also apparent that the earliest towns had very simple infrastructures, and although priests of various gods codified and monitored order and distribution of water and foodstuffs within these communities, they were not yet part of the complex bureaucracy that would mark Egyptian culture for more than two millennia.

The evidence is a bit shaky, reliable records being few and far between, but it appears that village warfare was comparatively rare in predynastic Egypt, and once the country was united, the need for such clashes diminished: Egypt had the Nile as its water source, and so long as it flooded its valley every year, agriculture was safe and more or less uniformly accessible. Until roughly forty-four hundred years ago, the range of arable land was significantly broader than it is now, although for some centuries the land had become steadily drier. After forty-four hundred years ago, the climate shift in northern Africa was more dramatic, and so it is after that point that the Nile became even more important to Egypt, for as much of the scrublands turned to desert, water became the most crucial factor in survival, and the life of Egypt concentrated along the banks and floodplain of the river: everything from the Egyptian calendar, to the cycle of religious rites, to major markets was planned around the annual innundation of the Nile, which determined not only feast or famine but the possibility of trade up and down the river.

It was roughly 2980 B.C. when Djozer, or Tsothros, became the first Pharaoh of the Third Dynasty and, through the genius of his

prime-minister and physician, Imhotep, developed a building program that has marked Egypt as profoundly as the Nile: Imhotep
invented the constructed pyramid, and after Djozer, for three centuries or so, Pharaohs built pyramids in profusion, improving the
construction over time. Snofru, or Snefre, the last Pharaoh of the
Third Dynasty, expanded Egyptian trade and developed copper
mines and extensive quarrying, leading Egypt in a time of height-
ened prosperity, as well as ordering not one but two pyramids to
mark his reign. By about 2900 B.C., the Great Pyramid of Khufu,
or Cheops, was under construction on the Giza plateau, and
within fifty years or so the second Giza pyramid, of Khafre, or
Chephren, had risen near the first, and at about that time the
Sphynx joined them, although some dispute this date. In another
fifty years, the third Giza pyramid, that of Menkure, or Mon-
choros, was erected and Fourth Dynasty Egypt had the symbols by
which it would be known from that time down to the present day.

In the Mesopotamian region, however, water rights were far less
predictable than they were in Egypt, leading to a volatility that did
not often touch the land of the Pharaohs; for the various cities in
the region water was more a matter of gaining control of wells and
rivers and meting out water to others in the form of irrigation. Because of that, intercity warfare, particularly over water, was fairly
common. From this, a complicated system of village/tribal alliances developed that continues in the cultures of the region to
this day, which still maintain strong kinship alignments within the
society for many generations.

Gradually the climate settled down, the Middle East slid into
aridity, and the various regions of the Middle East began to shift
from regional self-sufficiency to regularized commerce in order to
carve out trade-and-wealth niches for themselves. Not all the societies survived the transition, for many of the ancient cities disappeared into the encroaching desert, their populations dispersed

throughout the region as trophies of conquest, many of them as conquered populations. A few regions made the shift advantageously: in what is now Turkey, the region began its economic climb on herding and fishing; after about 5000 B.C., the various peoples in the mountainous regions of Anatolia increasingly exploited smelting and mining. The latter became so important that eventually a war with the Greeks was fought over the Trojan copper and tin mines, using Helen of Sparta as an excuse for their concerted campaign. Wives, even noble wives, in ancient Greek culture were relatively unimportant—certainly not reason enough to launch a thousand ships from states not directly affected by her kidnapping—but mines were good cause to undertake a long siege.

In Egypt, farming, especially of wheat and barley as well as legumes, not only created surpluses; it made significant reserves possible. With the emergence of a strong centralized government, preserving these surpluses and the distribution of them in times of famine became a stabilizing factor in Egyptian society. In addition to farming, masonry and goldsmithing became valuable, along with textiles and boatbuilding. A large part of the economic life of Egypt revolved around the funeral industry, from the creating of mummies, to the building of simple tombs, to the provisioning of the dead, to the honoring of the dead through religious ritual. Because of the closed nature of Egyptian society, exchange was managed by barter and by priestly recompense, not by the medium of exchange that was emerging throughout the Middle East—barter-tokens or, more concisely, the first money. There was one glaring absence in the rush to such exchange: Egyptian Pharaohs never minted coins. It was only after the Greeks took over the country, in 308 B.C., that coinage was introduced into Egypt as an accepted means of commerce.

In the Mesopotamian region, farming, textiles, and cart-and-chariot-making, with concomitant transportation services, including the breeding of pack and riding animals, became sources of wealth for the people. Beyond them, in the Persian highlands, lumber and quarrying provided the earliest foundations for riches beyond the most localized farming and hunting. The geographical advantage for Mesopotamia in terms of trade routes not only increased the region's wealth through commerce; it also added to the diversity of goods offered in Mesopotamian markets, thereby expanding the base of the region's wealth even more than surplus crops did, and creating ongoing agreements for trade with merchants from Asia to northwestern Europe. Thanks to Middle Eastern markets and their open policy to Asian traders, pre–2000 B.C. ornamental figures in Indian ivory and jade have been found in early villages along the Danube and in the ruins of a four-thousand-year-old fur-trading fort near modern-day Prague.

Over the centuries, city-states rose and fell—Babylon, Ur, Nineveh, and Susa among them—and certain major confederacies developed: Egypt's early consolidation into a single kingdom did much to establish it as the anchor to the southern end of the Middle East, and because of that, it came to dominate much of the eastern end of the Mediterranean, although Egypt was not a seagoing power as so many other city-states were: the Phoenicians at Sidon and Tyre relied heavily on trade and fishing for their success, so that much of their effort was directed to finding new markets for their goods—particularly textiles—and spices and dyes. The Phoenicians were also the first non-Egyptians to take on the newly "domesticated" cat as a protection against vermin, although, unlike the Egyptians, the Phoenicians did not worship cats as gods and did not stone to death anyone accused of stealing the holy animals.

Over many centuries the expansion of trade laid the foundation for true empires. The Egyptians, who in most matters were isolationistic, saw that controlling the borders of their kingdom was a necessary part of securing domestic peace and, in an effort to establish a protected kingdom, gained control of what is now Jordan and a swath of the Mediterranean shore west of Egyptian territory as a first step toward imperial status. Such actions commanded the attention of the Hittites far to the north in modern-day Turkey. The Hittites had developed a considerably advanced society encompassing the southern shores of the Black Sea, across the Anatolian mountains to the Ionian Sea and the Mediterranean, with their influence reaching well into Assyria, making them much too close to Egypt for comfort. Since the Hittite ambitions reached their height just as Egypt was entering one of her most prosperous and expansive periods, a clash seemed inevitable: it needed only a strong Pharaoh to attempt to contain the Hittites to set the buildup for war in motion, and in Rameses II Egypt had that Pharaoh.

Rameses II, known as The Great, was one of the longest-reigning Pharaohs in the long history of Egypt. His monuments are still seen all over Egypt, most of them erected at his order to his own glory or the glory of his regime. Coming at the height of the Nineteenth Dynasty, which began when Horemheb, or Harmhab, emerged as the winner of the squabble following the sudden and youthful death of Tutankhamen in 1350 B.C., Rameses II ruled sixty-seven years—remarkably long in modern times and positively mythic in ancient Egypt—from 1292 until 1225 B.C. Succeeding his father, Seti I, Rameses is credited with fathering more than one hundred children, many of whom predeceased him. This is significant because a fair number of the previous Pharaohs did not have more than one living son to succeed them, so Rameses' procreative success was seen as a powerful indication of his greatness, as well as insurance for his dynasty. Although Egypt had endured a period of turmoil, once the red-haired Rameses established himself as Pharaoh, for the greater part of his long tenure on the throne his rule was peaceful. However, early in his reign while there was still a degree of instability in Egypt, there were other problems from beyond their borders: Egypt was at war with the Hittites for control of the Syrian plain that lay between their respective territories, a rivalry that culminated in a series of battles near the Orontes River, the most decisive of them being the Battle of Qadesh.

The primary reason we know so much about Qadesh is that Rameses had at least two—there were probably more, but two have survived—massive inscriptions carved into the sides of public buildings about the battle and other, numerous, references were made to it throughout his long reign. That means that most of what we know about it now comes from the Egyptian and, specifically, Ramesean point of view. It is important to keep this in mind when assessing the campaign and the battle, for it is likely that the Hittites saw it differently than Rameses' assessment of the battle. Keeping in mind the biases inherent in the inscriptions that reflect the Pharaoh's outlook it is also important to factor in the great Egyptian cultural urge to be scrupulously accurate in their records of events: deliberate misrepresentation of things could imperil the soul's right to enter the afterlife, which was of paramount concern to Egyptians.

The Hittites at the time of Rameses the Great held most of what is modern-day Turkey and the northern part of Syria; they were the only serious competition to Egyptian power in the eastern Mediterranean Basin. Persia was too far away to undertake any serious campaigns against Egypt, and most of Persia's military attention at the time was focused to the east and south. A few Greek city-states were pesky, as were the African kingdoms to the south of Egypt, but none of those groups offered any substantial military potential to withstand the large Egyptian army. Egyptian territory extended through modern-day Israel, western Jordan, Lebanon, and southern Syria. What made the Syrian territory so valuable was the access to the Syrian plains, for the Persian trade-routes began there and some reached well into India. These were the spice-roads, as the northern trade routes into China were the Silk Roads, which, at this time in history, had not yet become the vast commercial highways they were to be but nonetheless moved goods from Central Asia, to the emerging trading city of Palmyra, to the Mediterranean. In this period, fortunes in spices, dyes, and slaves were traded along these Mediterranean/Persian routes. From Syria, the western end of a very profitable—if highly risky—merchant route opened the East to the West. Both the Hittites and the Egyptians strove to control these road-heads and the traffic on them, and both Hittite and Egyptian forces were prepared to battle for them.

The place where the two powerful regional influences overlapped was on the Orontes River at a small walled town with a ford then known as Qadesh. It was not particularly important, aside from its location, but that was enough to make it a bone of contention; it had no significant commercial value beyond the taxes for the use of the ford, which was low enough in the dry season to allow goats to cross the river—there were no brewers or weavers or stoneworkers in the village beyond the usual domestic kind and no major commerce beyond that of having a viable river crossing: only this physical situation gave Qadesh worth, and that was more than enough to make it of major importance in the Egypto-Hittite tug-of-hegemonical-war. Both Egyptian and Hittite forces wanted to take control of the village as a first step to ruling the area.

Warned of Hittite expansion in its southern territory, Rameses marshaled his army, broke it into four fairly equal divisions, and headed north, the Pharaoh himself with the leading, or Amun, division consisting of about one-quarter of his soldiers, with an additional unit that was composed mostly of chariots, which were the heart of Egyptian cavalry. This breaking up of his army was not as capricious a move as it might seem: the land through which they passed was barren, and providing food and water for his entire force at one time was a daunting task, one that if taken on in a body would slow down his march considerably, thus preventing him from seizing the advantage he was determined to have. As a result, Rameses decided to separate his army into more manageable groups, with the faster-moving cavalry in front, the foot soldiers immediately behind, and march them a day apart and approximately three miles from each other in line of march, bound to the north, knowing all would have a swifter passage and, after Hittite territory was reached, less exhausted soldiers would be available when the time came for the fight.

Given the demanding terrain and the harsh climate of the region, the Egyptian army—particularly the infantry, which comprised roughly 75 percent of the army—rarely marched in armor, because that would mean risking heatstroke and dehydration from armor-generated fevers; instead they carried their armor and weapons, along with their food, in simple backpacks. Even the charioteers in such a march carried their armor in their chariots and only donned it immediately before an engagement, which meant that the army was especially vulnerable on the march. The many scouts and couriers, most of them in chariots, not mounted, had only minimal armor, but that, too, was carried rather than worn except during active combat or prepared reconnoitering, when small companies of soldiers would be dispatched to assess the enemy, and ready to fight if challenged. This practice proved, in the case of the Battle of Qadesh, strategically prudent but tactically unwise.

Most Egyptian chariots were drawn not by horses but by asses. According to the inscriptions of the period, only the Pharaoh and his field commanders drove horses. Asses are not as fast as horses or as maneuverable, but their hooves are stronger—very important before the invention of the horseshoe—and their stamina and sure-footedness exceeds that of the horse; asses also are able to thrive on poor food, which horses are not, and suffer less from heat than horses do. Egyptian saddlery at the time was primitive, and working Egyptians more often rode donkeys, animals that did not need saddles, than horses, for although horses are faster than donkeys, they are not capable of carrying the per-pound loads donkeys can. The Egyptian horses of the time were small by modern standards, technically ponies, since their skeletons and occasional mummies show most of them stood under fourteen hands (the height dividing horses from ponies: four feet, eight inches at the shoulder), and their tack was quite simple. The Avars would not invent the stirrup until roughly A.D. 500, so accurately firing arrows or throwing spears from the saddle was not yet a workable tactic, and lances were not carried by mounted or driving Egyptian soldiers at this time, although spears and bows were.

Another indication that the Egyptians were not riders but drivers in military endeavors was their lack of trousers. Historically, in all societies where riding horses becomes an important form of transportation and the armies develop a significant ridden assault presence in military ventures, the invention of leggings quickly follows: from Asia to Europe, the riders of horses are also the wearers of trousers. Even the various native peoples of the New World when horses were introduced into the Americas invented simple saddles and leggings for riding. The image of horsemen without leggings is a film convention, not a reflection of actual riding conditions.

According to the vast inscriptions in Egypt made after the battle, Rameses spent April provisioning his soldiers and set out around the beginning of May; his chariot led the first of the four divisions of his army, the Amun division. He and his charioteer set a steady pace and arranged for frequent stops at any watering holes along the way, as much for their animals as the troops. By separating his divisions, Rameses was assured of making faster progress, as well as making it unlikely that he could be halted in his advance by an ambush attack or a concerted frontal assault; if a quarter of the army were engaged in battle, the remaining three-quarters could still advance and provide support for the part of the army under attack.

By late May, the Egyptian army was well into disputed territory. As Rameses sent scouts toward the Orontes to find a useful ford, two nomadic shepherds, or spies, depending on which account you believe, were encountered and taken to Rameses for questioning regarding the military activities of the Hittites and where the King, Muwatallish, was. The shepherds, or spies, said that the King of the Hittites was some distance to the north, near modern-day Aleppo, although how they knew this was not explained; it is possible that they were frightened enough to tell Rameses what he wanted to hear in the hope that the Pharaoh would spare their lives. Whatever their actual motives, the shepherds/spies claimed that they were looking for the Pharaoh to offer accords from their chief regarding territorial uses, since the Egyptian army was going to be passing through these nomads' grazing lands. Accepting the shepherds'/spies' accounts of the Hittite army's and King's location, Rameses, with the Amun division of his army, forded the Orontes and made camp to the northwest of Qadesh. As part of his usual campaign procedure, Rameses dispatched scouts to set up a workable perimeter, and it was at this point that things turned sticky: the scouts found Muwatallish and the bulk of the Hittite army encamped on the other side of Qadesh, troops rested and matériel at the ready.

Rameses summoned his officers as soon as this unpleasant news was related to him. The scouts described the Hittite army as fully prepared to fight, well supplied, and heavily armed, bad news all around. Rameses dispatched couriers to the next division of his army, one day behind his own men, urging the commander to hasten to join him. The Prei (one day behind) and Ptah (two days behind) divisions were expected to double their travel speed, the nearest of them—the Prei—having a possible arrival by midmorning the following day. The troops would be tired and there would be limited time to make camp and prepare for battle, but it was the best Rameses could hope for, and he made his plans accordingly. Rameses spent the evening setting up camp for battle and sending out small companies of men to reconnoiter; the Hittites in all likelihood knew that the first division of the Egyptian army was in the area and took that as fair warning, a warning that was confirmed shortly when Hittite scouts forded the river below Qadesh to size up the Egyptian threat. Between the Egyptian scouts and the Hittite scouts, both Rameses and Muwatallish soon knew that the Egyptians were seriously outnumbered.

In the later carved accounts of the battle, the Egyptian records claim the Hittites had twenty-five hundred chariots—a truly staggering number for the time. But this has been questioned by others; many later scholars believe the number was deliberately exaggerated to show Rameses' gamble as more heroic than it was. That is certainly a possible explanation, and there are elements in these huge carved accounts that are open to doubt, but in terms of numbers, the Egyptians had an almost superstitious commitment to accuracy, so that while it is unlikely, it is not impossible that the Hittite cavalry did indeed consist of twenty-five hundred chariots, which would mean five thousand asses to pull them, too vast a number to live off the land, so the other reckoning of numbers must be assessed now with an appreciation of the support such a large fighting force would require, and some of the numbers of combatants ratcheted down to account for support. The soldiers for the chariots consisted of one driver and two fighters each, making a total of seventy-five hundred chariot-cavalry, an amount sufficient to be cumbersome. That number of chariots would take many hours to cross at the Qadesh ford, and it is therefore likely, considering what happened that morning, that only a portion of the twenty-five hundred Hittite chariots were actually on the same side of the river as the Egyptians at the time the trouble started. There is some dispute about the number of Hittite infantry: according to the Egyptians, the Hittites did not have the numbers of men on foot that Rameses did in his full army, and it is likely that this is accurate, or that Muwatallish's infantry was considerably to the rear of his chariot-cavalry. Whichever was actually the case, the Hittites put the bulk of their fighting force in chariots and used infantry as backup while the Egyptians had fewer chariots but a large infantry with emphasis on archers.

First was the arrival of the first troops of the Prei division below Qadesh; they had answered Rameses' call and marched a good portion of the night. As they neared Qadesh, they encountered a company of Hittite chariots—by accounts, at least two hundred of them—and, being worn out, frightened, and unarmed, broke ranks in the face of the enemy, hardly surprising, given their situation. News of this rout was carried to Rameses, who was busy trying to choose where to place his troops to best advantage until his last two divisions could reach Qadesh. He was away from the body of the Amun division, apparently seeking places in the hills where his partial army could hold out against the Hittite chariots. Although not armed or with a large company of soldiers, Pharaoh made a quick decision, arming himself and preparing to stop his troops from fleeing before their panic spread to the Amun corps already preparing for battle against superior forces. Summoning his chariot, Rameses, in what was a colossal bluff, took the reins and charged the Hittite chariots by himself, protecting the Prei division while it could regroup and giving the Amun division time to get into position to fight. This daring move so astonished the Hittites that they hesitated to attack Rameses, and that hesitation cost them the advantage they had so clearly held.

During his solo assault, Rameses exhorted his troops to rally and appealed to Amun to protect his devout servant (Pharaoh) from harm. In the carved accounts, Rameses' condemnation of cowardice is extensive; Rameses saves his praise for his shield bearer, Menna, or Monneh, and his chariot horses, whose names have come down to us through the two vast accounts: Victorious Thebes and Muut's Favorite. Menna was understandably frightened but remained with Rameses throughout the whole of his daring—not to say reckless—single-handed onslaught, was apparently only superficially wounded, and emerged from the venture a military hero. Desperate the attacks might have been, but they were far from capricious, for it allowed Rameses' Amun officers to order their men into armor and to send out parties of men to halt the men of the Prei division in their attempted escape from danger, as well as throwing the Hittites into confusion. Six times Rameses charged the Hittite chariots, and he actually succeeded in forcing most of those chariots to retreat back across the ford. The ones left on the west side of the river had to contend with the Egyptians, for many of the Amun division had by this time sprung into action and were picking off those Hittites remaining, which significantly delayed an all-out attack of Hittite chariots.

Muwatallish had his whole army at his command and more than half the Egyptian forces were tired from their march, but he once again hesitated, possibly because he was aware more Egyptian troops were coming or because he was waiting for intelligence on the nature and placement of the main body of Rameses' army. During Rameses' attack, Muwatallish had dispatched his chariots to pursue the fleeing Egyptian forces and had ended up briefly victorious, but a second attempt to press the advantage turned into a standstill, so when a third opportunity seemed available, he remained cautious. By the end of the day, the Egyptians held the ground and Muwatallish withdrew. The next morning, Rameses mustered his army into battle formation, but apparently the Hittites did not reciprocate, for according to the records, the Hittites did not appear for battle at all that day. Rameses turned on the troops who had deserted him in battle, and when they came to plead for mercy he killed a great number of those men—the exact number, uncharacteristically, is not recorded—for their cowardice, a gesture that was not lost on the Hittites, who witnessed it. By the time the Hittites regrouped, rearmed, and prepared for battle the Ptah division had also arrived, and as a result, three-quarters of the Egyptian army faced the Hittites across the river, and that meant a much riskier encounter for Muwatallish's chariots, for they could only cross the ford three abreast, which exposed them to the Egyptian archers. Adding to this discouraging situation, many of the Egyptian companies, smarting from their poor showing during Rameses' attack, made it their task to keep up volleys of arrows at the ford to prevent the Hittites from trying another crossing; the Prei division was especially diligent in picking off straggling Hittite soldiers, and by nightfall, most of the soldiers were in camp and doing their best to make up for their earlier poltroonery.

The Egyptians, in order to make up for their initial poor showing against the Hittites, made a point of hailing Rameses a hero and praising his triumph, his courage, and his piety in gaining the protection of Amun, but this patriotic display was more to regain some of Rameses' good opinion than to celebrate a fact, for important as Qadesh was psychologically, it was not militarily decisive. As dramatic as Rameses' attack was, at the end of the day—literally and figuratively—no territory had been securely annexed to either side, and neither the Egyptians nor the Hittites held a significant advantage. Qadesh did, however, end up as an important draw in the long politico-military relationship between the Egyptians and the Hittites, and at the end of the battle-that-wasn't came a first in the military history of the Middle East: a peace treaty or, more accurately, a mutual nonaggression pact that provided for support for the two parties against external threats. This was sealed by Rameses' adding one of Muwatallish's daughters to his numerous wives. Oddly enough, given the volatile nature of Egypto–Hittite relations, the peace held throughout Rameses' reign.

But Qadesh left an important legacy to Egypt beyond the extended peace: since Rameses made a point of including depictions of the punishments of his troops as part of his record of the aftermath of Qadesh, it is clear that the point of such representation was not intended for the Hittites, who were unlikely to see them, but for the Egyptians, in particular the army, as a reminder of what could happen if the army failed Pharaoh again. It also made a useful cautionary tale to those officers who might become too ambitious, for it showed that Rameses was prepared to exact vengeance on his own men if they showed themselves to be disloyal in any way and to remind his courtiers that loyalty was required of them no matter what. Viewed in this light, the point of the explication of punishment becomes much clearer, and given the long reign Rameses had, he most certainly had times when such a reminder was not only useful but necessary.

Rameses II left another mark on history: it was reported—perhaps incorrectly—during his reign that Moses and Aaron led the Jews living in Egypt into the desert and toward the Red Sea, and although the Jewish accounts of determined pursuit are not reflected in Egyptian records, there was clearly a social disruption in Egypt around 1274 B.C. that may refer to the Jewish departure. Rameses himself apparently took no part in the event, although according to the accounts of the period, one of the regional governors attempted to keep his foreign servants from leaving the country but had to give up his pursuit when he reached the Red Sea at high tide, after the greatest number of refugees had crossed the tidal flats, some six hours earlier.

Throughout this period, the status of most women was constrained and circumscribed for almost all. There were a few highborn women who had visibility and influence, particularly at village-life level, where dependence on women's labor was particularly immediate; in the case of the Pharaoh Hatshepsut, major political power. There were a few important female religious leaders, but their influence tended not to penetrate beyond temple life; in terms of true influence, Hatshepsut stood alone—she was the only woman to lead Egypt until the Roman period, when Cleopatra IV claimed authority beyond her brother's and ruled as Pharaoh in everything but name; the distinction of being female and Pharaoh remains with Hatshepsut alone.

Most women in Egyptian culture held separate-but-equal status with the males—and you remember how well separate-but-equal worked in American schools, half a century ago—that made them something more than domestic livestock but not quite human, with the emphasis on the *man*. Village women were allowed to go to the marketplace without escort, to trade for goods on their own, to manage property for their underage sons, to make binding contracts for labor, and to be entitled to support from a deceased husband's family, provisions that applied until the gynophobic Greeks took over Egypt and imposed their culture of containment of women upon the Egyptians. Egyptian slaves had much the same status as household appliances do today and received similar treatment: they were expected to perform their jobs on demand and to fail to do so only when ill.

Arab women fared less well than the Egyptian ones, being sequestered to immediate family groups and occasionally in harems, assigned repetitive tasks, fed last, and punished for any slight infraction of the rules; they were valued only for their ability to give birth to sons, and in some Arab cultures of the time, failure to provide a husband with sons was ground for divorce or death—and given that women could not own property, divorce and death were often the same thing. Women were also treated as booty in raids, often captured and rarely ransomed, could be killed by husband or father without any criminal repercussions attaching to the deed, and were, with few exceptions, believed to be incapable of reason.

Mesopotamian cultures tended to fall somewhere between the Egyptian and the Arab models, some being more liberal, others more conservative, but most of those cultures assigned malign magical abilities to adult females and therefore had strict rules for their conduct and barbarous consequences for those females who failed to conform. Fathers, brothers, and husbands could, and usually did, have absolute control over their mothers, daughters, sisters, and wives. It was believed by a significant number of cultures that women could call down the moon and cause all manner of calamities, starting with impotence for men; it was also assumed that a man who slept with a menstruating woman would have "blood on him" and was at risk for being killed in battle. Except for professional prostitutes, women were expected to be unquestioningly faithful to their fathers and their husbands, to care for their children, and to bring credit to their sons. Although there is some debate as to whether or how much a woman could own in the way of property, once she was married, her husband became the administrator of anything his wife owned. Slaves, especially female slaves, were often captured foes and as a result were thought to be untrustworthy. Most were given routine work, treated fairly harshly, and considered an unfortunate necessity to life. The sole exception among captured slaves was scribes. In the vast majority of cases these were men, for most Mesopotamian cultures had respect, not to say awe, for the written word.

After the death of Rameses the Great, his son Merneptah expelled a Libyan invasion that seemed to be timed to coincide with the
shift in Pharaohs, and strove to continue the success of his father's
reign, but the Nineteenth Dynasty was winding down, and by 1198
B.C., following a dozen years of pharaonic squabbles and shifting
politics, the Twentieth Dynasty was established, beginning with
Rameses III, a name chosen to establish a nonexistent link to Rameses II. Over the next two centuries Egypt weakened, and in 945 B.C.
the Twenty-second Dynasty was founded by Sheshonk, a Nubian:
Egypt, gloriously isolationistic for more than a millennium, had
fallen into the hands of outsiders.

In 1194 B.C., the Greeks sailed for Troy, and ten years later they
gained control of the copper and tin mines the Trojans had
founded. Although militarily successful, the Greeks failed in their
intention of colonizing Troy despite efforts during their long siege
to do so, and for the next millennium Greek attention turned principally westward, away from the Middle East. The only concentrated
efforts to take advantage of the Middle East came from a question-
able source: Greek pirates regularly pursued Middle Eastern ships
for slaves and cargoes.

In 1170 B.C., Egypt, in the throes of an economic crisis, experienced a first at the city of Thebes: men working on constructing a
funerary temple, having been on short rations, were finally not
given food for their families, whereupon the men laid down their
tools and refused to work until their families were fed and their
full rations restored. After several days and many threats and
counterthreats, the authorities caved in and provided the working-
men most of what they demanded: Egypt had sustained a successful strike.

At Babylon in 1146 B.C., Nebuchadnezzar I began his rule as
king, marking a new expansionism among the Middle Eastern
city-states and creating another outburst of regional conflict that

was marked by small military scrimmages and raids. While the Israelites battled the Philistines (1141–1138 B.C.) and saw the Philistines decimated by plague before it ravaged their own people when they regained the Ark of the Covenant, the Assyrians were becoming restless: in about 1130 B.C., border skirmishes broke out with the Hittites, and by 1100 B.C., Assyrian forces under Tiglath-Pileser I conquered the Hittites and set their troops in motion toward the Phoenicians, the first serious step in their empire building.

In their continuing battles with the Philistines, the fractious tribes of Jews finally were forced, in 1025 B.C., to unite under a strong military leader, called king in later ages but more accurately an anointed military commander, in the person of Saul of Hebron, whose authority was constantly kept in check by influential priests and prophets; despite later accounts that implied mutual support, the comments of the time suggested that the military and religious factions were often at odds with each other. Saul's thirteen-year reign ended in his death and the death of his son Jonathan at the Battle of Mount Gilboa against the Philistines in 1012 B.C. The most ambitious and most charismatic of Jonathan's comrades, David of Hebron, carried on the fight, and in 1005 B.C. David took Jerusalem, was anointed military commander by the prophet Samuel, and began a thirty-three-year reign of military expansionism that saw the defeat of the Moabites, the Ammonites, and the Edomites as well as the final subjugation of the Jewish tribes under David's rule as David of Judea.

An astute military commander, David managed to secure Judean borders and maintain a high level of internal accord, but these came at a price, one that required a high level of military preparedness and a diligent public posture of combativeness. The former was expensive and the latter was risky, demanding that David respond promptly to any hint of internal or external aggression.

David's problems at home were as great as those in the field: his favorite son, Absalom, killed his half brother after Amnon raped his sister, and was banished for avenging his half sister. Although a degree of rapprochement developed between Absalom and his father, it was short-lived; in 978 B.C. Absalom attempted a rebellion against David and was killed for his temerity.

David's successor, his son Solomon, more diplomatically inclined than his father, spent a good part of his almost forty-year reign expanding trade, establishing commercial missions, securing mines, making treaties with Egypt and Tyre, erecting fine public buildings in Jerusalem, and acquiring a vast harem of wives and concubines. Upon Solomon's death in 933 B.C., his son Rehoboam ascended the throne, which was now a great deal more kingly than military, thanks to Solomon's long dependence on trade and statesmanship. Rehoboam was not up to the job, and so, when northern tribes broke away from Judea and established Israel with Rehoboam's brother Jeroboam as their king, the Jews suffered a strategic loss that made it possible for the army of Pharaoh Sheshonk to invade Judean territory and sack and pillage Jerusalem and Edom in 926 B.C. In an attempt to end the civil war and to once again unite the Jewish tribes, Jeroboam set up a Patriarchal sanctuary at Bethel, intending to shift power away from Jerusalem as well as to muster sufficient military support to drive out the Egyptians. Although this was militarily advantageous, it caused outrage among much of the citizenry and prolonged the civil war even while the Israelites warred with forces from Damascus seeking to achieve in the north what the Egyptians had done in the south. Jeroboam's son, Nabad, who sought to modify his father's policies, was murdered in 900 B.C. by Baasha, who took over rulership of Israel, restarted the civil war, and generally guaranteed continued hostilities for another quarter century.

Around 915 B.C. famine struck Anatolia, and for the next sixteen years the region suffered under its impact. Eventually, around 903 or 902 B.C., the King of Lydia, whose lands were among the hardest hit, ordered all non-Lydians in his kingdom to leave. The first to depart was a group said to come from the eastern Carpathian Mountains: the Etruscans took ship westward and settled in the northern part of the Italian peninsula, where they established hill towns and vineyards. Within three years, King Atys of Lydia had ordered a total of half his population to leave, be killed, or sold into slavery: the alternative was starvation for the entire country. While this was an expedient decision, it meant that the western end of what is now Turkey was seriously depopulated and that as soon as the famine ended, the region became a target.

First among those eager to make the most of this opportunity was the Assyrian King Assur-Nacir-Pal, who took over all Phoenician territory in 878 B.C., compelling the now-refugee Phoenicians to leave; they did, some of them going to the island of Tyre off the coast from the land-based city, where they bided their time. Others took the hint and went a much greater distance; they founded the city of Carthage on the north African coast. Assur-Nacir-Pal required all remaining Phoenicians to pay him tribute in ivory, gold, and precious stones, as well as provide him with slaves. He also ordered the young sons of Phoenicians to enter his army, allowing him to swell his ranks of soldiers without incurring the unpleasant expense of having to pay for their services. Assyrian expansionism continued throughout the eastern Mediterranean Basin, including, in 721, the conquest of the Kingdom of Israel by Sargon III, who dispatched his conquered foe to Central Asia, establishing the basis for the legends of the Lost Tribes of Israel, for the ten tribes Sargon relocated vanished from all subsequent records.

All through the 800s B.C., trade routes expanded and trading cities flourished. From Antioch, Sidon, and Tyre on the Mediterranean to the ports on the Black Sea, trade was becoming a mainstay of civic wealth and led to more focused military actions that were intended not to cut off trade entirely but to divert it to the coffers of rival cities and empires. Cities made dramatic improvements not only to show off their wealth and importance but to put their profits to good use; an example of this was found in what is now Yemen, where cities established impressive dams and waterworks along with fortifications to take full advantage of the profits of the incense trade. A number of these structures lasted a thousand years and more.

By 775 B.C. the Greeks had held the first Olympic Games; in 753 B.C. the city of Rome was officially founded. Western societies were becoming more independently established, and their interactions with the Middle East were changing as the Western city-states grew and expanded; although trade was still predominantly a Middle Eastern hegemony, the changes in the West were laying the groundwork for a mercantile shift, half a millennium away. Over the next two centuries, Greek agricultural colonies in Italy, Sicily, and Spain helped provide food to the prospering Greek city-states as well as markets for Greek merchandise. Through these Greek traders, the ports of the Middle East were increasingly accessible to Westerners. Greek colonization continued, and in 658 the city of Byzantium was founded largely to take advantage of the increased Greco–Middle Eastern trade. It also established a strategically important Greek presence on the Black Sea, which would prove continually significant to the present day; the city of Istanbul continues to be a crucial trading center and cross-road market.

Assyrian aspirations reached a zenith in 698 B.C., when the Assyrian King Sennacherib destroyed Babylon: he and his successors, despite vagaries of fortunes and changes of dynasties, rebuilt the city in grander form than it had been and held it as the most important center of their empire for more than a century behind newly strengthened walls; the Hanging Gardens of Babylon, one of the many improvements in the rebuilt city, was considered one of the Seven Wonders of the Ancient World. Making common cause with the Medes, King Nabopolassar of Babylon attacked the Assyrians on several fronts; the Assyrian capital at Nineveh fell to a combined force of Medes and Chaldeans in 612 B.C., and shortly thereafter the Assyrian Empire failed, sending military and economic ripples throughout the Middle East, as the Medean King Cyaxraes overran territory from the Tigris to modern-day Armenia.

Pharaoh Necho, a ruler with building projects worthy of Khufu in their scope, if not their execution, was also eager to fill the void left by the Assyrian collapse, and set out to battle the Chaldeans for control of the northern part of the Arabian Peninsula and Mesopotamia. Clever though he was, Necho bit off more than he could chew, and in 605 B.C. he was devastatingly defeated by Nebuchadnezzar II, who, making the most of his victory, in 597 B.C. went on to conquer Jerusalem, where he captured a large part of the population and took them back to Babylon; in the following year, his troops destroyed Jerusalem's Great Temple as part of his policy of subjugation of all conquered peoples. In 573 B.C. Tyre fell to the Babylonians, and five years later Nebuchadnezzar II continued his pursuit of world domination by invading Egypt. When he finally died in 562 B.C. Babylonian territory was more than three times the size it was when his reign began some forty-three years earlier.

Nebuchadnezzar II was succeeded by his son Evil-Merodach, a far more pacifically inclined leader than his father had been and one who saw Babylon as a more tolerant empire than Nebuchadnezzar had; Evil-Merodach indicated his more accessible policies by releasing the King of Judea, Jehoiachin, who had been imprisoned for more than thirty-five years, and generally attempted a less aggressive rapprochement with conquered and client peoples, which was probably why his own court conspired against him and, in 560 B.C., killed him and then began, predictably, to wrangle among themselves, weakening the court, the throne, and the country. In 536 B.C. the last King of Babylon, Nabonidus, began his reign, of just over sixteen years; faced with a depleted treasury, he raised taxes, imposed new ones, cut back services, lowered army pay, delayed maintenance and upkeep on the city's waterworks, and generally made himself disliked by anyone with property or entitlements, including many of the powerful priests and military leaders, none of whom wanted to give up a single iota of privilege that had been granted as a right to men in high positions back when Babylon was rich and powerful. The recalcitrance of the upper classes to accommodate any adjustment in their prerogatives created an impasse no emperor or empire could weather. Years before it fell, Babylon was doomed.

The year 550 B.C. saw the death of Anshan Cambyses I of Persia and the ascendency of his son Cyrus II, an empire builder of great vision and energy, who hit the ground running once he came to power: in 546 B.C. he surprised and killed Croesus of Lydia—a king known for his wealth—at Sardis and took over Lydia, then moved on to conquer Babylon and either killed Nabonidus or exiled him. Accounts vary as to what actually happened, although Nabonidus vanished completely. Cyrus then faced Nabonidus' son Prince Belshazzar and dealt him a decisive defeat. Before Cyrus destroyed Babylon, he allowed the captive Jews to leave the city and return to their homeland. He then turned his attention to more subjugation and earned himself the cognomen the Great; his death in 530 B.C. did not result in disruptive dynastic squabbles: his empire passed to his son, Cambyses, who in 524 B.C. conquered most of Egypt. His death, probably from disease, in 521 B.C. allowed his brother-in-law, Darius, to come to power after subduing a number of brushfire revolts and to go on to extend Persian control from the Indus River in northern India, to the Caucasus Mountains, to the Mediterranean. Aware of the problems confronting so vast an empire, Darius at once set about establishing and improving royal roads for couriers, building a canal between the Nile River and the Red Sea, and providing for a universal coinage; he also divided his territories into twenty satrapies, giving control of them preferentially to fellow Zoroastrians.

Because of a relatively calm fifty years, Phoenician trade had flourished, and by 510 B.C. ubiquitous slaves, Egyptian grain, Greek and Lydian linen, African ivory, Nubian pepper, Arabian dates and honey, Italian lumber and terra-cotta, Spanish silver, Cornish tin, Armenian lead, Russian amber, French wines, Slavic furs, Burgundian crockery, and Indian spices all traveled in Phoenician ships. Although plagued by Arab pirates, the Phoenicians were successful enough to maintain regular trading treaties throughout the Mediterranean, the eastern Atlantic, and the Adriatic, Ionian, and Black Seas and to weather the various exigencies of conquests and politics with their various trading associates. There is evidence that suggests that the Phoenicians had voyaged around the southern end of Africa and traded well into the Indian Ocean by 500 B.C. and that they had exchanged goods directly with Chinese merchants, including acquiring silks that had not come across the land route through Central Asia. Despite or perhaps because of this stunning success, various Middle Eastern powers were reluctant to attack the Phoenicians directly, for fear the damage this would do to trade would result in their own economic perturbation, a risk few were willing to take.

In 490 B.C. the war that had been simmering between the Greeks and the Persians finally erupted as the Persians strove to break up a revolt of Ionian Greeks living in what is now Turkey.

The revolt was crushed by the Persians at Miletus, but although the Persians, under Xerxes I, or Ahuerus, managed, after losing the Battle of Marathon in 490 B.C., to break Greek resistance at the Battle of Thermopylae in August of 480 B.C., his approximately 180,000 soldiers vanquishing the Greek forces of 300 Spartans and 700 Thespians, they had to face the main body of Greek soldiers—mainly companies of Boetians, Locrians, and Phocians—at their wall built across the Isthmus of Corinth, which was trickier. Still, the Persians broke the defenses and were able to take Attica, sack Athens, sending the Athenians fleeing to the Peloponnese, and gain control over a crucial part of the Greek territories. The Greeks retaliated in a naval operation that, less than two months later, trapped the Persians in the Bay of Salamis; although the Greek ships were outnumbered more than two to one, they nevertheless won the day by ramming the Persian ships after drawing them in between the mainland and the island of Salamis, where the larger Persian navy was unable to maneuver. Realizing the extent of the risk he was taking, Xerxes withdrew to Asia Minor, leaving behind a portion of the Persian army under the command of Mardonius, who was defeated the following August at the Battle of Plataea. The withdrawal of the Persians gave the Greeks the opportunity to fight the Peloponnesian Wars for the next several decades without significant foreign interference, and except for a devastating plague in 429–428 B.C., they were able to confine the bulk of their warfare to their own territories, although the Greeks did send troops to hot spots in the Persian Empire to encourage the Persians to stay away. This included aiding a revolt in Egypt and occupying part of Cyprus. Eventually, in 446 B.C., the Persians, now under Artaxerxes I Longimanus, and the Greeks signed a formal peace treaty, and for the time being, hostilities among their various military forces ceased.

Trade again was given the chance to flourish, and flourish it did. While the Greek city-states kept up their seasonal warfare, commerce continued more or less unimpeded with Middle Eastern ports, and with Italian ones as well. By now the Etruscans and, after their defeat in 509 B.C., the Romans were becoming active in trade as well, expanding into the Atlantic routes more routinely and going east into the Black Sea to reach such distant locales as the Sea of Azov and, beyond it, the Don River, Trapezeus and Colchis on the Black Sea, and the trade routes of Central Asia. The downside of all this trade was, of course, the spread of disease: for the next seventy years, epidemics came and went as commerce carried, along with goods, parasites, viruses, bacilli, and other infectious agents that left their marks on city-states from China to Europe.

The year 424 B.C. saw the assassination of Xerxes II by Sogdianus, who usurped the throne but was then assassinated and replaced by Darius II, who managed to hold the throne for twenty years, but upon his death in 404 B.C. another crisis arose as Cyrus, the satrap of Anatolia, rose in arms against his brother and emperor, Artaxerxes II Mnemon. With an army of Greek mercenaries, Cyrus attempted to march on Babylon but was defeated at Cunaxa in 401 B.C.; Cyrus lost his life in the battle, and the Greek soldiers accomplished a harrowing march to the Black Sea, taking the greater part of a year to accomplish it. In the meantime, another revolt in Cappadocia had begun, with the regional governor, Datames, at its head. The unrest in Egypt gained that country relative independence from Persia after 404 B.C., a state of affairs that inspired many regions with ambitions for greater autonomy. Over the next fifty years, other satrapies in what is now Turkey joined the revolt, rising against Artaxerxes II and Artaxerxes III Ochus. Artaxerxes III was able to end the rebellions and bring the satrapies back under firm Persian control, a control that lasted until Darius III Codomannus was conquered in 331 B.C. by Alexander of Macedon in the early phase of his march to world—meaning Middle East—domination.

Philip of Macedon had big dreams for his reign: tired of being considered an uncouth barbarian by the Greeks, he took pains to become more civilized. In 342 B.C., he hired Aristotle to tutor the children of his court as well as his son, Alexander, showing that he held learning in as high regard as he did skill at arms. He then, in 340 B.C., undid most of the good impression he was hoping to make by besieging the Greek city of Byzantium, a city whose symbol was the crescent moon, left over from Babylonian influences and allied to the moon goddess Hecate. Centuries later, Christians demoted Hecate to a demon, and the Turkish conquerors of the city took the crescent moon as the symbol of their religion, Islam. Philip did not succeed in his attempt to conquer Byzantium, but he made up for it by conquering the Athenians and Thespians in August of 338 B.C. at the Battle of Charleronea. His triumph was short-lived, for Philip was murdered in 336 B.C. at Aeges while attending his daughter's wedding celebration. Rumor had it that Olympias, the wife he had recently divorced and mother of his heir, Alexander, was behind it all, and she may well have been. Whether Alexander was implicated in the plot was— and is—open to speculation. Thanks to Macedonian ambitions, Greece was once again firmly in the Middle East. In response to the usual local revolts resulting from Philip's untimely and unseemly demise, several of the Greek states were brought back into the fold promptly by Alexander, who attacked and destroyed Thebes as an example of his intentions. The other states surrendered rather than risk such losses as Thebes endured.

In 334 B.C., at the age of twenty-two, Alexander III had about him an army composed largely of Greeks but also containing mercenaries from as far away as Africa. That spring, Alexander led across the Hellespont his army of approximately thirty thousand infantry, four thousand mounted cavalry, and one thousand chariots, augmented by about 150 naval ships. The Greek mercenaries of Darius attempted a retreat, laying waste to the countryside as they went in an attempt to slow the Greek advance. The regional satraps put a stop to this policy and ordered the mercenaries to take a stand, which they did at the Granicus River, where they were utterly defeated by Alexander's army, possibly because a fair number of the Greek mercenaries fighting for Darius saw the way the wind was blowing and changed sides, allowing for a more comprehensive triumph for Alexander. Taking this as a signal of change, the Greek cities in Asia Minor revolted against the Persians and hastened to ally themselves with the Macedonians. Things continued to go badly for the Persians: in 333 B.C. Alexander III beat Darius III at the Battle of Issus. Darius escaped, but only for a while; in taking advantage of the control of the coast of the eastern Mediterranean, Alexander turned south and conquered a large portion of Egypt and founded Alexandria, one of many cities he named after himself. The next year, 331 B.C., Alexander was once again in pursuit of Darius. At the Battle of Gaugamela in the fall of that year, Alexander became master of Mesopotamia and, by extension, the Persian Empire. To complete his capitulation, in 330 B.C. Darius III was murdered by his satrap, and shortly thereafter Alexander sacked the Persian capital of Persepolis. Some reports claim that as many as twenty thousand mules and six thousand camels were used to carry off Alexander's loot, although, as has been pointed out, the Greeks did not have such numbers of those animals to spare and while Persepolis might have had six thousand camels, it did not have twenty thousand mules.

Not content to control Egypt and Mesopotamia, Alexander began to dress in Persian finery and to believe his own publicity—that he was achieving divinity. Wanting to make the most of his legend, he headed east, conquering Maracanda, an early version of Samarkand, in Central Asia in 329 B.C., and continued on in 327 B.C. to northern India, where he stopped short of the Ganges Valley, because after the Battle of the Hydaspes, even though he won against Porus and had the support of Taxiles, a local ruler who had a long tradition of warfare against his neighbors, Alexander's troops had had enough and refused to go any farther, success or no success. Realizing that he was at an impasse, Alexander turned down the Indus River, going down to the ocean, where he dispatched Nearchus as commander of the eight hundred ships that Alexander had ordered built. As soon as the ships were ready, he sent them on an exploratory mission in the Persian Gulf while Alexander led his men back through the Gedrosian desert. Naval and land forces rendezvoused at Caramaina in 324 B.C. and went on to Susa.

In an effort to cement his conquests, Alexander ordered ten thousand of his men and eighty officers to marry Persian women. From Babylon, which he claimed as his capital, he sought to establish a blended Greco-Persian culture, with the Macedonians in charge and Greek customs prevailing. Where he found satraps had used their positions to exploit the populace and to found private armies, he ordered the armies paid and disbursed and replaced the satraps with Macedonian officers. He declared himself the son of Zeus, on a par with Heracles, and ordered that all Greek cities acknowledge him as such. But the strain was starting to tell, and after the death of his closest lieutenant and lover, Hephaestion, Alexander began to slip. By the end of spring of 323 B.C. he was ill and undergoing purges for what may have been intestinal parasites; whether from the treatment or the disease, Alexander III, the Great, died at Babylon on June 13, 323 B.C.

As large as Alexander looms in ancient history, it seems as if he occupies decades and decades of conquest and war, but in actuality, from his coronation to his death only a dozen years elapsed. By thirty-two he was dead and his empire fell apart. In the short time he ruled, the character of the Middle East was indelibly impacted and the uneasy relationship between Middle East and European West established for more than two millennia. In that, and in his relentless conquest, Alexander succeeded in attaining that one great Greek ideal of the ancient world: to perform deeds of such significance that your name is never forgotten—the deeds need not be good or bad, just great, and as Alexander III's cognomen indicates, even his own contemporaries hailed him so.

THE ROMAN PERIOD

Roman Expansion and Collapse

T HE death of Alexander the Great at Babylon in 323 B.C. left a vacuum in the power structure of the Middle East, and there was a scramble to occupy the empire he had created: most aggressive of these were the forces of an ambitious upstart city-state on the west side of the Italian peninsula that had been acquiring provinces and toeholds throughout the Mediterranean Basin. Although the Greek city-states were strong and rich, they also tended to fight one another more fiercely than any other opponents, and as a result, the potential of any Greek city-state to achieve regional control was never perceived as presenting a lasting military or commercial influence beyond its own walls. The internal bickering also created mutual suspicions that made eventual alliances difficult at best and outright impossible in some instances, which increased the opportunities for conquest by others.

Persia, still reeling from Alexander's occupation, was unable to restore itself to the prominence it had held in the past; there were border regions of the old empire that were in disarray, suspicious and contentious of one another and depleted of the resources necessary to rebuild what Alexander had exhausted. The Persian Empire became a broken state, composed of four principal kingdoms—the

Seleucid Kingdom in the west, the Arsacid Kingdom to the east of the Caspian Sea, the Bactrian Kingdom east of the Arsacid Kingdom, and the Kingdom of the Ptolemies in Egypt and along the Mediterranean. For the next several decades, Persia remained in a state of collapse, these various cobbled-together kingdoms warring among themselves, making it possible for outside elements to capitalize on Persia's misfortunes. The very commanders Alexander had intended to carry on his empire and conquest lost all he had gained and fractured his conquered territory beyond repair.

Aware as they were of the importance of trade, the Romans were keen on controlling the trade routes through the Middle East to Asia and so began a long program of conquest and occupation along the eastern end of the Mediterranean, beginning with attaining control of all of Italy, from which various ports they could strike out at Greece and then Syria; patient and determined, they did not allow setbacks to dull their aspirations, which turned out to be a good thing. Their first efforts were not particularly promising: they lost the Battle of the Caudine Forks to the Samnites in 321 B.C. and the Battle of Asculum to the forces of King Pyrrhus in 280 B.C., giving Pyrrhus the first pyrrhic victory in history, for although he won, his losses exceeded Roman losses by more than triple, leaving Pyrrhus with insufficient men to mount any real military presence against any opponent, a misfortune that keeps his name alive to this day.

By 270 B.C. Rome controlled all but a few isolated regions in Italy and was readying for the next step, which came in 260 B.C. off the coast of Sicily at the Battle of Mylae, Rome's first major naval victory over the Carthaginian navy but not its last. Rome had discovered an important truth about war as a result of their clashes with the Carthaginians: that war and conquest are not the same thing and that the success of a war is ultimately judged by what comes after it. As one Roman general of this period quipped, "Wars are won in the peace."

During this time, the Egyptians, after a long period of relative calm under Ptolemy II, once more became ambitious under Ptolemy III, who invaded Syria in 246 B.C. and the following year conquered Susa and Babylon. Only a revolt at home the following year arrested Egyptian progress in Mesopotamia and left the army without pharaonic support. By the time of Ptolemy III's death in 221 B.C., Egypt had lost many of its non-Egyptian holdings and made no serious effort to recapture them, Ptolemy IV and his sister/wife, Arsinoe III, having little interest in places beyond the Nile or in the expensive business of waging war.

In Carthage that same year, General Hasdrubal was murdered, and the command of his troops went to the sons of another Carthaginian general, the brilliant and impulsive Hamilcar Barca, who had been killed in battle seven years before, Hasdrubal and Hannibal. Although technically not truly part of the Middle East, Carthage, on the north coast of Africa to the southwest of Sicily, tended to be allied to the interests of the Middle East, and the actions of the Carthaginians were inclined to ripple across the Mediterranean to Syria and Greece, never more so than when Hannibal set out from Spain to take on the Romans in the Second Punic War (218–202 B.C.); in spite of early victories at the Ticino and Trebbia Rivers and at Cannae and a partial success near Rome, the Carthaginians lacked the war machines of the technology-minded Romans, which made effective sieges of Roman cities by less well-supplied forces difficult, and eventually, at the Battle of Metaurus in Umbria, in which Hasdrubal was killed, Hannibal was forced to abandon his Roman campaign in 207 B.C., and by 202 B.C. the Second Punic War was over and P. Cornelius Scipio, called Africanus for his military successes at Carthage, was a hero in all Roman territory. By 201 B.C.

the Carthaginians surrendered all their territory in the Mediterranean Basin, including their substantial holdings in Spain. Along with substantial reparation payments to Rome for fifty years, the Romans required that the Carthaginians make no war without Roman permission, essentially hog-tying the Carthaginians and preventing any effective insurgency from starting. Just to make sure that the Carthaginians wouldn't go back on the terms of their surrender, the Romans destroyed all but a dozen Carthaginian warships and imposed reparation payments on the people of Carthage.

With these new territories added to their control of Italy, the Romans were on a roll, and they made the most of it. At the Battle of Cynoscephalae in Greece in 197 B.C., the Roman General T. Quinctius Flaminius defeated Philip V of Macedon, thus gaining a considerable portion of Greek territory and an important corridor into the Middle East. The Romans allowed Philip to keep five ships for a navy, but they stipulated that Philip could not make war without Roman permission and required him to pay Rome one thousand talents over a decade and to provide harbor for Roman ships preferentially to others, guaranteeing an ongoing Roman presence in Macedonia. This policy of balance of payment and reduced military matériel worked well for the Romans for several centuries.

The Syrians had not been idle during the Roman expansion, and in 191 B.C. the Romans, holding Thermopylae in much the same way the Spartans had, but with far greater numbers, defeated Antiochus III, who, undeterred by his losses, continued the war against the Romans and Roman possessions. Antiochus had taken in Hannibal, and between the two of them disgust and hatred of Romans became required sentiments in military and aristocratic Syrian circles. To augment the army's activities, a large number of spies were dispatched to report on any weaknesses that could be discovered in the Roman Legions, and two of the spies—both Greeks—were

able to report on a problem in the supply line. Unfortunately for
the Syrians, these men were captured and exchanged their knowledge for their lives, leaving the Romans more prepared than before
and more determined to make the most of their intelligence. In 190
B.C. the Battle of Magnesia was another Roman success over Antiochus III and his Syrian army. The Roman General L. Cornelius Scipio (called Asiaticus, to differentiate him from his brother, Scipio
Africanus) crossed the Hellespont and sent his Legions after Antiochus, finally and roundly defeating him. From this victory Rome
gained all Antiochus' Asiatic and European territory, and in addition, the Romans required the Syrians to pay fifteen thousand talents
to Rome over twelve years and to surrender Hannibal. Although Antiochus III agreed to the terms, lax security on his part allowed Hannibal to escape before Rome could take him in charge. Hannibal
finally ended up at the court of Prusia I of Bithynia, where in 183
B.C. he committed suicide when he learned that his host had agreed
to sell him out to the Romans.

Rome encountered a setback in 172 B.C. when Philip V's son,
King Perseus of Macedon, defeated the Romans in the first sally
of a war that would last until 168 B.C., when, at the Battle of
Pydna, General L. Aemilius Paulus brought the Macedonians to
their knees. For his victory Paulus was granted a full triumphal
procession through Rome, with captives and loot on display to the
populace; for a time, the bounty of the Macedonian campaign so
swelled the coffers of Rome that the Senate suspended the tribu-
tum, or income tax, on the residents of the city.

It was at roughly this time that the city of Rome began to pave
her streets, a technological improvement that spread quickly to other
Roman cities; with it went a significant improvement in road building throughout the burgeoning empire, which not only served to
help military movement but also stimulated trade by making travel
easier, both of which usages were to have far-reaching implications

as the Roman presence expanded. Paved streets became a standard of civilization throughout the Roman Empire, as did another Roman determination of roughly the same period: in 153 B.C. the six hundredth anniversary of the founding of the city, January 1 became the official date on which the year began, a decision that remains in effect to this day.

In 167 the King of Syria, Antiochus IV Ephiphanes, in a forceful and arrogant attempt to bring Greek culture and values to Judea, where they were not wanted, attacked Jerusalem, destroying the Great Temple and proclaiming Judaism illegal. He then set up statues of the Olympian gods throughout the ravaged city and ordered the people to direct their worship to these gods. Used to the polytheistic Greek view of religion, Antiochus IV Ephiphanes was wholly unfamiliar with the monotheistic zeal of Judaism and its strictures against any form of idolatry. Antiochus IV was shocked at the response his orders received: there were riots and then open rebellion. One priest, Mattathias of Modin, took his family and escaped Antiochus IV. Over the next year Mattathias and his five sons became the center of a Jewish revolt against the Greco-Syrians, and in 165 B.C. Mattathias' sons took back Jerusalem, restored the Great Temple, destroyed the Olympian statues, and, by keeping their one-day supply of oil going for eight days, established the Dedication Feast known as Hanukkah. By 163 B.C. Antiochus IV Ephiphanes was dead and his ten-year-old son, reigning briefly as Antiochus V, concluded a peace with the Jews under the direction of his regent, Lysias. Three years later, Antiochus V was murdered by adherents of his cousin Demetrius I Soter, a heavy-handed politician, who reigned for twelve years. This volatile state of affairs held the Romans at a wary distance, at least for a while.

But the instability in Judea was not over. In 160 B.C. the new governor died in battle with the Maccabees, the followers of the sons of Mattathias of Modin, whose leader, Judah Maccabaeus, died not long after in the Battle of Elasa. Judah's older brother Simon, with his younger brother Jonathan, took over the Maccabee forces and continued their resistance to any Greco-Syrian presence in Judah, killing the new Syrian governor and keeping up their resistance to the Syrian presence so that by 143 B.C. Judah was a largely independent client state to Syria rather than a subject one. Not that Syria had only Judea to contend with, for Alexander Balas usurped the throne on the somewhat shaky claim to being the son of the late Antiochus IV and, with Roman backing, ruled Syria until 145 B.C., again increasing the Roman presence in the Middle East.

In 150 B.C. the Romans also embarked on the Third Punic War with Carthage, this time after forming an alliance with the eighty-seven-year-old King Masinna of Numidia, who sought Roman support in his war with Carthage, providing the Romans a plausible excuse to attack Carthage, which they besieged in 149 B.C.; three years later, the city was destroyed by Scipio Aemilianus' troops. Where cities were concerned, sieges were still the usual means of occupation: starve out the occupants, then raid the city and plunder it for goods as pay for the siege. It was a nasty business, but it required very little in training of troops for either side, and, if the siege succeeded, then the besiegers usually had something to show for their efforts. If the besieged city had allies who would drive off the besiegers, the demands for rewards could be as devastating to the city as those that would have been made by the original besiegers. Gradually, as defenses improved and conquest became harder, the degree of training and preparation on the part of the besiegers required more trained troops—men who would do more than camp around the walls and wait for the city's inhabitants to run out of food and water—and the business of sieges became riskier for those planning sieges.

In the same year that Scipio destroyed Carthage—146 B.C.—the Romans also annexed Macedonia and Achaea in Greece as Roman provinces, setting up a garrison and governor there and furthering the cause of Roman territorial ambition as well as testing their policies of occupation: remove the leaders; impose and enforce Roman law and Roman leadership under a local authority; tolerate local religions, unless they suborn rebellion; offer protected markets to the farmers, craftsmen, and merchants; stamp out insurrections but provide the Legions to guard and defend those loyal to Rome; interfere with the culture as little as possible; offer the client nation a voice in Roman decisions, not only to avoid trouble but also as a means of maintaining goodwill and clout; and avoid getting involved in internal squabbles except when such squabbles threatened Roman suzerainty. It took a while for them to get rid of the rough edges, but once it was in place, the formula was successful for four hundred years and held the Roman Empire together under stresses that might have torn many others apart.

In 145 B.C. Syria was once again disputed. This time things went badly for Alexander Balas, who was killed in battle and his army routed by the combined forces of Demetrius II and Ptolemy VI Philometor, whose son was advanced to the throne and ruled through a regent until 142 B.C. as Antiochus VI. His death brought Demetrius II Nicator to the throne of Syria, and under his rule, a more lasting truce was hammered out with the Judeans, permitting them to dispatch their own ambassadors and coin their own money. By 141 B.C. Jerusalem was liberated from the Syrians completely. Simon Maccabee led his army against a reduced Syrian garrison while Demetrius II Nicator was on campaign against Babylon. The new Judean state proved unusually durable for the region at that time: it lasted until 63 B.C., in spite of the murder of Simon Maccabee in 134 B.C. at the instigation of the governor of Jericho. Simon Maccabee's surviving son, John Hyrcanus, became ruler of Judea, and until his death in 104 B.C. he expanded Judean territory east of the Jordan and into the Samarian and Idumaean regions.

Upon John Hyrcanus' death in 104 B.C. his son Aristobulus I, in his very short reign, added the Galilee to Judean holdings and compelled the Hurae to become one with Judea. In 103 B.C. Aristobulus I was succeeded by his more violent and demanding brother, Alexander Jannaeus, whose reign, which lasted until 76 B.C., was marked by cruelty and strife.

The Romans had been concentrating on pushing back their European boundaries from roughly 130 B.C. until the rise of the energetic and autocratic L. Cornelius Sulla in 86 B.C., when Roman attention once again swung eastward. The Romans, during this European phase of empire building, had devoted some of their considerable energies to improving technologies, including the development of the water-driven mill, the formulation of concrete, the creation of grander public buildings in the Forum Romanum, and the improvement of radiant central heating in Roman homes. There had also been political strife, including a short-lived breakaway republic (91–88 B.C.) marked by a civil war and troop rebellion, which ended only when the King of Pontus, Mithradates VI Eupator (not to be confused with Mithradates the Great of Parthia, who died in 88 B.C., the same year as Mithradates IV Eupator began his first of three wars with Rome), annexed a number of countries in what is now Turkey: Bithynia, Cappadocia, Paphlagonia, and the majority of ports on the south side of the Black Sea all came under his rule; in the following two years, he took over a few of the eastern ports on the Black Sea as well. In 87 B.C., having brought the Roman rebels to their knees, Sulla turned his attention to Asia Minor, and in 86 B.C. Athens fell to the Roman Legions. By 84 B.C. Sulla's army had not only stopped Mithradates' conquests, it forced a peace on Mithradates that required him to give up all his conquests to Rome, that he pay a reparation of three thousand talents, and that he hand over more than eighty warships to the Romans. As an indication of Roman determination to maintain control of the region, Sulla left two legions in Syria and appointed L. Licinius Lucullus to collect more than twenty thousand talents from the occupied territories, while Sulla returned to Rome to regain the city in the Battle of the Colline Gate, which his forces won against local rebels, and then make himself dictator, a post he held for roughly three years before retiring from public life in 79 B.C. Sulla imposed reforms on the Roman Senate and established a new set of regulations for the Roman civil service; had he done so in a less high-handed way than he did, they might have lasted a little longer, but Sulla was not a man to do things by halves, and his governing style reflected this.

Rebellions, insurrections, and other opposition to Rome sprang up during the next five years: M. Aemilius Lepidus attempted to undo Sulla's reforms and raised a small army to challenge Rome. Q. Lutatius Catulus' loyal forces met him in battle in 78 B.C., and Lepidus was defeated. Still undaunted, Lepidus tried again the following year, but this time he faced Gnaeus Pompeius, whose skilled tactics drove Lepidus' men from the field and then harried Lepidus as far as Spain. Pompeius, or, as he is more usually called in English, Pompey, was now an important figure in Roman politics as well as a major political figure with an empire-wide reputation, who, four years later, at the onset of the Spartacus Rebellion, found himself with a rival for public approval: M. Licinius Crassus, who in 71 B.C. managed to defeat and capture the ragtag army of slaves, many of them former arena fighters, and gain the effusive gratitude of Rome. Pompey hastened back from Spain to help with the cleanup and then to negotiate privately with Crassus.

With such turmoil in Italy, the Middle East quickly became restive. The Parthian King, Phraates III, made several attempts in 70 B.C. to rout the Roman Legions from his land yet ultimately failed. But in Armenia, Tigranes II cemented his recent conquests and declared himself King of Kings; to cap off his achievements, he began to build his new capital on the Tigris. Whether this was intended to challenge the Romans was apparently unclear to everyone but the Romans, who dispatched L. Licinius Lucullus to deal with him. Lucullus defeated Tigranes II in 69 B.C. and marked his victory by sending vast quantities of black cherry trees from Pontus on the Black Sea back to Rome, introducing the fruit to Europe. Whether or not the cherry trees had anything to do with their discontent, the Roman troops in Armenia mutinied the following year, compelling Lucullus to retreat and emboldening Tigranes II to reassert his claim on his territories, and leading to another war, or at least a resumed one, at the end of which, in 65 B.C., Rome had five new client kingdoms (Lycia, Eastern Pontus, Cappadocia, Galatia, and Judea) and four more provinces. During the Armenian portion of this campaign, Pompey subdued Tigranes II in 66 B.C.; Tigranes II was required to pay six thousand talents for waging war on Rome. Although he agreed to the terms, he fled north into what is now Crimea the following year, where in 63 B.C. he committed suicide when he learned that his son had attempted another revolt against the Romans.

Like Lucullus, Pompey celebrated his victories by sending fruit trees and berry bushes back to Rome: Armenian apricots, Damascan plums, Trojan raspberries, Persian peaches, and other exotic provender became part of the upper-class Roman diet, as well as a constant reminder of Pompey's successes in the Middle East and an incentive for Romans to support the continued occupation. It was perhaps a fortunate thing that Q. Caecilius Metellus had rounded up many of the pirates who had been preying on Egyptian grain shipments to Rome, for the prestige of bringing new foods to Rome depended on the foods actually arriving safely. Losing trees and amphorae filled with fruit could damage the social standing of the man sending them as much as suffering a military setback could harm his reputation as a leader. Pompey's conquest in 63 B.C. of

Palestine, which he added to Syria, would have been less significant without his constant additions to Roman orchards and larders, as well as dispatching beasts to the Great Games in the Roman arenas.

By 57 B.C., thanks to the creation of a ruling triumvirate with M. Licinius Crassus, Pompey, and his father-in-law, G. Julius Caesar, the latter two had more or less squared off against each other in a bid for public popularity, political power, and military prestige. Because Caesar was popular with the common folk, he was seen as particularly untrustworthy and therefore was encouraged to build his reputation away from the city, where it was hoped he would have less political impact. Caesar's invasions of Gaul were part of his gamble to gain the kind of general support that would make it possible for him to deal with the vastly popular Pompey on equal footing. Pompey was old-money and an elitist, Caesar was nouveau riche and a populist, so they were never on the same footing, despite their making common cause with each other. By sending Caesar to Gaul the Senate hoped he would be out of the public eye and through his absence lose some of his support in Rome. This might have succeeded had Pompey had the chance to provide for Rome in the manner that Romans expected: grain shortages for Rome were looming due to piracy and a small harvest in Egypt, so Pompey was put in charge of Rome's grain supply, making him much more crucial and more visible to the city at large. Crassus was more or less allied with Caesar but knew better than to challenge Pompey in Rome when shortages were under his control. This unsatisfactory situation could not be sustained for any length of time.

The next two years, things muddled along in much the same fashion as they had been, relatively tranquil on the surface, but seething beneath. In 55 B.C. the Roman Senate made Pompey and Crassus consuls, giving Crassus all of Syria to administer and enlarging Pompey's districts in Spain; they also extended Caesar's campaign in Gaul for another five years but did not make him consul, a slap in the face that was a calculated attempt to keep him in his place. In response to his promotion, Crassus left for the Middle East at once, but Pompey remained in Rome, where in 54 B.C. Pompey's wife, and Caesar's daughter, Julia, died, a tragedy that shook both men, but for different reasons: Caesar seemed to have truly loved his daughter; Pompey lost not only a wife but also his tie to Caesar, who was then in Britain, establishing a Roman presence and setting up Roman camps, trading ports, two major roads, and supporting towns. Crassus was off plundering Jerusalem, so for a time Pompey was virtual head of Rome, but, of course, it could not last.

By 51 B.C. Caesar finished his conquest of Gaul and determined to return to Rome. The Senate, under Pompey's influence, discouraged this. Caesar pressed the matter and in 49 B.C. crossed the Rubicon to challenge Pompey's authority and begin a civil war. Pompey withdrew to Thessaly in Greece; Caesar pursued him and, in 48 B.C., defeated Pompey roundly at Pharsalus. In his hope of rallying another front of opposition to Caesar, Pompey set sail for Egypt, dispatching reports to those he thought would support him. Arriving in Egypt, Pompey was captured by the Egyptians and beheaded while Caesar pursued him, taking troops from his forces besieged through the winter at Alexandria by Ptolemy XII's troops until the spring, when Roman Legions from Asia lifted the siege; Ptolemy XII died during the winter, creating difficulties in the Egyptian nobility and disunity among the military commanders, a situation that threatened to become a long-term stalemate. Not wanting to become bogged down in Alexandria, Caesar made the young Cleopatra IV Queen of Egypt along with her younger brother Ptolemy XIII as coruler. Caesar was fascinated by Cleopatra, and their affair fed rumor mills from Britain to the Persian

Gulf. How much of their relationship was passion and how much was politics is open to conjecture, but it was clear that the Greco-Egyptian Cleopatra did change Caesar's view of Roman activities in the Middle East in general and in Egypt in particular. She clearly realized she had a formidable ally in Caesar, and as long as he remained powerful, she revered him as a leader and mentor as much as—or more than—her lover.

Knowing that the Middle East was crucial to maintaining Roman preeminence in the world, in 47 B.C. Caesar turned his forces against Pompey's supporter Pharnasus II, King of Pontus. Caesar reported his victory over Pharnasus with the terse and memorable summation: "Veni, Vedi, Vici"—I came, I saw, I conquered. With his position firmly established, Caesar returned to Rome the following year and set about a vigorous program of reforms, including a rectification of the calendar, the enlargement of the Senate to include a more balanced representation of the population, expanding the land grants available to retiring Legionaries, and extending Roman citizenship to certain Greeks, including physicians and mathematicians. By 45 B.C. he had decreased the grain dole to Romans by about half, one of the few actions he took directly against the group that had most supported him at the start of his rise to power. He reformed slave laws to avoid another Spartacus-like uprising, he increased the legal rights of women, he instituted new penalties for illegally tapping the aqueducts for irrigation, and he undertook to improve Roman relations with the Middle East. More pragmatically, he adopted his great-nephew G. Octavius as his heir, received a state visit from Cleopatra with their baby son, Caesarion, and in 44 B.C. was made dictator for life, an ironic title as it turned out, for on the first day of the Senate session in 44 B.C., the Ides of March, March 15, he was assassinated by a group of men who had given every appearance of loyalty to him.

Of course, the conspirators, having rid themselves of Caesar, took to bickering at once; M. Antonius, better known today as Marc Anthony, Caesar's master of horse, managed to come out on top for a while. When Octavius came to Rome as Caesar's heir to claim the fortune left to him, Anthony refused to provide it, fearing—correctly—that some, if not all, of the money would go to finance Anthony's overthrow. By the summer of 43 B.C., Octavius' forces had driven Anthony into Gaul and Octavius called for a special election, which resulted in Octavius and Pedius being made counsuls; this was soon modified to a second triumvirate, of M. Lepidus, M. Antonius, and G. Octavius, to reorganize the government, an arrangement that worked about as well as the first triumvirate, of Crassus, Pompey, and Caesar. The three men jockeyed for position for the next twelve years, culminating in the Battle of Actium, September 2, 31, B.C., in which the fleet of Octavius (now known as Octavian) met the Egyptian fleet, commanded by Marc Anthony, who had married Cleopatra in 36, although he had neglected to divorce his Roman wife, Octavia, sister of Octavian, which only provided Octavian with justification for his pursuit of Marc Anthony and his Egyptian queen.

The Romans succeeded in driving both Anthony and Cleopatra from the site of battle, gaining a victory for Rome and Octavian; the following year, both Anthony and Cleopatra were dead, officially from suicide, and Rome gained full control of Egypt. A document purported to be Marc Anthony's will left Egypt and half the Roman holdings in the Mediterranean Basin to Cleopatra, an interesting, if futile, gesture and one that permitted Octavian to press for a greater Roman presence in the Middle East so such an embarrassment to Rome could not happen again. In 27 B.C. Octavian had another name change when he became Imperator Caesar Octavianus, and he then modified this still further to Augustus

Caesar, by which name he is still known to history, although he himself usually preferred the less grandiose title of Princeps— "prince" and "principal" both devolve from this.

In 20 B.C. Augustus achieved peace with Parthia and recovered the standards of Crassus and Anthony and embarked on a two-pronged campaign of military expeditionism and diplomatic expansionism that would mark the Roman Empire for three centuries. One of his first endeavors in this drive was his decision to annex the Arabian Spice Kingdoms (most of the Arabian peninsula), ostensibly to reduce the exorbitant prices demanded for spices in the markets of the Roman Empire. To this end, in 24 B.C. Augustus ordered A. Gallus, Prefect of Egypt, to bring the Spice Kingdoms into the Roman fold. This first attempt in Arabia was not successful— disease and hunger exhausted the Roman troops, who were further encumbered by poor maps, inadequate or nonexistent roads, lax navigation, and simple exhaustion of men and resources. Not one to beat his head against a stone wall, Augustus abandoned his appropriation of Arabia until he and his Legions were better prepared for such a difficult undertaking. For the next several years, Gaul, Germania, Hispania, and northern Africa, where roughly two-thirds of Roman grain came from, demanded the greatest part of Augustus' attention; he left the Middle East to prefects and governors, and the presence of the Legions to maintain the status quo.

In the spring of 5 B.C., a supernova appeared in the night sky; documented by Persian, Indian, Chinese, and Korean astronomers, this two-month-long phenomenon came to be known as the star in the east that marked the birth of Jesus of Nazareth. In Rome it was interpreted as an indication that Rome's fortunes were to come from the east and its appearance was regarded as fortuitous, indicating that the setbacks in Arabia and Syria were only temporary and Rome would eventually triumph there. Some prefer to date this event to a conjunction of Saturn and Jupiter, two years before, but that event was not viewed as particularly remarkable at the time, since planetary movements were well-known and such conjunctions were interesting but not novel. The supernova was completely unexpected and therefore caused a great deal of excitement among stargazers, especially in Asia. The long-term ramifications of this event were to send shock waves through the Roman Empire two centuries later.

Upon Augustus' death in A.D. 14 at the age of seventy-six, the reins of power passed to his stepson Tiberius, who determined to carry on Augustus' policies, giving them his own spin. One of Tiberius' areas of personal interest was the Middle East: in A.D. 17 Tiberius sent his nephew Germanicus to Armenia, out at the eastern edge of the Roman Empire, to oversee the establishment of a new king there. That same year Cappadocia and Commagene in what is now eastern and central Turkey became a Roman province. During his stay in the Middle East, Germanicus behaved in such an obnoxious way that his death in Syria was considered suspicious. At first speculation was rife that the remaining royals in Armenia and Cappadocia had conspired against him, but then Piso, the Roman Legate of Syria, was accused before the Senate as having done it, and retaliation against the Syrians, Armenians, and Cappadocians was canceled. Since Piso committed suicide shortly thereafter, the accusation against him might have had some truth in it.

Events in Europe loomed over Rome, with rebellions in Gaul and Germania. Aside from skirmishes in the Dacian region near the Black Sea, in what is now eastern Romania, the Middle East remained comparatively quiet in the Roman territories. Although technically a client country, Dacia was in fact an independent buffer state receiving money from Rome to keep the border secure, an arrangement that lasted for more than a century. The Romans did begin a program of road building and the construction of fortresses at seven-league intervals (approximately twenty-one miles) along the Silk Road for the protection of merchants and the advancement of trade. Manned by Roman soldiers, these small fortresses were the beginning of a successful plan to encourage commerce and protect the Roman hegemony without interfering with local governments too intrusively.

For the Roman military, maintaining the Roman presence un-challenged was the goal for which they all worked, and most of their military organization had evolved to suit that end. The basic Roman fighting unit, the century (meaning one hundred), consisted of eighty fighting men and twenty for support, including engi-neers (seven to ten per century) whose job it was to organize and supervise the building of walls, roads, barriers, bridges, ballistae, siege machines, fortifications, and whatever else their officers or-dered. Each century had its own armorers (two or three), wheel-wrights (one or two), wagoner/harness maker (one), cooks (one or two), farrier/smith (usually one), tent maker (one), master of horses/mules (one), cobbler (one), and physicians (one was standard except in contested regions, where two were needed). The exact composi-tion of the support personnel for each century was adjusted for the locale and political climate of the Legions' service. Most Legions had separate walled camps in which they lived, with barracks, mess halls, taverns, infirmaries, storehouses, baths, smithies, stables, and wells, to minimize exposure to the populace and to ensure the safety of the soldiers, always an important consideration with Romans.

Another important improvement in Roman military equipment was the development of interlocking shields, which meant that a century, with its eighty fighting men arranged in the hollow Roman square, could lock their shields and present a nearly impregnable wall to the enemy or raise their interlocked shields over their heads and withstand barrages from above. With the shields interlocked, maintaining the line was easier, even if men were injured, for if the soldier fell, the shield would continue to be part of the defense. The Roman square allowed for uniform advancement or entrenchment, as well as providing a zone of protection in the center, where troops could be held in reserve as well as guarded during combat if they were injured. With such comprehensive support, from equipment to backup, the century was an effective, self-sufficient unit that was highly mobile, tactically adaptable, and well prepared. The other significant innovation of the century was the noncommissioned officer in charge of the unit—the centurion, or sergeant. By providing a leader for each century, a man in charge of the troops under him and responsible to the tribunes and other officers above him, the Roman chain of command from soldier to general was assured.

In Rome, Tiberius had come increasingly under the influence of the Prefect of the Praetorian Guard, a fellow named L. Aelius Sejanus. Depicted as a nasty combination of Uriah Heep and Rasputin, this relentlessly ambitious man fed Tiberius' increasing paranoia while securing the emperor's trust so absolutely that Sejanus' authority was almost the equal of Tiberius'. From A.D. 24 on, Sejanus encouraged Tiberius to retire from the demanding and dangerous city of Rome in favor of the pleasant isolation of Capreae (now Capri). In A.D. 26 Tiberius finally agreed to deputize Sejanus to represent him in Rome and took up residence on the island in the Bay of Naples, where, according to gossip, he was free to indulge himself in all manner of excesses, ranging from sexual perversions to throwing his slaves to the sharks and watching the feast, to hunting men like animals. Just how much of the scandal was true and how much conjecture is a matter of debate, but publicly at least Tiberius presented himself as a man of probity, deeply committed to Augustus' vision for the Roman Empire, and worn out in the pursuit of that vision. While a little debauchery was not seen as detrimental in an emperor, the sorts of vices attributed to Tiberius were well beyond anything the Roman public at that time would tolerate, and so it is likely that some of what was said about him was intended to keep him away from Rome, a move that was highly advantageous to Sejanus. When Tiberius finally realized what Sejanus was up to, he arranged for his arrest and execution in A.D. 31, although Tiberius declined to leave Capreae to resume his duties as emperor in Rome itself, a decision that did nothing to improve the internal state of the empire. Abroad it was another story.

Despite, or because of, Tiberius' absentee rule, diplomacy flourished in all parts of the Roman Empire. Governors were encouraged to exercise their authority without constant approval from the emperor, but they were also held accountable for all they did. In some cases this backfired, as it did in Gaul, but in the Middle East it allowed for a more adaptable posture that averted open warfare in a number of instances, most notably in treating with Artabanus, King of Parthia, who, after decades of internal dynastic strife, made peace with Rome, thereby securing the south end of the Caspian Sea as well as the borders of Armenia, Assyria, and Mesopotamia for Rome. A few prominent senators began to speak openly of the possibility of reclaiming Alexander's empire for Rome, a stance that created unease in the Middle East, and not without cause. It also fostered mutual suspicions among the major Middle Eastern kingdoms and provinces, so opposition to Rome continued sporadic and localized.

During Tiberius' long isolation, the Roman games expanded and flourished and the Middle East became important as a supplier of exotic animals and unusual fighting men. Tigers from the Caspian Sea region and India, horses from Central Asia, Bactrian camels, Asian wolves, wild boar, bears, wild cattle and goats, Indian as well as African lions, Nile crocodiles, asses, zebras, antelope of all sizes, even seals and dolphins, as well as skilled performers with animals, all were fodder for the Great Games.

Supplying men and beasts for the games could advance those willing to bear the risk and cost of acquiring and transporting this
living cargo to Rome; governors, legates, and procurators all vied
with one another in meeting this tremendous demand. Distant
Bactria, out in the wastes of what is now northern Afghanistan,
although pursuing resolute isolationism, did cater to Rome to the
extent that the animal dealers regularly shipped horses, tigers, wild
goats, and steppe ponies westward for use in the Roman arenas.

When Tiberius died in A.D. 37, he designated two heirs: his
grandson Gemellus and Germanicus' surviving son, Gaius, known
popularly as Caligula for his custom in childhood of wearing soldiers' boots (caligulae). The two seemed to get along well enough for
a time, but then Caligula fell ill—an illness that went undiagnosed
and that he attributed, upon his recovery, to an attempt to poison
him—and his cordial relationship with Gemellus was at an end.
Caligula was always a bit eccentric, but after his illness he was thoroughly unhinged. His behavior was well documented, and he
quickly made himself odious among the Roman elite, never a wise
move for an emperor. He extended his outrageous whims to propos-
ing that a godlike statue of himself be erected in Jerusalem, where
the people would be ordered to worship him. This highly incendiary notion was quashed by Petronius, then Legate of Syria, who did
his best to check another of Caligula's intended extravagances—the
systematic castration of all Jewish slaves. None of this eased tensions in the Middle East, and gradually those tensions spread to
Rome, where, on January 24, A.D. 41, a conspiracy led by Cassius
Chaerea ended Caligula's short but hectic reign.

Because of the disastrous impact Caligula had had, the Senate
proposed bringing back the old Republic, but the Praetorian Guard
wanted an emperor, and they finally turned to Germanicus' younger
brother and elevated Claudius to the purple. Scholarly, compulsive,
a stutterer, and unused to the rigors of power, Claudius steered a

somewhat erratic course through the confusion of Roman politics. He was fairly well informed about the various parts of the Roman Empire, the client nations, and the state of commerce associated with all of them. He was not always prudent about those he selected to work most closely with him. His immediate staff and his four wives all reflected this skewed judgment and contributed to the Roman perception of him as dependent and foolish. Dependent he may have been, but foolish he was not. Claudius undertook a significant reorganization of the provinces, particularly those in Greece and the Middle East, including restoring to Judea its status of procuratorial province and once again putting Macedonia and Achaea under the Senate's control. His capacity for work was formidable, and he made it a point to gather his information from more than one source, a practice that stood him in good stead except for his determination to Romanize the Britons, which he pursued doggedly but with no real success, even with the Roman conquest of Wales in A.D. 48. The most lasting impact the Romans had on the British Isles was the system of roads they built and a few impressive settlements that remain to this day.

While Claudius worked to shore up the borders of his empire, the Parthians were taking advantage of Roman road and fortress building to formalize and lock in favorable trade agreements with India and Mongolia. Travel was still a risky business, but no longer so dangerous as it had been a century earlier, thanks to guarded trade routes and walled market towns. Since the western borders of Parthia were reasonably secure and the trade fortresses were maintained by the Legions, the Parthians were able to improve their situation through improved roads and protected trading centers. While the nobility scrambled to improve their position and fortunes within the court, the government put its emphasis on commerce and on expanded markets. By strengthening its commercial ties, Parthia guaranteed it would not be wholly bound to Roman

economics, a position that stood them in excellent stead over the
next few centuries.

When in A.D. 54 Claudius died from eating poison mushrooms—
said to have been provided by his wife, Agrippina, to allow the
advancement of her sixteen-year-old son to the position of
emperor—the character of the Roman Empire had been established. In spite of various bickerings among the aristocratic and
military leaders, the empire was fairly stable and nothing more intrusive than the occasional insurrection disturbed its accord. For a
time this continued under Agrippina's son, the vastly popular
Nero, whose capacity for grandiose gestures endeared him to the
people. He did order a ban on killing animals in the arenas of
Rome, but this proved so unacceptable to the Roman people that
after just over two years he lifted the ban, to the acclaim of Rome.

As trouble erupted in Parthia, which had moved to annex Armenia, in A.D. 56, Nero sent his trusted general G. Corbulo to deal
with the problem there. Corbulo, a career military man, began by
rebuilding the Legions posted to the region, restoring morale along
with resupplying the Legions' camps. That done, he set about reclaiming Armenia and by A.D. 59 had largely accomplished the job.
Things were looking up, which added to Corbulo's reputation at
home, distressing Nero, and in A.D. 61 Nero sent his general Paetus
to relieve Corbulo and to keep him from engaging any more Roman support. Paetus suffered an embarrassing defeat at Rhandeia
in A.D. 62, and the Romans had to fall back on the resolution Corbulo had already arranged: a negotiated peace that was endorsed
when the King of Parthia, Tiridates, came to Rome to be crowned
in A.D. 63, ensuring Parthian ties with Rome and saving Roman
face at the same time.

Matters were also becoming difficult in Judea, with various
Jewish factions, including the self-identified Christians, growing
restive under Rome's demanding presence. There had been hopes

of a regional uprising that would have the support of more than four of the six major Jewish sects of the time, but neither the Libyans nor the Egyptians were inclined to try to rise against Rome, and so the Judean opposition was forced to retrench. But the Romans were aware that the Judeans were not happy and began to detain Judeans in Rome for the crime of sedition. That at least half of these Judeans followed the Christian sect meant less to the Romans than that their loyalty to Rome was suspect.

Following the catastrophic fire of A.D. 64, during which Nero did not fiddle, the fiddle not having been invented yet, but may have exclaimed Greek poetry about the fall of Troy, the young emperor set about a vigorous program of urban renewal. Since more than half the city was ashes, Nero hired architects to rebuild and improve the city. Spending lavishly (his usual style), Nero approved straightened streets, established building standards, and provided a better system of fountains. Although the Senate generally supported the rebuilding, they balked at the price until the Vestal Virgins intervened on the side of the city and Nero. Of course, this took money away from certain crucial border conflicts, most notably in lower Dacia and in Colchis, but not even the most militarily ambitious senator was in a position to thwart the Vestal Virgins, so the rebuilding of Rome continued on its magnificent   ·
realization while the people of the city rejoiced and senators muttered about neglect of the empire.

In A.D. 66 a revolt in Judea—the result of years of misgovernment by a succession of greedy bureaucrats—required military action along with careful diplomacy. T. Flavius Vespasianus, known to history as Vespasian, was dispatched, along with his son T. Flavius Vespasianus, known to history as Titus, to bring the situation under control without causing more trouble than they already had in the region, a dodgy proposition at best, but one Vespasian rose to handle in a canny way that resulted in a slow but steady campaign that ended in the recapture of Jerusalem. This careful prosecution of the reconquest improved Vespasian's status at home, and his clever manipulation of the Judeo-Egyptian grain supply to Rome increased his power on several fronts. While Rome struggled through the chaos in the wake of Nero's ordered suicide in A.D. 68, then began the next year with the execution of G. Calpurnius Piso, a Caesar so short-lived that he is usually left out of the official list and the dreadful Year of the Four (actually Five, counting Piso) Caesars, A.D. 69, Vespasian waited and bided his time while first S. Sulpicius Galba, M. Salvius Otho, and Aulus Vitellius briefly took power. Finally the Senate sent for Vespasian, proclaiming him Caesar. Leaving his son Titus to continue to deal with Judea, Vespasian returned to Rome in A.D. 70, when he, with characteristic purpose, revised the tax codes, improved the pay and provisioning of the Legions, ordered more ships built for the navy, rebuilt the Capitol, and began a spectacular new arena, the Flavian Circus, known today as the Colosseum, and in the wake of his son's triumph in Judea ordered the building of the impressive Arch of Titus in commemoration.

On August 24, A.D. 79, Mount Vesuvius erupted at about 2:00 P.M.; it had been smoking and grumbling for three days, and the wisdom of the time said that so long as the volcano smoked, it would not erupt, for that had been the pattern for more than a century, so the two towns had not bothered to evacuate, and only those worrisome people who disliked the soot actually left. The pyroclastic flow covered Pompeii and Herculaneum and sent a series of small tsunamis across the Tyrrhenian Sea that disrupted harbors along the Italian coast, Sicily, Sardinia, and Corsica. The harbor at Pompeii was lost, and the Neapolis (modern Naples) harbor was filled with ash that persisted well into the winter months. Volcanic ash covered a good portion of central Italy, and crops were damaged as far north as the Alps. For the next year Rome had to double its imports for food, and for the next dozen years the area around the volcano remained empty and devastated. The harbor at Neapolis was enlarged and improved to take the shipping no longer going to the vanished Pompeii, and gradually the disaster passed into legend as more pressing problems demanded Roman attention.

Judea remained a flash point throughout the reigns of Vespasian and his son Titus, but a kind of uneasy balance was achieved until Titus died in A.D. 81 after two years of rule. He was succeeded by his younger brother, T. Flavius Domitianus, known today as Domitian. More brusque than his father or brother, Domitian disliked the Middle East and its peoples and alternately ignored or persecuted them. Like many other emperors, Domitian grew increasingly paranoid and often banished those he felt were plotting against him or supported his enemies; he usually sent those he banished to the more backward ports on the Black Sea, where he was sure no Roman could mastermind a conspiracy without being discovered, thereby assuring himself against any danger, real or imagined. Domitian ignored the eastern side of the empire and paid little attention as Armenia slipped away from Roman control, as he believed that the people there were beyond governance and therefore deserved to be excluded from Roman protection. He also had a horror of disease and was appalled at the ongoing anthrax epidemic sweeping through the Roman Empire, seemingly unstoppable. Domitian ordered the disease be halted, but no one managed to produce a cure, and the pandemic continued. Breaking out in A.D. 80, by A.D. 83 it had reached every part of the empire and had killed in excess of eighty thousand people, according to the records in the various Roman provinces. As the disease spread eastward beyond Roman borders, it impacted the lives of the nomadic peoples of Central Asia, killing their flocks and herds as well as their human populations. Forbidden by the emperor to treat any Mongol barbarians for the disease, Chinese physicians did not provide any of their medicines, some of which were fairly effective against anthrax. Marginalized and panicked, gradually these tribes and clans banded together and began a westward migration, reaching the easternmost portions of the Roman Empire by about A.D. 120 in a trickle that would become a torrent.

In A.D. 90 the improved Roman navy finally ended the Arab monopoly of the spice trade. By building their largest cargo ships at Roman-controlled ports on the Red Sea in Egypt, then escorting them with fighting ships, the Romans made routine trade with India possible. Taking advantage of the shifts in prevailing winds, Roman ships could leave Egypt, reach India, and return to Egypt in less than a year, a vast improvement in dealing with the Spice Kingdoms. This had the effect of expanding markets once again, although in time the balance of trade proved detrimental to the Roman economy. This greater trade also spurred piracy as independent Arab, African, and Indian ships realized the huge profits to be made in taking Roman spice ships. Of all the Arab kingdoms of the time, Yemen was the most openly hospitable to pirates, and many were openly welcomed in the kingdom at the entrance to the Red Sea. A low-level arms race developed between the Roman navy and the various pirate groups, each attempting to find weapons that would give them the necessary advantage in a sea battle.

In A.D. 95 an outbreak of malaria in central Italy added to the rising mortality rates in Rome. For once the aqueduct system that had so benefited Rome now became part of the instrument of disease, providing breeding grounds for mosquitoes to carry the infection throughout the city. To escape the fever, many market farmers abandoned their fields and came to the city, swelling the ranks of the semi-employed and at the same time driving up the cost of produce as more and more of it had to be brought in from greater distances. Shortages of various fruits and vegetables made

Romans more dependent than ever on the dole, which increased the grain-and-oil rations to more than a third of the city, imposing another drain on the treasury and increasing Roman dependence on the Middle East for foodstuffs, a cycle that continued for almost two decades. This explosive state of affairs exerted itself on the Senate and the emperor, who became more paranoid as the death toll in Rome rose and dread of contagion became far more pervasive than fear of invasion. For the next decade Rome was caught up in a cycle of annual outbreaks of fever and anthrax, which faded after time but did not disappear, imposing more demands on the Roman public health system and on the capacity for Rome to care for its stricken people, a state of affairs for which many blamed the emperor.

But Domitian was not, as it turned out, paranoid enough: in September A.D. 96 Domitian was assassinated at the instigation of his empress and her confederates in the Senate. His successor, M. Cocceius Nerva, a former Roman consul, began by rescinding the exile of most of Domitian's so-called enemies, restoring as much of their lands and fortunes as remained; he also reformed the Roman postal system, establishing a more regular course of delivery to the outlying regions of the empire. In A.D. 97 he summoned General M. Ulpius Trajanus to Rome and officially made him his heir, a move that proved almost providential, for Nerva died the following year, at age sixty-three, and M. Ulpius Trajanus became Trajan, a Caesar of good sense and sound fiscal policies, at least for the first fourteen years of his nineteen-year reign. He began domestically with a beautification project for Rome, having many of its public buildings, made of brick and/or concrete, clad in marble, and provincially by bringing Dacia firmly into the Roman fold, making it a province, not just a client nation, upon the defeat of King Decebalbus in A.D. 106. Aware that the Black Sea had been neglected during Domitian's and Nerva's reigns, Trajan adopted a much more hands-on policy for the region. Once again he sent Legions to annex rambunctious Armenia to Rome (A.D. 114) and made provision for the garrisoning of the country; this entailed raising taxes in Italy, a move that was offset by the potentials for commerce expected to develop from the Armenian trade routes. Next, in A.D. 115, he ordered troops into Mesopotamia and claimed land all the way to the Tigris River.

After making Syria a Roman province, Trajan went on to the Persian Gulf and established the Roman province of Parthia. He guaranteed the Parthians a degree of autonomy usually not granted to Roman provinces, but he was persuaded to accept the unique situation Parthia had and relaxed the terms of the treaty, permitting the Parthians to maintain their own army next to the Roman Legions stationed there. Convinced that the east was secure, Trajan, now sixty-three, headed for home. He never made it. At Selinus in Cilicia, in what is now southern Turkey, he died August 8, A.D. 117. His successor, P. Aelius Hadrianus, was informed of Trajan's death and his elevation at Antioch in Syria, three days after Trajan died. News of the emperor's death spread rapidly, thanks to Roman courier services. In response to the news of Trajan's demise, Jews living throughout the Middle East attacked Greeks and Romans, in some instances killing significant numbers of them and claiming the end of Western rule, a move that was somewhat premature.

Facing this crisis, Hadrian took the most direct step he could think of and debased the Roman coins as a means of getting money without increasing taxes, a fine method in the short run but creating a long-term problem that would see the Roman denarius lose half its actual value in less than a century. Hadrian took a cohesive approach to rule and in his first year gathered assessments and reports on the state of the empire, including the readiness of Legions and the state of Roman administration, restoring the uniformity of Roman law throughout the empire, and once again standardizing customs regulations, as well as instituting new ordinances for harbors. From Britain to the Red Sea, Hadrian began a vigorous attempt at creating cohesion throughout the empire. He ordered a wall built in the north of Britain to hold out the fractious Picts, then the most aggressive of the Scottish tribes; Hadrian's Wall is still there today. In Parthia, he negotiated a peace with the king in order to avert rebellion and war, although the hawkish Senate decried his efforts. He attempted to create a commission on public health to evaluate the whole empire, but this met with such vehement resistance that he was forced to abandon his plan, which proved to be poor timing for everyone.

Just as things were steadying down, in A.D. 125, northern Africa was struck by a locust invasion that left everything from the Red Sea to the Nile stripped, which meant that half the grain dole for Rome was gone. This alone would have been disastrous, but the locusts were followed by an outbreak of disease that may have killed as many as five hundred thousand in the course of a year. This renewed Roman fear of epidemics and, soon after, of famine, and the city suffered some of both. For the next dozen years Romans were understandably skittish, and the increasing need for imported food only made the situation worse.

With a degree of quiet restored to the Middle East, Hadrian devoted himself to completing temples in Greece, improved harbors in Pontus and Byzantium, and ordered repairs to the trade-route fortresses protecting the Asian roads. Thinking that he had secured the Middle East, he was unprepared for the Jewish uprising in A.D. 132, led by Simon Bar Kochba, and did not move quickly enough to keep the rebellion from spreading as two Roman Legions were fought to a standstill and another was defeated. Three years later, Bar Kochba was killed and his movement soundly vanquished. In retaliation for allowing the insurrection to occur, Hadrian ordered Jerusalem destroyed and a new, Roman city built in its place. He ruled that Jews were not to be allowed into the new Jerusalem, unless they were of a sect that did not support the rebellion. The most prominent of these sects was the Christians, now composed not only of Jews but with a strong admixture of Greeks and Romans.

In July A.D. 138, Hadrian died, providing not only a heir but also a line of succession: T. A. F. Boionus Arrius Antoninus and M. Annius Verus; as his original heir, L. Celonius Commodus, had predeceased him six months before, securing the Antonine line seemed a much more immediate concern than it had been. Antoninus was ordered to adopt L. Celonius Commodus' son, A. Aurelius Commodus, as well as M. Annius Verus, to guarantee the succession. In order to honor Hadrian and to make the succession official, Antoninus, as one of his first deeds, went to the Senate to ask that godhood be granted Hadrian, for which affectionate devotion Antoninus was given the appellation Pius. He remained in Rome for almost all of his reign and proved a capable administrator—not particularly imaginative, but thorough and even-tempered. His devotion to public works included repair of sewers, aqueducts, roads, walls, and baths, which brought down the instances of malaria within the city. Both arts and sciences advanced during this time, not just in Rome but in most of the empire. The formidable Roman system of roads was extended and improved, and for a time the debasement of Roman coins was stopped, with a silver content of the denarius remaining steady at 75 percent. He authorized a restructuring of the tariff schedules for all imported goods and standardized customs regulations. Trade flourished throughout the empire, and only two years of bad weather marred the general prosperity of Antoninus' reign.

Antoninus' adopted sons served as co-emperors: M. Annius Verus took the name of Marcus Aurelius for his reign; L. Aurelius Verus took his first name, Lucius, as his imperial name. The two worked fairly well together, which was crucial, since this was a more turbulent time than Antoninus' reign had been; Legions returning from the Middle East brought with them a disease, which may have been smallpox or possibly bubonic plague, that spread rapidly through the empire, causing a great loss of life everywhere, as well as causing localized famines, disrupting trade from China to Britain, and damaging the economy. Epidemic disease had hit the empire before, but never so calamitously as at this time. The Senate wanted to halt all dealings with the Middle East until the contagion had passed, but it proved impracticable to do this, since Rome was so heavily dependent on the Middle East for food. When trouble broke out in Parthia, in A.D. 162, Lucius Verus was sent to deal with it and, after a violent, broad-fronted campaign, set up a puppet king in Armenia, as well as bestowing provincial status on Mesopotamia, assuring the Middle East a greater say in administration. It was a reasonable quick-fix solution, and one that provided the Middle East some needed support for its plague-depleted armies.

From A.D. 165 to 167 outbreaks of this epidemic crippled various regions of the empire. In spite of this, Rome was able to hold off the first serious barbarian assault on the city by the Marcommani in A.D. 167, during which some of the aqueducts and other water-support systems outside the walls were damaged. In A.D. 168 Marcus Aurelius and Lucius Verus undertook an intensive campaign to contain the Marcommani, pulling troops out of the Middle East to tend to the situation in Italy. A peace of sorts was concluded in the fall of A.D. 168, but it proved inadequate, for the following spring, shortly after the death of Lucius Verus, from either poison or appendicitis, another campaign against the Marcommani was undertaken, this one lasting for three years, ending only when disease had reduced the Marcommani soldiers to nothing more than a few squads of sick men. The Legions also suffered from the sickness, and the two armies were exhausted in every sense by the time a more stringent peace was concluded.

But pulling soldiers out of the Middle East proved a poor strategy. Not only did it lead to a deterioration of Roman authority, it left the various client governments without necessary support, and that created a climate ripe for insurrections. Had the peoples of the Middle East been culturally inclined to undertake unified action, the Roman presence might have ended before A.D. 170. Between epidemics and crises in Europe, the Legions were spread dangerously thin in the eastern provinces. But since most of the various groups distrusted one another as much or more than they distrusted Rome, the opportunity was lost in a number of small, regional brushfire conflicts. Then, in A.D. 175, in answer to rumors that Marcus Aurelius was dead, the Legions in Asia under Avidus Cassius rebelled against Rome. Cassius was proclaimed Marcus Aurelius' successor and emperor. Upon hearing that Marcus Aurelius was alive, the same officers who had supported Cassius now killed him and sent his head to Marcus Aurelius as proof of their loyalty. Parthia, which had hoped to gain total independence from Rome and a slice of the eastern empire, was especially disappointed by this turn of events, and the Roman presence once again became problematic.

Although Rome was noted for its religious and cultural tolerance, in A.D. 177 Marcus Aurelius took action against the Christians in Rome—now no longer a sect of Judaism but a separate and distinct religion—because the Christians refused to worship the deified emperors, a stance that undermined civil authority and was seen as a form of sedition. Christians were not forbidden to worship their God, but they were expected to honor the Roman emperors in the name of civic duty; their refusal to do so constituted a serious crime, and they were treated accordingly. By that time, Roman Christianity had split into two sects: Peterine (essentially

Jewish, communal, and Messianic) and Paulist (essentially diverse, hierarchical, and Apocalyptic). Over the next century, the Paulists became the authority of the Church, and the Peterine branch survived only in the Middle East, associated with the Gnostic Christian sects.

Other than the two primary western sects of Christianity, there was the Coptic form of the faith principally in Egypt, Abyssinia, and Ethiopia. In the Middle East, Christianity was absorbed into the teaching of Mani in the third century. According to his biographer, Mani was born near Babylon in 216 in a Christian community. At the onset of puberty, Mani experienced a vision and became a Gnostic holy man. Mani preached the messages of his angelic visions—much as Muhammad did four centuries later—gathering followers. Mani's religion contained Christian elements as well as Buddhist ones, and many aspects of Persian religion based on Zoroastrianism. Because of the spread of Mani's faith, after its initial regional impact Christianity never became much more than localized communities in the central Middle East.

Marcus Aurelius died of epidemic fever in A.D. 180 near modern-day Vienna and was succeeded by his son L. A. Aurelius Commodus, a man who proved as reckless as his father was restrained. Three years later, Commodus survived the first of several assassination attempts—this one supported by his sister and a group of powerful senators—and dealt with those guilty with utmost ferocity. He went on to court the people of Rome by offering them extravagant and increasingly violent entertainments in the arenas of Rome, which drained the public treasury. He ordered taxes raised in the provinces to cover his expenses, and he confiscated lands and goods of those he identified as enemies, using that wealth to replenish the depleted treasury. Because of his profligacy, the shipments of grain to Rome from the Middle East were cut back, and in A.D. 189 bread riots in Rome resulted in the killing of Cleander,

Prefect of the Praetorian Guard, who supervised the distribution of grain and oil in Rome. On the last day of A.D. 192, Commodus was killed by his Praetorians, whose Prefect, Laetus, was on the emperor's latest execution list.

Another year of multiple emperors followed: P. Helius Pertinax was elected by the Senate, reportedly against his wishes. His reign was short due to his draconian economic reforms, and upon his death in March, this time the imperial leadership was auctioned off to the highest bidder, thereby avoiding another financial crisis. Didius Julianus paid over 300 million sesterces (roughly the modern buying power of $4 billion) to become Caesar, and his rule was immediately challenged by legates in Britain, Syria, and Pannonia; the governor of Mesopotamia declared the advancement of Julianus to be illegal and offered his support to a qualified successor. L. Septimus Severus, then posted to the Danube region of Pannonia in what is now Croatia, offered his troops generous bonuses for accompanying him to Rome. They covered more than eight hundred miles in forty days, arriving at Rome on June 1, arrested Julianus, who was taken to the baths and killed, and Septimus Severus declared himself Caesar. Most of the European possessions of the Roman empire accepted this new leader without too much dispute, but the Legate of Syria, C. P. Niger Justus, continued his resistance, with help from Arab merchants and Greek landholders. The next year, 194, Septimus Severus took his troops to Antioch, captured Justus, and executed him, then authorized an inquiry into who had supported Justus. As a result of Septimus Severus' discoveries, in 196, Byzantium was sacked by Roman Legions, its walls pulled down, and its harbor reduced in punishment for giving aid to Justus.

Once all challenges to his rule were over, Septimus Severus proved adept at dealing with economic affairs, particularly those of the Middle East and north Africa. He instituted court reforms that streamlined civil suits, and he expanded the rights and responsibilities of regional magistrates. In addition, he enlarged the advisory capacity of the ambassadors from the provinces and client nations, all of which proved useful. Not all his decisions were equally wise: he devalued the Roman coins, the silver in a denarius dropping to 50 percent by the end of his reign. This helped to avert a general downturn in the economy throughout the empire, but it paved the way for greater debasements during the third century, a move that overall damaged the fortunes of Rome.

Although Septimus Severus was inclined to be helpful to northern Africa, since he came from there, he was wary of the Middle East and made a point to make sure his legates and governors did not get along. He wanted to avoid another opportunity for rebellion and believed that so long as the Romans serving there were at cross-purposes, he and his supporters would be safe. In order to streamline the government and reduce costs, he privatized the civil service, instituting a 4 percent surcharge on all legal transactions, from the recording of transfers of goods, to probating wills, to validating marriage contracts, which became the source of income for all clerks and bureaucrats and quickly led to widespread corruption. By the time he died at Eboracum (modern York) in Britain in February of A.D. 211, Septimus Severus had largely stopped the erosion of imperial power, but at a cost that continued to escalate.

His oldest son, Augustus, called Caracalla for his fondness for the hooded tunic worn in Gaul *(caracallus)*, became Caesar and began his reign by extending Roman citizenship to all free men of the empire, with a few specific exceptions, such as Egyptians and the Mythras-worshippers on Cyprus. This made for more uniform taxation throughout the empire and led to an increase in Romanization of much of the Middle East. Caracalla left an impressive monument to his reign in Rome: the Baths of Caracalla, a huge complex covering six acres is the most impressive group of public buildings outside of the Forum Romanum and the Colosseum.

Once again there was trouble in Parthia, and once again the emperor prepared to take to the field to enforce the Roman claim on the country. But the officers who were to accompany him instead killed him on April 8, A.D. 217, and elevated M. Opellius Macrinus, who quickly made himself odious by reducing the pay to the Legions and was killed not far from Antioch on June 8, A.D. 218. Before the Middle East could revolt, a fourteen-year-old boy said to be Caracalla's son and grandnephew by marriage of Septimus Severus, V. Avitus Bassanius, who took the name of his Syrian sun god for his reign: Heliogabalus. In his four short years as Caesar, he exhausted the treasury, debased the coins to 43 percent silver, and increased taxes on merchants to almost double what they had been in the reign of Septimus Severus. Heliogabalus' extravagances were monumental, and his conduct was scandalous, even to the Romans who claimed to be inured to such things. His capable mother and grandmother wielded the real power, but as a figurehead Heliogabalus left a lot to be desired, and as his popularity eroded, his family shifted support away from him. When the Praetorian Guard murdered him in March of A.D. 222, he was succeeded by another fourteen-year-old—his cousin and adopted son, Alexander Severus, who further devalued the denarius to 35 percent silver, a move that brought crushing inflation to the Roman Empire. Dominated by his mother, Julia Mamaea, Alexander Severus was apparently content to leave the hard parts of ruling to her and to devote himself to grand occasions and beautifying the city.

Because of the lack of attention from Rome, Persia finally made itself independent of Roman influence in A.D. 226, when Ardashir, whose grandfather had been able to seize the region around Persepolis from Artabanus and to hold it against repeated attempts to reclaim it, finally killed Artabanus and became the founder of the Sassanian dynasty, which ruled Persia for almost four centuries. This led to a more restive state in the Middle East and some dismay in Rome, as the taxes and tariffs from the eastern ends of the empire dropped off and not only less money but also fewer goods made their way from Asia to Rome. Small revolts against taxation began to erupt sporadically throughout Syria and Mesopotamia, none so widespread as to constitute out-and-out rebellion but sufficient to disrupt trade and increase the rising rate of inflation.

Severus Alexander's reign ended in March of A.D. 235 when his troops killed him and proclaimed G. J. Verus Maximinus Caesar. This rule was challenged three years later when Roman citizens in northern Africa declared their proconsul, M. A. Gordianus Africanus, to be Caesar. While the Senate supported Gordianus and a majority of the Roman provinces also endorsed his claim, those who allied with Maximinus took their argument directly to Gordianus, besieging him at Carthage for over a month. Upon learning that his son had fallen defending him, Gordianus committed suicide. At that point, the Roman populace settled on yet another fourteen-year-old boy to be Caesar—Gordianus' grandson M. Antonius Gordianus III—and left it to the Praetorians to dispose of Maximinus.

Instability on this scale took a major toll on the Roman Empire: the borders were eroding as a number of the client nations and buffer states began to pull away from Rome. This was particularly apparent in the Middle East, with Persia as an example to follow. Armenia once again broke most of its ties with Rome, permitting only a minor Roman presence within its borders and minimizing the role of Roman magistrates to matters of Roman trade, not local dealings. Faced with the debased Roman coinage, some of the more distant provinces began to issue their own money as a way of protecting their regional economies.

Taking advantage of the spreading disorder, the Persians in A.D. 243 began an assault on Roman territory, which Gordianus III met the following year, his Legions not only holding their own but also pushing the Persians back across the Euphrates River. The Persian defeat at the Battle of Resaena capped the Roman triumph. But the Legions had not been paid their salaries for some while, and now, flushed with success, the troops demanded their money. When none was forthcoming, they killed Gordianus III and hailed M. Julius Philippus of Arabia Caesar. In order to keep the support of his troops, Philippus made peace with the Persians, accepting terms ultimately damaging to Rome, but it provided money to be paid to the Legions. With the Roman denarius now composed of only 1 percent silver, pay in the form of loot was increasingly necessary.

Upon reaching Rome and in an effort to solidify his position as emperor, Philippus sponsored a lavish display of games, chariot races, musical competitions, and grand civic processions to mark the one thousandth anniversary of the founding of Rome (in 753 B.C.). The grandiose Roman celebration of A.D. 248 was one of the last to be held to mark an imperial occasion. But it proved insufficient to gain the loyalty of all Romans. The following year, an uprising in the Balkans among Roman troops was contained; loyal Legions proclaimed G. M. Q. Traianus Decius emperor, and he and his troops marched toward Rome, meeting Philippus at Verona, where Decius emerged victorious. One of Decius' first official acts was to send back pay to Legions throughout the empire and to initiate a system of bonuses for actions above and beyond the call of duty.

Several of the Roman provinces in the Middle East had now become virtual fiefdoms of their governors and legates, operating with only the most minimal supervision and support from Rome. Many of the Roman authorities had married their sons and daughters to local aristocrats, cementing the bonds between Middle Eastern clan and Roman gens, and while gaining more support for Rome from the clans involved, this practice also committed the Romans to the tribal allegiances that still continued as the base of Middle Eastern politics.

Not that things were much better in Europe. Decius, on campaign against the Goths in A.D. 251, was betrayed and killed by his general G. V. Trebonianus Gallus, who claimed the title of Caesar only to lose it less than two years later to P. Licinius Valerianus, who, as Valerian, reigned for seven hectic years marked by epidemic disease, unstable prices, increased banditry and piracy, and obduracy in the Senate. To make things worse, a minor climate shift added to the stresses on the Roman Empire, with cool summers and dry winters once again throwing Rome back into dependence on the Middle East for food. But this time the Middle East was also caught up in the change in weather and was in no condition to supply food to Rome, lacking sufficient amounts in any of the provinces to feed its own populations.

In an attempt to hold the eastern empire, Valerian led his troops at Edessa, where he not only lost against the Persians, he was taken prisoner while engaged in peace negotiations. This time there was no chance of ransoming the emperor, and his son, P. L. Egnatius Gallienus, tried to carry on in his father's stead, but that proved increasingly difficult as a swarm of would-be Caesars continued to make their claims from the various provinces, usually with a Legion or two to support them. In the meantime, the epidemic—one that caused bleeding from the nose, the eyes, and the lungs—continued to spread, taking an especially heavy toll in Egypt, where a quarter of the population succumbed over a period of six years. With its apocalyptic visions and promises of salvation, Christianity saw a dramatic increase in conversions during the epidemic; those accused and condemned for sedition were now officially designated martyrs to their faith.

Gallienus, in what was becoming a tradition, was killed by his own soldiers in A.D. 268. The self-proclaimed Caesar, Aureolus, had barely celebrated his victory when he was killed by another claimant to the office—M. Aurelius Claudius, known as Gothicus for his successful battles against the Goths. Gothicus died of plague in A.D. 270 and his brother Quintillus was hailed as Caesar in his place, just shortly before his own Legion deserted him. Committing suicide rather than face execution, Quintillus was eventually succeeded by L. Domitius Aurelianus.

With such bloody chaos in Italy, the Middle East began to pull away from Rome and Roman organization. In A.D. 273 Palmyra was sacked by the Romans to stop its revolt from spreading along the trade routes. The Legions were allowed to pillage and plunder as compensation for short pay, but this did not ensure their loyalty as it had in the past. Roman installations in Transylvania and along the Danube were abandoned rather than permit them to become outposts for regional insurrections. With the grudging support of the Senate, Aurelianus managed to push forward improved fortifications of Rome's walls and gained authorization to lead his Legions on an invasion of Persia. Continuing in the now-ordinary style of advancement, Aurelianus was killed by his officers before he could depart for the Middle East. His successor was the elderly Senator M. Claudius Tacitus, who managed to rule for almost a year before the Praetorian Guard killed him for ordering the Guard to escort him to Antioch, where an epidemic was raging, having spread in three years from Mesopotamia to Byzantium, where, between illness and desertion, the Roman Legions were reduced to less than half of their original numbers. Tacitus was followed in office by his brother M. Annius Florianus, who had a reign of less than six months; he was murdered and succeeded by M. Aurelius Probus.

Under pressure of invasion by the Alans, the garrisons of Pontus and Cappadocia were on the edge of mutiny, but this time the

Romans had found an emperor who could deal with the demands made of him: he refortified Roman Legions along the borders and drove a number of barbarian groups out of Italy, Greece, and modern-day Turkey. But it was not to last. His troops, possibly out of political habit, assassinated him in A.D. 282 and supported the Praetorian Prefect M. Aurelius Carus, who died of illness the following year and was succeeded by his son M. A. Numerius Numerianus, who had an equally short reign, being killed in A.D. 284. Finally, G. A. V. Diocletianus Jovius was proclaimed emperor by the Legions at Chelcedon. Diocletian was content to remain in Turkey for a good portion of his reign, and his appointed co-emperor, M. A. V. Maximianus Herculius, took up official residence in Mediolanum (Milan today), away from the turmoil and disease of Rome.

By A.D. 293 the long decades of debased coinage caught up with Rome, and the empire suffered a monetary collapse that spread throughout the empire and beyond. The damage to trade was immediate and severe. Roman coins were no longer accepted currency, and as a result, tariffs dropped and taxes, even when collected, were without value. From his luxurious villa in Bithynia, Diocletian issued limits on the prices of goods and services, with the intention of ending the erosion of the economy, but his orders made little impact in the Middle East and none whatsoever in Italy, and the spiral continued. Not even the building and opening of the Baths of Diocletian in Rome was sufficient to save his reign, and so, in A.D. 305, Diocletian abdicated in favor of co-emperors Galerius Valerius Maximanus, a Greek, and F. Valerius Constantius, from what is now Serbia.

As is often the case during political meltdown, the major wealth and power was now in the hands of landowners and successful merchants. Due to the monetary failure in Rome, many of these men based themselves away from Rome: in Hispania, Gaul, Egypt, and the Middle East, where they found protection for what little remained of Roman wealth and the opportunity to consolidate what they had preserved. Many of these landowners controlled whole crops within a region and became food brokers of tremendous importance. Merchants with ships and caravans rose to prominence within trading cities and as often as not profited from the regulations they themselves enacted. Locally, trade had fallen off, a victim of epidemics as much as collapsing currencies, and long-distance trade was once again a very risky business, requiring significant investment in protection. The Senate no longer had the administrative authority it had once commanded, and Rome itself was open to attack due to the shrinking size of the Legions and the corruption rife in the Praetorian Guard.

Upon the death of Constantius in northern Britian in 306, his troops proclaimed his son, F. Valerius Constantinus, Caesar. In response, Galerius in Rome advanced F. Valerius Severus as his co-emperor, which resulted in the Praetorians supporting M. Aurelius Valerius Maxentius as Caesar. The next year, Severus died, of either disease or poison, and Galerius, with another military man from the Balkans, F. G. Valerius Licinianus, held on to power until A.D. 324, largely ignoring anything beyond the Italian peninsula, including F. Valerius Constantinus, more or less ruling Gaul and Britain without opposition. By A.D. 311, upon the death of Galerius and the revelation of plots against Constantinus, that indifference to matters beyond Italy brought Constantinus south. In late October of A.D. 312 at the Battle of Milvian Bridge, Constantinus was victorious over Maxentius and became Emperor of Rome. Flushed with his accomplishment, in A.D. 314 Constantinus took on his co-emperor, Licinius, and regained a significant portion of the Balkans for Rome but was unable to capture Licinius, who continued to cause problems for the next decade. Constantine secured his rule as quickly as possible with a few timely executions and orders of exile. He then set about rectifying the abuses of the past six decades. He issued new, full-value coins, restored the dole, standardized taxation, and brought the civil service back under governmental pay and control. After a long history of changing religious affiliations to suit the occasion, Constantine became a Christian and recognized the Church as the spiritual authority for his reign, including forbidding labor on the Sabbath.

In A.D. 324 Licinius was executed and Constantine's rule was no longer disputed. But Constantine knew which way the wind was blowing, and in A.D. 330 his new capital, Constantinople, which had been the Greco-Roman city of Byzantium, was dedicated. Rome was no longer the center of its empire, as power and money shifted eastward, to the city at the link of Europe and Asia.

Byzantium and Islam

*The Byzantine Empire, the Crusades,
and the Mongol Invasion*

WITH the Roman Empire fatally divided, the Middle East again asserted itself to gain independence from what had become a social, military, and economic burden. Regional rulers no longer strove to support the Legions, or to collect taxes and customs duties for the imperial coffers, and did so with the knowledge that the Romans had internal problems to occupy them and thus would not be inclined to impose upon their now-reluctant client countries. By 333, the western Roman Empire was pulling back from its farthest eastern and northwestern borders, leaving Britain and the outer reaches of Gaul and Germania in an effort to preserve those provinces closer to Italy, where the barbarians were gathering to make all-out assaults on Rome; a quarter century after Roman withdrawal, the Picts crossed Hadrian's Wall and began bloody raids in York and Northumberland. Only the hope of making the eastern and western empire into a unified body again gave solace to the people of Rome.

Constantine died in May 337, and the empire remained split on a north–south line through the Balkan Mountains and the Adriatic Sea to Libya. There would be no reunification of the Roman Empire, although the co-emperor status continued with Rome for another eighty years. Since Constantine had executed his son by his first wife, his half—the eastern or Byzantine half—of the empire was left to his sons by his second wife, Fausta, and these young men had to vindicate their claim at once, which, thanks to their mother, they were ready to do. The Byzantine Empire was in its infancy, but it was plagued by all the problems the Roman Empire had encountered in the Middle East. There was already trouble brewing with Persia, and this was beginning to demand the full attention of the Byzantine army, which was a restructured version of the Legions, organized along more authoritarian lines, with fewer support personnel included in the companies. Most of what had been the engineers of the old Legions were now a separate body of men, and the Byzantine army was dominated by its fighting units, similar in structure to the Persians' armies. Most construction was left to slaves and contracted local work gangs.

Roman laws were changing to accommodate this new Roman Empire in the East: slaves no longer had the right to purchase their freedom or to sue their masters for abuse. Women could not control their own property or money unless specifically provided for by their fathers under terms approved by a magistrate. Once a woman married, her estates and fortune passed to the hands of her husband. Foreigners could not become Roman citizens—which meant Byzantine citizens—and only men who owned property were allowed to vote. In addition, bishops were given certain magisterial powers, granting civil power to the Christian Church.

In order to stop the religious monopoly of Christianity, which he felt damaged the people, in 361 the Byzantine emperor Julian attempted to reintroduce paganism, but since almost all the middle-level bureaucracy was controlled by Christians, his success was limited and short-lived. Those Byzantines who did not support Christianity began to be excluded from advanced posts, and the approval of Church authorities was increasingly made a condition of promotion. Commercial negotiations now favored Christians above members of any other religion, making for a two-tiered tax base and creating outposts of the faith throughout the trading world to take advantage of it. The Apostle Thomas had gone to India to preach, and between his expansion and the slightly later missionary zeal of the Nestorians, small enclaves of Christians reached along the Silk Road from Constantinople to Bei-jing.

But just as the Byzantines managed to make a less-than-satisfactory peace with Persia, a new peril arose in Asia: the Huns were headed west, and by 360 the first companies of this fierce migration had reached the Carpathian Mountains and had begun to fan out into Europe. This was not simply military adventurism; it was the wholesale movement of a large population, most of which came from Mongolia. Initial reports described ferocious fighting, but against fairly small mounted armed companies, which led the Byzantines to suppose the Huns could be contained without a great expenditure of money or military personnel, so they provided only minimal reinforcements of their border installations, which quickly collapsed as the Huns increased in numbers and came hurtling into Europe, driving those in their path westward before them. By 372 they had crushed the Alans and the Ostrogoths and driven the Visigoths away from their towns on the Dneister River, sending the surviving Visigoths ahead of them into the heart of Europe, where the Italian Romans were unable to stop their advance, and in August of 376, at the Battle of Adrianople, the Visigoths killed the western emperor, Gratian, further weakening an already weak Roman military hold on the crumbling western empire.

The next year, Shah Shapur II died, leaving Persia with more power and securer borders than it had had since before Alexander, with Armenia and the ancient city of Susa now firmly back in Persian hands. Thanks to diplomatic missions to China, trade was on the increase through Persia; the fur traders from Russia had begun to bring their goods to market at ports on the Caspian Sea, which benefited Persia still more. With so many developments in their favor, the Persian Empire, at the edge of the Huns for a time, flourished despite continued clashes with the Byzantines, but by 390 the Huns were beginning to invade Persian territory.

The eastern and western Roman empires were now almost at each other's throats, and in 395 the split was made official, although theoretically temporary. By mutual consent, the Byzantine Empire was politically and militarily separate from Rome, and the rulers of each no longer shared duties and responsibilities with each other. In the most immediate repercussion, this allowed more expansion for Persia as the remnants of the Legions were withdrawn from the eastern provinces and replaced with the Byzantine army. It also brought a new level of internal strife to Syria, as the Roman presence continued to fade and to be absorbed into the Syrian culture even as the Byzantines sought to establish their empire as separate and distinct from the Roman one. Syrian cities burgeoned as the trade routes brought the treasures of Russia and Asia to their markets and as scholars came to study as much as they could of these new traders.

Money, goods, and culture had been bound to Rome from Europe, northern Africa, and Asia for almost five hundred years; now the Middle East became the center toward which commerce and learning flowed. The transition was a gradual one, but by 406, when the Vandals crossed the Rhine bound for Spain and then northern Africa, which they reached in 429, the tip of economic and cultural balance was clearly in place, and Rome sank into a decline that would mark the city for about seven hundred years. In 406 the Visigoths under Alaric besieged Rome and breached the walls, demanding tribute not to destroy the place (they sacked it in 410); in 408 the Byzantine Emperor Arcadius died and was succeeded by his seven-year-old son, Theodosius II, making the break between the two empires final and irrevocable, little as either side wanted to admit it.

With the Huns moving farther into Byzantine territory, the need to defend the northern provinces became paramount; more Byzantine troops were pulled from the southern forts and cities to shore up the fortifications against the Huns and other barbarian bands wanting to get their piece of the Roman Empire before it was picked clean, which put an intense demand on the Byzantines, not only to hold on to what they had but to stem the invading tide. The Huns were slowed at last in 425, when their advance on Constantinople had to be abandoned due to an epidemic disease that ravaged their numbers and made military forays impossible. The illness reached Constantinople, but by that time it was on the wane, and the city suffered only minor outbreaks. The main body of the Huns continued westward toward the center of Europe, driving the remaining Goths before them.

As Rome slowly succumbed to increasingly violent waves of barbarian invaders, Byzantium not only held on to its half of the Roman Empire; it expanded its holdings and, from the capital of Constantinople, continued its dominance of the Mediterranean Basin from Syria and northern Africa through the Black Sea to the western shores of the Caspian Sea. This created a powerful quasi-theocracy in the Middle East, one that was tied to every Greek and Armenian Orthodox community throughout the region, giving the Orthodox Christians an edge over the various other groups: Arabs, Syrians, Egyptians, Armenians, Albanians, Cappadocians, Dacians, and Georgians all found themselves under fairly constant attack from many directions. Increasingly they relied on Byzantine communications and organization left over from the Roman occupation, keeping the alliances that Rome had established as a means of maintaining their security against various groups of barbarians who were coming out of Central Asia and into the greater Mediterranean Basin, fleeing the general collapse of their homelands and seeking more viable lands to settle.

In 433 Attila became leader of the Huns, and for the next twenty years he continued an aggressive campaign through central and western Europe. Bribed by the Pope to spare Rome (and advancing the Church's prestige politically), Attila's forces sacked major centers in Germania and Gaul. At the Battle of Châlons in France in 451, Attila was defeated by a combined army of Romans and Visigoths. Battle was not the only cause for the defeat: once again the Huns were suffering from an epidemic that may have been cholera, and the number of fighting men was reduced, as was the population in general. Owing to the disease, the Huns were dangerously low on food as well, and upon the death of Attila in 453 the Huns were run out of Italy by Roman, Visigothic, and other barbarian forces. Those Huns remaining went eastward, toward Byzantium, where in 466 they were met by the army of Emperor Leo I and driven out of Dacia.

Leo I created a temporary truce with the Romans by making his best general Roman emperor for long enough to take on the Vandals, now invading from their positions in north Africa. Leo ordered a fleet of Byzantine ships to intercept the Vandals on their way to Italy, but the fleet was ambushed by the Vandals, resulting in the loss of half the ships in the Byzantine fleet. The Vandals, with the help of the Goths, now turned their attention from Rome to Byzantium. Reluctant to take on another naval battle, the Byzantines came up with another tactic: as the Vandal navy made its approach to Constantinople, the Gothic leader Ardaburius was murdered and the attack was called off.

Persia, profiting by the unresolved upheavals in the west, secured its Caspian territories and began a program of forced conversion to Zoroastrianism; Christians unwilling to convert were sold into slavery, usually in the Central Asian markets. Those who were obdurate were killed or sent to work in quarries or mines, which amounted to the same thing. With Persian support to the regional centers, the campaign against Christians spread to Mesopotamia, and only an outbreak of smallpox in 460, followed by three years of famine, halted the religious conflict in favor of putting the Christians to work in the fields to make up for the depleted workforce. Under Firuz, the farsighted and charismatic emperor, the Persians were able to get through a difficult period with minimal social upheaval. As things improved, the ever-fractious Armenians revolted, and in 481 Firuz took to the field to contain the rebellion. Rumors of more insurrections sent him to contain his eastern provinces, but he and his army were too worn out, and he was killed in battle in 483.

Balas, who succeeded Firuz, adopted a more pacific approach to the problems confronting him. In his short reign of slightly more than two years, he established a policy of tolerance for Christianity and, due to this policy, made Armenia a province of Persia and Nestorian Christianity the court religion of Persia, much to the disgruntlement of the Zoroastrian majority of the population. All this came unglued when Balas was succeeded by his son Kobad, a devout Zoroastrian, who sought to impose the austere branch of that religion to which he subscribed on the people of the Persian Empire. The army, unwilling to give up their religions, rose against Kobad and installed his brother Zamasp, who banished his brother and ruled until 501, when Kobad returned and, in a show of uncharacteristic clemency, allowed Zamasp to abdicate. Kobad's second reign lasted until 531 and was marked by insurrections, rebellions, and massacres, as well as two major wars with Byzantium.

The mid-530s were marked by four years of uncharacteristically cool weather throughout Asia and Europe. Crop failure was common, and this led to starvation and the spread of epidemic disease. In the Middle East, the Kurds were particularly hard-hit, losing both orchards and flocks to the encroaching cold even as their borders were being attacked by Syrian and Greek forces made desperate by the weather shift. Recent studies of ice cores and tree rings have revealed that the climate change was in all likelihood worldwide and that it may have caused the death of as much as 20 percent of the total population. The one region that appeared to benefit from this was north Africa, and for the next decade the farmers from Egypt and Ethiopia to Morocco commanded high prices for their crops. This, in turn, promoted shipping to get grain, fruit, and salted meats to markets where food was scarce. Nomadic tribes fragmented in order to survive, and this provided many larger provinces and kingdoms in the Middle East the opportunity to bring these nomads into their control in exchange for protection and a share of what food there was.

Now that the Huns were contained, a new group out of western Mongolia began to make its first appearances on the edges of the Persian Empire; these were the Western Turks, who, two centuries later, would be reinforced by a larger group—the Celestial Turks. While the migration did not actually occur until 540, small raiding parties attached to nomadic clans were first mentioned in 537, presaging things to come. While the ancient province of Colchis at the eastern end of the Byzantine Empire struggled to free itself from Constantinople, other eastern provinces and protectorates recorded the progress of the Turks into Persian territory. What started as a trickle eventually became a torrent and brought new stresses to the Middle East as that region fell into famine. Persia, caught up in an ongoing campaign against Byzantium, soon had to deal with another threat on the opposite side of the empire from its Byzantine borders, a divisive problem that would have serious ramifications for Persia as the might of Byzantium grew and the Turks continued their advance. At first, Byzantium claimed the greater part of Persian military attention, in a series of conflicts that grew steadily more acrimonious.

During the early years in power of Justinian, the Byzantine Emperor (reigned 527–565), the dramatic climate shift that caused famine throughout Asia and the Middle East diminished the grazing lands in that wide swath of land once called the Fertile Cresent, a change that reached all the way to northern China and Manchuria. Although the Turks were at the forefront of the migration, this climatic shift drove many of the tribes from Mongolia westward, seeking pasturage and protection from the marauders from the Siberian north who had begun moving into the Mongol territories. The Middle East, already seriously depleted thanks to the past centuries of increasing aridity and resultant overgrazing, now lost all but a very few regions of savannah lands and had to make do with scrub-desert conditions, which persist to this day; these new conditions made for many groups of desperate people contending over increasingly unproductive land. Although Justinian was counted as a great emperor and a saintly man, he was, by present-day standards, a martinet and a bigot, embracing religious intolerance as a high virtue and judging those around him in terms of the degree of adulation they offered him. That was the nature of his culture and his time, and by the lights of his social environment he was indeed admirable, but his view of the world was not—and could not be—the current one; in any attempt to evaluate his policies, his context is as important as his decisions within it.

In an attempt to shore up his eastern borders and to support his campaign to conquer Italy for Byzantium, Justinian signed a perpetual peace agreement with Persia (532), and in spite of dramatic unrest at home, he sent his armies, under the great General Belisarius, first to north Africa to deal with the Vandals there and then to Sicily as a jumping-off point for the Italian campaign against

Vandal strongholds and the conquering Ostrogoths. The Italian campaign was going quite well until the perpetual peace with Persia ended and the twenty-three-year-long Byzantine–Persian War broke out in 539. This war was complicated by an epidemic of Plague in 541 that spread throughout the Middle East and Europe during the next two years, cutting back Justinian's military ambitions in the West. By 546 the Ostrogoths, under the very persistent Totila, recaptured Rome, and although the Byzantine navy defeated the Ostrogoths at sea in 551, this was insufficient to swing the balance in favor of the Byzantines in Italy. Belisarius was summoned home in disfavor, and General Narses was appointed in his stead, and achieved only a slightly better record of success, although his victories were reported grandly back in Constantinople.

As much as he wanted to continue his campaign in Italy against the Vandals and Ostrogoths, Justinian was forced to deal with the more pressing threats from the East instead of attempting to reassemble the Roman Empire in the West, which had been his stated goal. By 559 an army of Huns and Slavs attacked Constantinople itself, and Belisarius, who had been retired from service and was still out of favor, was called back to lead the defenders of the city, which he did successfully, though his success did not restore him to favor. Justinian feared—with some justification—that Belisarius' popularity with the army and the people made him a danger to the emperor and kept the aging Belisarius under house arrest for the remainder of his life. Myth said that Belisarius had been blinded and crippled and left to beg in the streets, a move that would have been very risky for Justinian; although it makes a good story, it is more metaphor than fact.

In 572 a second Byzantine–Persian War began, which would last nineteen years, handled badly for Byzantium under a succession of emperors whose policies resulted in a prolonged war, this in spite of an invasion of Persia in 589 by a combined army of Arab, Turkish, and Khazar men, who by now had united into a formidable military force. The Persians emerged victorious from the attacks and put their attention to making Arabia a Persian province. They also drove the Abyssinians out of Arabia and went on to create four large satrapies. Under Anushirwan the administration of the empire was reorganized and roads were improved, all the while keeping up the pressure at the borders with Byzantium.

Italy, abandoned by all but a skeleton force of Byzantine forces, was finally occupied by the Lombards, who in 580 managed to drive the Ostrogoths back over the Alps and claimed control of most of the peninsula, which they held until 744. They did not occupy Rome or Naples, but their presence influenced military decisions and politics until Charlemagne came to power and added the Lombard kingdom to his empire.

Matters did not go well for the Emperor of Persia, either: after the canny Anushirwan, the volatile Hormizd, having lost territory and men to the Byzantines and unable to enlist the assistance of Arabs or Khazars or Kurds in Persia's defense, was deposed and executed in 589. His successor, his son Khusru Parviz, called Chosroes III by the Byzantines, established a less bellicose relationship with Constantinople and the Emperor Maurikios and began to restore Persia, undertaking necessary agricultural reforms and expanding trade once again. Khusru reigned for thirty-nine years, far longer than Maurikios, who in 602 was killed, along with all his family and supporters, on the order of Phocas, who was proclaimed emperor by the Legions of Byzantium. Phocas had managed to slow the Alans at the Danube and was determined to stem the tide of barbarians, from those who had begun their encroachment over a century ago to the most recent upstarts. Phocas himself was supplanted by Heraclius in 610, which brought a new dynasty to Constantinople and another layer of extended-family politics to the Byzantine Empire.

The Huns, among the most destructive of the many invaders from the East and among the most persistent since the first on-slaught in the fifth century, now found themselves with signifi-cantly reduced numbers and up against Byzantine forces in many locations, including the line of fortresses the Romans had built along the western half of the Silk Road at roughly twenty-mile or seven-league intervals—a day's walk for merchants with pack animals—for the purpose of protecting travelers from the many groups of robbers that made their living from plundering travelers. These fortresses not only provided safety to travelers; they also had lookout towers that were used to signal back and forth along the trade route and kept the level and speed of essential communica-tions moving ahead of events, a purpose they continued to serve even when the Byzantines turned them into military installations with the intention of monitoring the activities of the many tribal groups moving west. They had difficulty maintaining a full com-plement of soldiers at these outposts and over time the fortresses were abandoned as being too costly to be effective, and a crucial warning system was lost. A good number of them were taken over by Huns and Persians and used defensively when, a century later, the main body of Turkish forces arrived from Mongolia; by that time, many Huns were mercenary soldiers for the Byzantines.

In 608 the Persians occupied Syria and Mesopotamia and an-other perpetual peace with Byzantium was over. By 611 the Per-sians had reached the Mediterranean and Antioch was sacked by Khusru Parviz' armies; this last Sassanian Emperor was determined to carve out a kingdom as vast as the Persian Empire was when Alexander the Great usurped it, almost a thousand years before. With Antioch firmly in his grip, Khusru turned his attention to-ward Damascus with similar results. After that, in 619, the Persians sacked Jerusalem. Byzantium braced itself for a long and costly war with the Persians.

But another potent force was rising from the Arabian Peninsula, and an unanticipated element was thrown into the mix: a former caravan guide, camel driver, and merchant of the Koreish tribe called Muhammad began to preach a new religion, rooted in Judaism and aimed at the division and superstition he had seen tear the Arab Middle East apart for all his life, as it had done for almost all recorded time. Until Muhammad introduced his teaching, the Middle East was a hodgepodge of paganisms of many sorts, Mithraism, Judaism, Zoroastrianism, Christianity, assorted local totemic religions, as well as remnants of the old Egyptian polytheism and Babylonian moon cults. In the eastern reaches of the region there were also small enclaves of Buddhism and Mongolian sky-worship. Muhammad's call to unify under one god and to obey the laws of that god was met by fierce resistance by established authorities throughout the Middle East, in part because the religion was so appealing and so much adapted to the prevalent cultural conditions of the time that it was readily embraced by vast numbers of people and where Muhammad's teaching took root the socio-governmental structures tended to be severely shaken; yet that very resistance helped the new religion to spread with astonishing rapidity, particularly into areas battered by war and privation, where conditions created a social vacuum into which Islam flowed with the inevitability of a tidal surge.

Unlike the Christian gospels, which—with the exception of the ancient gospels recovered in Egypt about fifty years ago—were cobbled together some three centuries after the death of Jesus of Nazareth, most of Muhammad's visions were written down in his lifetime, in the *Q'ran,* which means "Recitation." Muhammad's work was therefore subject to much less editing than were the accounts of Jesus' teachings. And although Jesus was recognized as a prophet in the *Q'ran,* which also endorsed both the virgin birth of Jesus and the virginity of his mother, Mary, Muhammad was perceived as the culmination of Jewish and Christian thought, an understanding that the churches of the time thought intolerable temerity and that fueled early animosity between these two religions.

Over the next decade conflicts escalated throughout the region, with the Persians and Avars (a loose confederation of nomadic tribes from Mongolia and Central Asia) attacking Constantinople in 625 following the Byzantine invasion of Armenia eighteen months earlier; the forces following the prophet Muhammad besieged Medina in 627. In the same year, the Byzantines extended their invasion to Assyria and Mesopotamia itself, where in December Heraclius was victorious in the Battle of Nineveh; the Persian Emperor Khusru was compelled to give up his war with the Byzantines, and then, to assure there would be no more trouble with him, in 628 Khusru's son murdered him and took over as Kavadh II, securing yet another perpetual peace with Constantinople, exchanging prisoners and seized goods and returning Jerusalem to the Byzantine hegemony. It was also 628 when Mecca surrendered to Muhammad's forces and Islam became a politico-military force as well as a religious one, so that by the time of Muhammad's death in 632 his followers were ready and able to spread the faith from India to western Africa, starting with an attack on Persia in 632 under Muhammad's father-in-law, Abu Bekr, the first caliph. In 634 Omar became the second caliph, and for the next decade Islam spread in a holy war through Syria, Persia, and Egypt, beginning in 635 with the fall of Damascus, which was named the seat of the caliph and remained so for more than a century. That year also saw Gaza fall to Islam.

The Byzantines, harried and shaken, entered into an alliance with Kuvrat, King of the Bulgars, hoping to stop the advance of the Avars; this spread Byzantine forces very thin over the limits of their empire. The Avars proved to be seriously persistent foes, conducting war by raids and forays rather than the kind of ongoing campaigns that marked the Byzantine conflicts with Persia. But things weren't going well for the Persians, either. Islamic victories at Ualula and Tunis, then Jerusalem in 637, paved the way for an unhampered assault on Mesopotamia, with Persia the next target of opportunity. The Persians were so worried about Arab success that they appealed to China for support.

All this conflict was bad for trade and farming, and the general population suffered because of it. Throughout the Middle East there were sporadic famines and, along with the famines, outbreaks of cholera, dysentery, smallpox, and bubonic plague. Northeastern Persia was among the hardest-hit areas, war and disease reducing the population by a quarter over a three-year period from 637 to 640, leaving towns and villages deserted, crops unharvested, animals starving, and the entire region rife with banditry and lawlessness.

In 642 the armies of Islam conquered Persia, ending the reign of the Sassanian Dynasty after more than four hundred years of capable, not to say ruthless, rule. Pleas for Chinese assistance proved fruitless in spite of the many trade advantages offered, and Persia was added to the Caliphate. The grandson of Khusru, Yezdigerd III, became a fugitive and was killed near Merv almost a decade after his family fell from power, and Islamic attention was then concentrated on the Byzantine Empire, a standoff that would continue for almost eight centuries. Only an anti-Islamic backlash in Egypt and Mesopotamia against the blatant nepotism rife in Islamic government in 645 and 655 slowed the astonishing success of the new religion.

In 642 the Arabs overthrew Alexandria and completed their domination of Egypt, a development that sent dread through the few remaining European powers in Egypt and north Africa, for Alexandria was the primary city of access to the Middle East for

many of them; Cyrus, the Patriarch of Alexandria, negotiated surrender terms that permitted the people of the city free exercise of
religion and security of their persons and property, all in exchange
for a hefty amount of gold—accounts of the actual amount of the
tribute vary, but even the lower figures are staggering: twenty
thousand sequins is one of the more frequently mentioned sums.
Alexandria managed fairly well under Arab rule for three years, but
in 645 the Byzantine fleet arrived and the city's populace revolted,
aiding in its recapture by the Byzantines, a short-lived victory: Abdallah ibn Saad organized his Arab forces and in a three-pronged attack forced the Byzantines to retreat. Once he had the city firmly
in his grip again, Abdallah ibn Saad, in 646, began to build a major seagoing fleet and to prepare to wage war for the Mediterranean. Within two years, Cyprus was taken by Arab forces and
Islam established as a religious presence on the island. Occasional
sea skirmishes broke out among Byzantine and Arab naval forces,
but most were small engagements, at least for a few years, while
both sides reorganized and developed new strategies for this expansion of engagement. When, in 655, the Byzantines and Arabs
met in battle off the coast of Lycia, the Byzantine Emperor Constans II, who personally commanded the Byzantine ships, was
roundly defeated. Arab attentions now expanded toward Malta and
Sicily.

The inner strife of the Arabs intervened in the drive to conquer
territory held by Christian Italians: the caliph Othman was assassinated while visiting Medina in 656, leading to five years of near
civil war in Arabia and Arab-held regions and a polarization
among Islamic groups that sharply divided the political groups in
the conflict. Unaware of the extent of the internal hostilities among
the Arab factions, in 663 Constans II, still smarting from his defeat
in 655, precautionarily moved his court from Constantinople to Italy
but was unable to claim Rome from the Lombards, and after five

years, and Constans II's suspicious death at Syracuse on Sicily, the Byzantines withdrew to Constantinople, losing their opportunity to secure Malta and Sicily against the Arab navy. No Byzantine emperor ever occupied Rome again.

That same year, 663, at the eastern end of the Middle East, Kabul was attacked by the first of two Arab armies, and the following year the city fell after a bitter siege that left a third of the city in ruins and a quarter of the population dead. Arab forces now had control of lands from the borders of India to half of northern Africa, and the Byzantines were encountering difficulties at every turn. In 669 Constantinople was besieged by Arab forces fresh from their victories in Chalcedon; the city proved hard to bring down, and so a naval blockade was imposed, which lasted until 678, when a perpetual peace was reached—it lasted until 709.

Other encounters yielded more equivocal results: in 677 the Arab fleet bound for Sicily was met by the Byzantines, who routed the Arabs so comprehensively that the Arabs abandoned for the time being any plans to attack Europe; the superiority of Byzantine weapons demonstrated the folly of marine campaigns against them, at least for some decades to come. Chief among their weapons was the napalmlike Greek Fire, a substance that was dreaded by all who encountered it. But that ordnance superiority did not extend to the land: three years later, the Byzantine army suffered a staggering defeat at the hands of the Bulgars, then allied with the Arabs, who had occupied a good portion of the territory between the Danube River and the Balkans as well as the Carpathian provinces of Bessarabia, Moldavia, and Wallachia in present-day Romania. The Byzantine vanquishing provided the first real access to the Carpathians for Arab forces, and it gave Islam a toehold in the region, a development that was to have long-lasting ramifications.

As Constantine IV's seventeen-year-old son, Justinian II, ascended the Byzantine throne in 685, more divisions were taking place within Islam: in 680 the Battle of Kerbelah, in what is now Iraq, ended the life of Hussein, until then one of Muhammad's few surviving cousins and a rallying figure for many converts to Islam. His murder was seen as an act of treachery by the Kurfans, who had offered hospitality and political support to Hussein and provided him an escort but had apparently abandoned him on his journey from Mecca, allowing his enemies to attack and kill him. Hussein's followers still celebrate his martyrdom and form the heart of the Shiite sect. Conflict between the Shiites and other Islamic sects, already simmering, erupted after this incident and has been ongoing almost constantly to the present day.

Meanwhile, a new city had emerged in the roster of ports-of-call: a group of islands at the northern end of the Adriatic Sea, originally dealing in salt and dried fish, now merged—literally and figuratively—into the city of Venice, electing a Doge for the first time in 687. This humble beginning heralded the arrival of a true mercantile giant; within a century Venice took its initial steps to making the Most Serene Republic into a formidable empire.

In 689 Justinian II's army fought the Slavs in Thrace. After a weak beginning to the battle, the Byzantines achieved an unexpected victory, one that resulted in a roundup of the remaining Slavic forces and the deportation of more than half the captive soldiers into what is now Turkey, where the able-bodied were sold as slaves, some of whom were taken into the Byzantine army to man the most vulnerable outposts along the Silk Road and the Persian Gulf, away from Slavic territory. Although desertion was high at those forts, the risks of capture by Syrian or Arab forces was generally sufficient to keep the Slavs at their posts.

Convinced he was on a roll, Justinian II determined to beat back the Arabs around the Black Sea and, with that in mind, dispatched his army to drive the Arabs out of Crimea, but in so doing he overstepped himself; at the Battle of Sebastopol in 692, Justinian II suffered a major defeat—one from which he was unable to recover and which, three years later, led to his generals' deposing him, cutting off his nose, and exiling him, ironically to Crimea. In 705 Justinian II, now called Rhinometus (the Noseless), regained his throne, which he held for six more years until another uprising of troops in Crimea and Anatolia. This time his luck ran out, and he was killed in December 711, ending the century-long reign of the House of Heraclius.

The Arabs had not been idle in this time. In 697 they destroyed Carthage, driving out the Byzantines and asserting their claim to the ruined city, which they used as a base from which to expand their presence in Africa, a ploy that worked well for them, for in 700 Algiers capitulated to Arab armies and Islam came to north Africa to stay. It was from their north African ports that the Arabs launched their assault on Spain in 711. Under the leadership of the freed slave Tariq, an army of Berbers and Arabs advanced through the Iberian Peninsula; in July, at the Battle of Wadi Beqqah, Tariq's men killed Roderich, the Visigothic King of Spain, after which most resistance in the south collapsed and Tariq took over the Visigothic capital city of Toledo and occupied Cordova as well before preparing his men to march on Seville. By 716 Lisbon was in the hands of the Arabs, and by 720 the Moors of Spain had spread over the Pyrenees and taken the French city of Narbonne as well as occupying the island of Sardinia; only the northeastern part of Spain remained in Christian hands, creating a bitter rivalry that would last for seven hundred years. Not that all Arab efforts were confined to the West: in the East, in 651, there was an Arab uprising against Persia, one that reclaimed Arabia and added parts of Mesopotamia. Taking advantage of this powerful position, the Arab army expanded east-by-northeast, spurred on by religious fervor. In 712 Arab forces occupied Samarkand and crossed the Indus Valley and took over the northwestern section of India.

Fighting styles were changing, favoring cavalry over foot soldiers. Once the Avars introduced the metal stirrup into Middle Eastern saddlery, the advantages of this stabilizing device became immediately apparent. The Avars, being bowmen as well as horsemen, found that they could shoot arrows from a considerable distance accurately if they had stirrups to stand in, and soon their opponents were using stirrups as well. In Persia, this brought about scaled armor not only for cavalrymen but also for their horses. For the first time a massed cavalry assault could be used to break infantry lines without imperiling the horses. Persian armies began to use such tactics against both the invaders from the east and the entrenched Byzantines in the west. Arabs quickly adapted the stirrup to their tack, but they never took on the horse armor that the Persians developed, not only because it slowed down their horses but because the heat of the bards (horse armor) was counterproductive in battles fought in the desert, as so many Arab battles were. Bards also proved less than effective against the Turks toward the end of the eighth century when their ongoing incursions began to demand serious military opposition. Turkish skill on horseback was legendary, and Turkish compound bows were perfect mounted weapons. As the presence of the Turks increased, the Persian bards grew lighter, with scale limited to the highly vulnerable parts of the horse, but in time even this proved insufficient as the Turks increased in numbers.

While Islamic forces were spreading throughout the Middle East, western Asia, northern Africa, and western Europe, the Byzantine Empire was bogged down in heresy battles that managed to cause a serious rift in the Orthodox Church. The Iconoclasts (literally, breakers of images), favored by the Byzantine Emperor Leo III, aroused the Greeks to rebellion, and, assembling a fleet, the

Greeks sailed for Byzantium. Encountering the Byzantine navy and its formidable weapon, the incendiary, oily Greek Fire, the Greeks were completely defeated, and the movement to preserve icons had to wait for abler champions to change imperial Byzantine policy, although Pope Gregory II in Rome endorsed the veneration of icons and encouraged the Greeks to continue their resistance to Leo III, which only served to prolong the conflict.

The Moors continued their activities in Spain and France without significant checks until 732, when they suffered a staggering defeat at the Battle of Tours; they had captured and burned Bordeaux and were eager to take Tours, not only for the wealth of the nearby monastery of Saint-Martin but also for control of trade routes. Charles Martel drove them out of Tours and back to the Pyrenees. With the Berbers of northern Africa in open rebellion, Moorish attention was required elsewhere, and France endured no more concerted attacks from Africa or the eastern Mediterranean. Charles Martel, who gained lands and political clout through his successes against the Moors, in 739 was approached by Pope Gregory III and asked to lead Christian forces against the Christian-but-encroaching Lombards, the Greeks, and the Arabs. For two years Martel provided some of the protection the Pope requested, but in 741, Martel and the Byzantine Emperor Leo III died, and the potential for upheaval in both Europe and Byzantium became a reality within the year.

Constantine V, the new Emperor of Byzantium, had to put down an uprising within six months of his ascendancy. Charles Martel's sons Pepin and Carloman received roughly half their father's kingdom each, a division that neither was entirely pleased with, thus creating internal squabbling that required their attention be focused on issues within their own borders rather than looking beyond for outside threats.

In 745, having successfully stopped the insurrection at home,

Constantine V—an energetic and pragmatic man who was more concerned with the economy and infrastructure than religious practices, a stance that turned the clergy against him—ordered the Byzantine army into Syria, and the following year the Byzantines retook Cyprus and destroyed the Arab fleet anchored there. But just as the Byzantines seemed to be on a roll, bubonic plague broke out in Constantinople, and the army of Constantine V was soon after decimated by the disease. The deadly epidemic made its way westward, arriving in Spain in 750, on the heels of the establishment of a new dynasty holding the caliphate with Abu-I-Abbas al-Saphah, which almost all in the Islamic world recognized, with the exception of Islamics in Spain and northern Africa. In 762 the caliphate was moved to Baghdad, and that city entered a period of expansion and building that lasted the greater part of a century, but the most significant fortifications and palaces were finished by 770, creating a political center for Arabs as Mecca and Medina created religious ones.

During this time, the Venetians were setting up trade routes, establishing contracts with various governments and port authorities throughout the eastern Mediterranean, the Adriatic, Ionian, Aegean, and Black Seas, and the Sea of Marmara. They were also building escort ships to accompany their trading vessels; pirates were always a hazard, and by providing escorts, the Venetians ensured a degree of safety to their merchants that was unusual for the time. The Venetians were also beginning their navy, which would in time become one of the most formidable marine fighting fleets in the world. Although they had no formal trade agreements with various governments in the Middle East—and very few traders did—the Venetians were remarkable for a Dark Ages society in that they had a national policy of putting trade above military considerations and in adapting their military efforts to the support of trade.

Upon the death in 775 of Constantine V Copronymus, he was succeeded by his son Leo IV Khazar; this comparatively young man (he was about twenty-five when he became emperor) continued and enlarged upon his father's efforts to drive back the encroaching Arabs and Bulgars. Leo had more success against the latter than the former. Upon his death in 780 his widow, Irene, became the regent for the ten-year-old Constantine VI, and she remained in that position for a decade. One of her first acts was to ban Iconoclasts from government and to restore the worship of icons throughout the Byzantine Empire; the followers of Islam, for whom the representation of any living thing was abhorrent, were deeply offended by this restoration of sacred images, and what little goodwill had been developed among the religious leaders on both sides eroded. In 782, with Arab forces advancing on Constantinople, Irene, in a stratagem reminiscent of the Pope's buy-off of the Huns at Rome three centuries earlier, arranged a payment to their leaders that kept the Arabs on the south side of the Bosporus. The following year, the Byzantine army undertook a largely successful drive against the Greeks and Slavs, although Byzantine losses were higher than expected.

Haroon al-Rashid, who became caliph in 786, created a far more stable presence at Baghdad than his Abbasid predecessors had: he established diplomatic relations with China while at the same time he continued to push Arab forces eastward; in the West, he reinforced Arab holdings in northern Africa even as he exchanged gifts with Charlemagne. He understood how crucial a central government was not only to achieving military goals but to maintaining an established capital for the sake of the governed as well. A devout man, Haroon al-Rashid was also keenly aware that his religious agenda could best be accomplished by a strong governmental structure that could support the religion within Islamic territory and create a tolerance for the religion in other countries, particularly those bordering the lands of the Caliphate. The establishment of the independent Moroccan Empire in 788 only served to underscore the need for centralized power in the Islamic world, and to encourage al-Rashid to keep a firm hold on the reins of power.

Religious and political tides were also changing in Byzantium: monasticism was making a major comeback in response to the ousting of the Iconoclasts; the Armenian Orthodox Church remained split from the Greek Orthodox Church; Constantine VI's army had mutinied against him in 790, so that in less than two years he was compelled to restore his mother to co-regent of the empire. It was a gamble, and one he lost, for in 797 Constantine VI was arrested and blinded on his mother's orders. With the army behind her, Irene became the first Byzantine Empress to rule wholly on her own, and while she could, she made the most of it, until her deposition in 802. She was exiled to the Greek island of Lesbos and reduced to making a living as a spinner of yarn. Within the year, she was dead, some said from starvation, others hinting at more sinister causes.

About 780, shortly after the death of al-Mansur, the energetic second Abassid caliph, the area controlled by the Muslim Arabs was fairly secure. Incursions from Georgia and Byzantium had been put down, communications improved, towns fortified, schools established, and centers for the arts endowed. Works of scientific interest from India and China were translated into Arabic, and libraries of scientific writings from Egypt and Greece were created. Advances in chemistry, metallurgy, glassmaking, and distillation were made and recorded. But it was also a time of religious fervor: Manichaeans were persecuted, and various Islamic sects in Mesopotamia and Persia were all but wiped out in a drive to establish "correct" worship. In addition, friction with Byzantium was building, and by 791 it became official warfare again, this time under Haroon al-Rashid, who ruled until 809.

By 800 most central and western Europeans were using the three-field crop rotation system, and for the first time since the fall of Rome there were surpluses on a regular basis, expanding trade and increasing the raising of livestock as much to replenish the fields as to provide wool, milk, and meat. Since roughly 85 percent of the population farmed, and only 15 percent, living in cities and towns, were artisans or merchants this surplus provided a formidable advantage to farmers that they had not enjoyed for centuries. Between the advantages of three-field crop rotation and the development of the standardized horseshoe, agriculture was looking up in most of the Western world, developments that led to a steady but gradual increase in population.

Among his many accomplishments, Haroon al-Rashid succeeded in restoring the Arab fleet, and in 807 this formidable body of new, heavily armed ships attacked the island of Rhodes and subjected it and its inhabitants to battle, rapine, pillage, and the taking of slaves. In answer to this attack, Nicephorus, the Byzantine emperor, invaded Arab territory the following year, and although his armies made some initial successes, they were eventually brought to a standstill and then a partial withdrawal. Emboldened by this success, al-Rashid expanded his military ventures to include putting down an insurrection in Khurasan, where he was killed in the spring of 809; the caliphate passed officially to his son al-Amin. However, al-Amin's brother, known as Mamoon, claimed the caliphate in Persia and took up arms against his brother, and in 813 al-Amin surrendered to his brother's general at Baghdad, after a peace was negotiated. Shortly thereafter, al-Amin was accidentally murdered (that was what the records said), and Mamoon went on to a cultured and literate reign of about twenty years.

Islam had spread rapidly for a century, and now it reached from

India to Spain and France and from the entire coast of north Africa, through most of Egypt, over the entire Arabian Peninsula, to the eastern shores of the Black Sea. Most Christians were not forced to convert but were compelled to keep to Christian villages and enclaves, except for those young men drafted into the army or those men who had been made eunuchs. The same was true for Zoroastrians. As a result, there was a small but steady trickle of Christian refugees into the Byzantine portion of what is now Turkey, a population shift that continued for two centuries and resulted in a posture of guarded uncertainty among those displaced. As the Middle East flourished, many Christians converted or adapted their style of Christianity to something more in accordance with the tenets and practices of Islam. The exceptions were the Nestorian Christians, who were found along the Asian trade routes and who functioned as record keepers and bankers for merchants, services that made them valuable enough to allow them to preserve their own manner of worship, which was substantially different from that of either Roman or Byzantine Christianity.

Just at the time that the Arab government was undergoing such a splendid revival, the Byzantine Empire was struggling with a series of short-lived and incompetent emperors. From the removal of Irene to the advancement of Leo V in 813, the Byzantines floundered, and the empire suffered for it at a time the empire could ill afford it. This political muddle was complicated by an epidemic of what was probably malaria in 809 that struck on the north shores of the Black Sea and ranged as far as Bulgaria and Thrace. Called the African Fever by physicians of the time, the much-traveled army was hard-hit by the disease, which did not help the plight of the ineffective emperors. By the time Leo V was murdered in 820, the ravages of the epidemic were behind them; Michael II Psellus reigned for nine years.

Striking out from Spain, Islamic pirates took the island of Crete in 826; attempting to follow their example, Saracens from north Africa attempted to conquer Sicily the next year—it took them over fifty years to gain the foothold they sought. The opposition they encountered was as determined as it was unexpected, the island being reinforced by a detachment of Byzantine ships. By 837 Saracens were also attacking Neapolis (Naples), with the intention of gaining control of southern Italy; the Neapolitans succeeded in ejecting the Saracens and inflicted sufficient damage on them to force them to confine their raids to Sicily, at least for the time being.

By the time the Byzantine Emperor Theophilus died in 842, his cruelty was legendary: not only had he waged unrelenting war on Islam, he had subjected his own people to religious persecutions, condemning idolators and heretics to imprisonment, torture, slavery, and anything else his overly zealous mind could conjure up. When Theophilus was succeeded by his baby son, Michael III, under the regency of his mother, Theodora, the empire was once again in the hands of ineffective leadership, and although the religious intolerance lessened, the wars continued. As the Byzantine Empire drifted, the kingdoms around it, particularly Bulgaria, grew stronger, so that by the time Malamir, Tsar of Bulgaria, died in 852, his successor, Boris I, controlled not only Bulgaria but parts of Macedonia and Serbia. Over the next decade, Boris devoted himself to maintaining his hold on the new territories, and although his attempts at expansion were not very successful, he did keep a good grasp on what Bulgaria had added to its empire in spite of Byzantine and Arab efforts at conquest and reaquisition. In 864 Boris converted to Christianity and declared it to be the religion of the country, a decision that would have a lasting impact on Bulgaria and its burgeoning empire, for among other conflicts there was disagreement from the first as to whether the Bulgarians were part of the Roman Catholic or the Greek Orthodox community, creating rancor among those truly observant Christians, as well as sowing dissent among those whose religious profession was only pro forma. In this instance, the debate had no impact on Bulgarian territory: only a major earthquake near Corinth in 856 resulted in significant Bulgarian losses in the region at the time, due to a reluctance on the part of the army to occupy forts in areas affected by the quake.

In that same year, in Constantinople, Theodora was forced from power by her brother, Bardas, who took over running the Byzantine Empire through his skilled manipulation of his nephew. Bardas' rule lasted until his murder in 866, a crime committed at the instigation of his nephew, Michael III, who rewarded the assassin by making him co-emperor; the next year, this co-emperor became the only Emperor, Basil I, when he murdered Michael III and founded a new Byzantine dynasty. One of his first acts, among many that restored Byzantium to glory and prestige, was to order new ships for the navy and funds to restore the army to full power, and not a moment too soon, because in 869 Malta fell to the Arabs, as island conquests were once again high Arab priorities; naval skirmishes increased and piracy on both sides was encouraged.

The year 867 brought the conflicts between the Roman Church and the Greek Church to a head; the Patriarch Photius accused the Pope in Rome of all manner of crimes and sins and ended by declaring that the Roman Church had no authority over the Greek Church. The Great Schism sundered the two most prominent branches of Christianity, ending the one shared tie left between the two states. From this time on, the Catholic (Roman) and Orthodox (Greek) Churches were two separate and distinct bodies. A brief reconciliation was attempted in 868 at the urging of the new Byzantine Emperor Basil I, but it did not last, and in 877 the break was recognized by the Eastern churches and became official. Leo VI tried another reunification of the Churches in 887, but it was more cosmetic than substantive and tended only to have impact on the churches of Constantinople and Rome—elsewhere the Schism held.

In 858 an Arab-held port on the Black Sea was attacked and sacked by Vikings, who were beginning to roam a long way from Scandinavia in search of loot and adventure. Arab forces drove them out and put their allies on the alert for more such incursions. It was also about this time that the Byzantine records show an increase in trade with Russians; fur and amber were among the most valuable goods brought from the north to Constantinople. The world was once again expanding. With the Arab capture of the island of Malta in 869, the balance of power shifted once again, giving Arabs clear control of the southeastern Mediterranean and making trade a significant component of the Arab presence.

From 871 until 880 the Byzantines fought a constant stream of border conflicts with Arab forces, none of them decisive in the ongoing campaigns. The Byzantines were also dealing with a pair of Christian sects within their empire that were opposed to the power and influence of the Orthodox Church and were striving to return to what they saw as the simplicity of Christianity. The two sects disagreed with each other as to how that simplicity was to be practiced and so were unable to make common cause and eventually suffered the fate meted out through divide-and-conquer tactics. As the Byzantine navy was rebuilt and expanded, there were a number of important engagements with the Arab navy as well as Arab pirates in which the Byzantines triumphed and continued to maintain the advantage they had secured. It also created a naval arms race that continued until the latter part of the sixteenth century.

Piracy had been on the rise since the Arabs, who had a long tradition of independent sea raiding, had come to dominate so much of the Mediterranean, and as a result the Byzantines suffered many trade losses. In response to this, a new fleet of ships was designed and given the task of containing the Arab pirates. In late 880 the

campaign began. For three years the Byzantines made real headway against the pirates, but by 884 the pirates had changed their
tactics and the Byzantine navy had its hands full just to keep matters
even. By 904 the corsair Leo of Tripoli attacked Thessalonika with
a fleet of pirate ships. His men plundered the region and took a reported twenty thousand captives as slaves, although the ineffective
Byzantine navy said the pirates only got half that number. It took
until 915 for the Byzantines to regain control of the Byzanto-
Italian trade routes, and even then there were ongoing problems
with pirates.

To make matters worse for Byzantium, Tsar Symeon of the Bulgarians was building an empire for himself, modeled on the Byzantine one, with his own Patriarch to add to his authority. Symeon
had waged a successful war against the Avars in what is modern-
day Hungary and in 913 turned his attention on Constantinople,
ruled by Constantine VII Porphyrogenetos, who was still a child
and therefore assumed to be weak. The next year Symeon took
Adrianople but was unable to hold it. In 917 he was victorious
against the Byzantines at Anchialus. The war continued indeci-
sively for years, ending only when Symeon died. Bulgarian attacks
on Byzantine territory did not stop with his death, but they tapered
off significantly and during the famine of 927 stopped entirely
while the crisis raged.

Both Persian and Byzantine traders did business with the Russians, and that finally brought military action to the Greeks. In 941
the Byzantine navy met the Russian navy in a battle for Black Sea
ports. The Byzantines won the encounter, but they realized they
no longer could assume their Black Sea ports were safe. The need
to protect these ports led to the need for a larger naval force, an
expense that hit the Byzantines hard, since their long campaign
against the Arab pirates was proving to be costly. Only a slightly
covert deal with the Venetians, who agreed to provide extra armed

escorts for their ships in Byzantine waters, made it possible for the Byzantines to enlarge their fleet on the Black Sea. The Russian standoff was negotiated to a less belligerent relationship in 955 when Princess Olga of Russia visited Constantinople for the purpose of being baptized into the Christian faith.

The Byzantines had other disruptions to deal with: in 944 Saif al-Dawla took Aleppo from the Egyptians holding it and began a drive to push the Byzantines out. With the support of the Syrians and mercenary Turks, he kept the city firmly in his own hands. He then established a cultured, educated, and magnificent court at Aleppo, which lasted for about eighty years and might have endured against the Byzantines but was finally struck down by two rival Arab clans, leaving the way open for more Byzantine incursions and for an increase in piracy. By 1050 the rival clans had joined together with the Turkish Seljuk Empire, centered at Mosul and Baghdad, and had begun to expand the territorial borders to include not only Aleppo but most of the region from the Mediterranean Basin to the edge of the Persian Empire.

After the brief reign of Constantine VII's debauched son, Romanus II (959–963), his seven-year-old son, Basil II, became Emperor of Byzantium, and for the first thirteen years the military decisions of his reign were handled by the great generals Nicephorus II Phocas and Ioannes I Tzimisces. Ioannes was Armenian but had been part of the Byzantine army since his youth. Nicephorus, known for his victories at the eastern edge of the Byzantine Empire, supervised four years of land grabbing in what is now Turkey and Syria. By 968 the Byzantines had gained control of Aleppo and Antioch and retaken Cyprus. Nicephorus pushed his luck, however, and was killed by a group of his officers, who claimed to be afraid that Nicephorus had designs on the Byzantine throne.

Byzantine fighting continued against the Bulgarians. In an unusual alliance with Sviatoslav of Russia, the Greeks finally forced the Bulgarians to the peace table, and in 969 a treaty was signed with great pomp, leaving the Russians in charge of Bulgaria but with the support of Byzantium. But the goodwill did not last: the Russians crossed the Balkans, and Ioannes set out to stop their advance. Although the Byzantines were defeated at Philippopolis, they held Adrianople and pushed the Russians back, annexing part of Bulgaria as a Byzantine province in the process. Ioannes then devoted his attention to Syrian and Arab territories; under his generalship, the Byzantines took Edessa in 974 and Damascus and Beirut in 976. Heartened, the Byzantines marched on Jerusalem and were only prevented from taking it by reinforcements of Muslim soldiers from Egypt. Only the sudden death of Ioannes in 976, apparently from disease, but possibly from poison, kept the Byzantines from enlarging their territory even more.

Byzantium had more challenges that demanded attention. In 983 much of what is modern-day Turkey was taken over by the powerful warlord Bardas Phocas, who was defeated two years later. In 987 Bardas Skleros, claiming the region for himself instead of continuing allegiance to Basil II, marched not only through Anatolia but toward Constantinople. Basil appealed to Bardas Phocas and supported his efforts, promising a return to high position for the contentious warlord if he would halt Bardas Skleros. The two armies met and the Byzantine claim remained undefeated until in 989 Bardas Phocas and Bardas Skleros made common cause against Byzantium in a rebellion that lasted under two years but strained the Byzantine military situation throughout the Middle East. When Bardas Phocas died of wounds sustained in battle, Bardas Skleros surrendered. Both Bardas Phocas and Bardas Skleros had a significant number of Huns and Turks in their armies. By this time, the Huns were part of the larger Byzantine culture, but the Turks were not, and this uprising only served to whet their appetite for conquest.

In 992 the Byzantine Empire and the Most Serene Republic of Venice entered into official trade agreements, opening many new western markets to Byzantium and bringing about improved relations with many European states. This was one of the first formal trade agreements enacted between governments, and it served as model for many to come, including one a century later made with Venice's great rival, Genoa. The Byzantine control of the western end of the Asian trade routes, already important, now became crucial to continuing Byzantine prosperity. Since Venice was already dealing with many north African and Syrian ports, this trade agreement spurred the Byzantines to occupy all of Syria and to gain control of the eastern Mediterranean. Emboldened by this success, Basil II ordered his armies into Bulgaria and Macedonia, gaining control of more crucial ports as those territories were brought into the empire in 1002.

As Byzantine forces continued their expansion, the Islamic forces of Mahmud the Idol-Breaker, who was the son of Subaktagin, a Turkish slave who became a prince and founded the Ghanzavid dynasty, controlled most of what is now northern Afghanistan. From this strategic location in 1004 he began a campaign to gain control of northern India. By 1008 his army had defeated Indian forces at Peshawar. In two years he extended his kingdom from the Tigris in the west to the Ganges in the east. The Ghanzavid dynasty was overthrown in 1037 by the Seljuk Turks, who were in the process of annexing Persia and needed the eastern outposts on the edge of India to put pressure on the Persians.

At the invitation of the King of Armenia, Basil II sent his armies to reclaim the kingdom in 1021, a campaign that bogged down early and continued to be challenged not only by Armenians but by the Turks and the Arabs as well as the Persians. Armenia had always been something of a flash point, and now the region was so contested that although the Byzantines kept it under their control, it required constant vigilance to maintain the occupation. Tensions remained high in that region for the next dozen years, and as a result, the Armenian court, worried about its security, relocated to Constantinople and in three generations of marriages melded into the Byzantine aristocracy of the Greeks.

In 1075 the Seljuk Turks took over Syria and Palestine and began to build wealth from their acquired cities, which brought them into the complex Mediterranean world. Trade in the Mediterranean Basin was on the rise, as was Christian pilgrimage. In cities such as Alexandria, Tyre, and Antioch there were districts for foreign merchants, many of whom also sponsored pilgrims' hostels: Venetians and Genoese, along with Pisans and Constantinopolitans, kept homes and businesses in these districts, paid local taxes, and were regarded as legitimate residents, useful as well as economically convenient. It also brought the Middle East back into the political attentions of Europe. Had Europe not been divided into small, warring principalities and had there been a less restrictive religious climate, there might well have been a successful rapprochement between the Middle East and Europe, or at least some move toward common understanding through the offices of pilgrims who had begun to flock to Jerusalem to pray for salvation. But neither region was in any social, religious, or military state to do so. In fact, the single most obvious result of this development of trade was the run-up to that most catastrophic series of follies, the Crusades.

The end of the tenth century saw a revitalization of the papacy in Rome and a spread of Church influence throughout Europe. Public acts of devotion were encouraged, and in some cases required, for amid the political and military carnage the Church had become the champion of unity under the banner of Christ. Since the Church was now a major landowner in Europe, it held tremendous feudal authority through the land; its feudal estates, or *vidames,* provided a great deal of leverage to the Church in its dealings with the nobility of the time. The Church had even supported the Orthodox Church and the Byzantine emperor in resisting the advances of Islam, since Spain was still largely under Islamic control and no Christian wanted to lend even the appearance of tolerance to Islamic expansion. The first significant change in the military balance came in 1087, when Genoa and Pisa, in a combined assault, took Madhyah in north Africa, effectively reclaiming the western Mediterranean for Europeans and breaking the already politically fragile ties of Islamic Spain and the Middle East. This, coupled with the appeal from the Byzantines, encouraged Middle Eastern military adventurism on the part of Europeans. Endorsed and encouraged by the Cluniac Pope Urban II, who cloaked imperialism in religiosity, the call to save Jerusalem from Islam was made primarily to the French—Urban II was a Frenchman—and controlled by them throughout most of the messy events that followed.

The First Crusade, begun late in 1095, was a wave of disorganized general migration of Christians to the Holy Land. Some seven thousand followed Peter the Hermit, and another four to five thousand under Walter the Pauper arrived in what is now Turkey, where they were killed or taken as slaves by the Turks and Syrians. In response, a loose body of knights and men-at-arms under French commanders headed off to Constantinople in three groups: the Lorraine contingent was commanded by Godfrey and Baldwin of Bouillon, the southern French under Count Raymond of Toulouse, and the Normans under Bohemund of Otranto. The entire army numbered between twenty-seven thousand and thirty-one thousand men. The wily Byzantine Emperor Alexius I Comnenus, who had forced his predecessor, Nicephorus III, to abdicate in 1081, gave the Crusaders housing and food, punished any of them who broke the law, and provided them escort in exchange for their pledge of fealty and the promise to hand over any formerly Byzantine territory to him that the Crusaders might recover.

Alexius regarded the Crusaders as mercenaries and misunderstood the intensity of their zeal.

The Turks, garrisoning but not actually colonizing much of what is now Turkey, were still outsiders to the local populations and as such could not easily rouse the people to resist the invading Crusaders. Islam was fragmenting, and the last rallying figure of Islamic unification, Malik Shah, had died in 1092, leaving the region to flounder as the Crusaders captured the Seljuk Turks' capital of Nicea and, in 1098, Antioch. In both campaigns, the Byzantines turned the Crusaders' acts to their advantage, treachery that the Crusaders resented. Finally goaded into action, the Turks and Syrians under the Emir of Mosul counter-sieged Antioch with only partial success. The battles for Antioch were marked by atrocities on both sides, but certainly the Crusaders were the more barbaric.

In 1099 the Crusaders marched on Jerusalem, occupied and viciously sacked it, then set up a kind of government under Godfrey of Bouillon, who, although offered the title, did not style himself King of Jerusalem but Defender of the Holy Sepulcher, given authority under the Pope. Godfrey's brother Baldwin, who succeeded him, accepted the royal title willingly. Most of the Crusaders, having reached their goal and being allowed to keep their loot, returned home, leaving Godfrey to deal with the various factions among the remaining Europeans, the upshot of which was that Jerusalem soon became not a theocratic state but a feudal kingdom with close commercial ties to Genoa and Pisa (Venice's long alliance with Byzantium made the Venetians suspect to the French-dominated courts in Jerusalem). Godfrey himself died in an attempt to take Damascus, leaving the remaining Crusaders in disarray. Only the continued rivalry between the Sunni and Shiite sects of Islam prevented Jerusalem from being retaken by Islamic forces. Crusaders still held Edessa and Antioch as well and through them controlled crucial trading ports.

In 1104 the Crusaders, under Baldwin I, took Acre, which became an important Crusader center, while a Norman army was beaten near Rakka. Raymond of Toulouse besieged Tripoli. Not to be outdone, Bohemund of Otranto took an Italian army to Epirus and pressed the Byzantine emperor for control of the southwestern region of modern-day Turkey, a move that was devoid of any religious excuse but was nonetheless supported by the Pope, who understood it was payback for Alexius' double-crossing the Crusaders at Nicea, as well as the Byzantine attempt to take Antioch after the Crusaders had secured it.

There was trouble brewing on the northern and western flanks of Byzantine territory, and in 1122 the Emperor Ioannes II Comnenus sent his armies to wipe out the Patzinak Turks, then holding a good portion of the Balkans. The Turks were massacred, and an outbreak of Shivering Fever—probably typhus—claimed most of the rest. The poor remnants of the Patzinak Turks were rounded up and sold into slavery. In the wake of the elimination of the Turks, the Serbs rose against Byzantium and were defeated, but not before dragging the Hungarians into war with Byzantium, which resulted in the Hungarians being contained. Just as the Balkan conflict was calming down, the Byzantines entered a four-year-long war with Venice over trade agreements, resulting in a concentration of military forces at crucial Byzantine ports, leaving other regions open to more European adventurism, while Byzantium took over Antioch once more as part of maintaining its ports and the access to major trade routes.

By politicizing the First Crusade, Baldwin and Bohemund made the Second Crusade, which had only the faintest trapping of religion to justify it, not only possible but desirable for European chivalry bent on looting the treasure-house of the Middle East. With the consent of the Knights of the Temple, founded in Jerusalem in 1120, the Second Crusade had a guarantee of backup, for the

Templars, unlike most religio-monastic Orders, were allowed to process money and to warehouse goods—for a price. The Templars also admitted illegitimate sons of noblemen, unlike the Hospitalers of St. John, officially established in 1198 but begun at Jerusalem and Tyre in 1129, who allowed only legitimate sons in their ranks. Under the encouragement of Pope Eugenius III, Bernard of Clairvaux preached the Crusade in 1145. In 1147 the Crusade set out, Conrad III and Louis VII leading two separate armies, totaling about 450,000 men. In the excitement, the greedily ambitious Roger of Sicily, a Norman warlord, used the Crusades as an excuse to seize the Greek islands and to try to take Athens, Corinth, and Thebes, attempts that forced the Byzantines to make a solid peace in 1148 with the Venetians, who then helped the Byzantines to repel Roger of Sicily from Greece. Except for plunder, little was changed in the Middle East by this blatant grab at land and money. Conflict about the papal succession between Innocent II in 1130 and the anti-Pope Anacletus II (the better candidate but a semi-converted Jew) claimed the religious loyalties of Europe for the next decade.

Over the next twenty years, the Arabs and Berbers drove the Sicilian Normans out of their various toeholds in north Africa and renewed their ties with Islamic Spain. In Syria and along the eastern Mediterranean, Crusaders continued to establish and maintain fortresses for the protection of pilgrims coming from Europe. Turkish expansion continued and spread from what is now northern Afghanistan to the southern shores of the Black Sea. The first paper mill in Europe was established in Islamic Spain around 1150, using technology first developed in China and brought along the Silk Road to Baghdad and Damascus. Egypt was taken over by the forces of Salah-al-Din in 1171, a military hero from Damascus, and the Fatamid dynasty ended its almost three-hundred-year sway; making Egypt his home base and himself sultan, Salah-al-Din conquered Syria in 1176. Striking out from Persia, Mohammed of Ghor invaded India in 1175 in a campaign that continued for nearly a decade and ended with his conquest of the Punjab in 1187. During this time, Salah-al-Din attempted to drive the Christians out of Jerusalem, while attempting to force the Byzantines to withdraw from their centers in Aleppo and Damascus.

Sentiments against the Europeans were growing in the Middle East. Even in Constantinople there was open distrust that boiled over. In 1182 a mob attacked and butchered the Romans who had been employed by the Regent Maria of Antioch. The distrust of Europeans extended to merchants and officials and ended in the proclamation of co-emperors Andronicus I Comnenus and his young nephew. The new co-emperors soon discovered how seriously depleted the treasury had become and how enmeshed the empire was in all manner of diplomatic skulduggery, which Andronicus attempted to address. But in 1185 some of these deals brought a Norman attack against the Byzantine Empire, beginning at Durazzo and going on to Thessalonika, where there was a heavy loss of life among the Greeks. Rallying under Isaac Angelus, the Greeks defeated the Normans on sea and land. Andronicus was tortured and executed, and Isaac II Angelus was hailed as emperor, one pledged to check the Europeans and to stem the widespread corruption that had permeated the Byzantine court and civil service for two centuries. He did fairly well with the former but made little or no headway against the latter.

Salah-al-Din continued to press Jerusalem, and in 1187 he succeeded in taking it and inadvertently stirred up European chivalry to try to take it back, setting the spark for the Third Crusade. Philip III of France established a Saladin Tax to pay for France's participation in the Crusade, which was endorsed by the Church but disliked by the people who had to pay it. The Third Crusade got off to a rocky start in other ways: in June of 1190, the Holy Roman Emperor Frederick Barbarossa drowned while crossing the river Calycadnus in Cilicia at the head of his army bound for the Holy Land. This left the Crusade without a leader and the other kings to scramble to fill the vacancy. By autumn Philip III of France claimed to be too ill to continue and withdrew from the Crusade, taking his men with him. Philip had clashed with Richard Coeur de Leon of England and Aquitaine. In order to bring a large army to the Middle East, Richard had mortgaged England to France—leaving his brother John to make the payments—and then had slighted the French king, causing hard feelings between the two, despite Richard's early victory at Arsuf.

The Third Crusade is probably the best known one, the glamorous one—if something so deadly can be glamorous. In 1192, following unreliable guides into the desert east of Antioch, many Crusaders were struck down by famine and an outbreak of dysentery, a disease that killed more men in the Third Crusade than all the deaths and wounds in battle. Desertion ran high, and not just among men seeking to get back to Europe: the Third Crusade had a very high instance of men "going native," joining the Islamic forces and remaining in the Middle East. Finally, Richard Coeur de Leon made a truce with Salah-al-Din, who allowed the Crusaders to keep their coastal cities and fortresses. He also granted the Crusaders access to the Holy Sepulcher in Jerusalem, provided that they entered the city unarmed, a condition Richard found so unacceptable that he himself never actually entered Jerusalem. Bound by oath to break off fighting, Richard headed for home through present-day Austria, where he was captured and held for ransom, becoming the only King of England to bankrupt the kingdom twice. Of his ten-year-reign, Richard spent about a year of it in England. By the time of his death in 1199, at age 42, Richard was in the process of losing a third of his French holdings.

Sultan Salah-al-Din predeceased Richard by six years, and his vast empire was divided up between his relatives. He had been able to hold most of the western Islamic Middle East together against the attacking Crusaders, but once the bulk of the Europeans had gone home, the unanimity was over and ancient rivalries asserted themselves, leaving the Middle East ill prepared for the Fourth Crusade in 1202, promulgated by Pope Innocent III, who sought to bring the Orthodox and Catholic churches under his Roman banner. The Pope had managed to persuade the Venetians to endorse the Crusade, although the ninety-four-year-old Doge Enrico Dandolo demanded a high price for the use of Venetian men, ships, and ports. It was a price too high for the European kings to meet, so Dandolo struck a bargain—Venice would lower the price if the Crusaders would sack the port of Zara on the Dalmatian Coast on their way to the Holy Land.

At Zara the Crusaders were met by the son of the deposed Byzantine Emperor Isaac II Angelus. Alexius offered handsome rewards to the Crusaders if they would continue their detour as far as Constantinople and reclaim the city for him. The Crusaders agreed to help out Alexius although they were informed of their entire excommunication for the sacking of Zara, a technically Christian city. In July of 1203 the Fourth Crusade arrived at Constantinople to the news that Alexius III had fled, leaving the way open for Alexius to return his father to the throne. Just for good measure, the Crusaders sacked part of Constantinople and then accepted a generous bribe from the rescued Isaac to stop. Many Crusaders hired on as mercenaries in the Byzantine army rather than return to Europe as excommunicants, all of which made it easier when in 1204 a new court was established in Constantinople under Baldwin IX, Count of Flanders, and the Venetian Tomas Morotinople was elevated to the position of Patriarch of Constantinople as a first step toward reuniting the Greek and Latin Churches.

Not that Alexius Comnenus was through: a number of Byzantine nobles who had accompanied him out of Constantinople established a small Byzantine-style empire centered at Trebizond at the southeastern end of the Black Sea, with ties to Bithynia, Sinope, and the island of Rhodes. Another Greek, Michael Angelus Comnenus, took over Epirus and attempted to establish a dynasty there. His efforts and those of many of the Crusaders were undermined by an outbreak of bubonic plague that reduced the numbers of the Byzantines and Crusaders by about 25 percent in the space of two years, making it possible for the Crusaders, with Baldwin and the now ninety-seven-year-old Enrico Dandolo, to attack the Bulgarian King Kaloyan near Adrianople and to be roundly defeated. Hope of a Middle East dominated by Crusaders began to fade.

On the eastern side of the Middle East, the Persian sultan, Mohammed of Ghor, was assassinated at Delhi in northwestern India. His throne was taken by his former viceroy, Kuth-un-bin-Aebach, who declared northern India independent from Persia. There were enough concerns about Central Asian forces at the eastern frontiers of Islamic territory that it was generally accepted that an independent Islamic state in such a strategic location was not a bad idea, for it provided the possibility of protection from the Mongols who had been expanding all over China and Central Asia and seemed to be looking westward.

This threat brought Central Asia into the purview of the Middle East in a way that it had not been in the past; over time, events at the eastern edge of the Middle East cast long shadows into the west, and never more than during the Mongol campaigns that began in the early part of the thirteenth century, when the Crusades were finally losing steam. With Islam already spread through Persia into northern India and Persia itself in disarray, the pressure from the Mongols added to the pervasive unease of the time. As the astonishing tactics of Jenghiz Khan spread the Mongols from China to Baghdad, the already unstable politics of the Middle East became more chaotic.

The long career of Jenghiz Khan was marked by constant warfare, both as a subordinate to his Kiyat family's and Jagatai clan's ambitions when he was young and later as an expression of his own. His ancestry gave him extra status among his contemporaries: he was a descendant of the Borjitin (Blue-Eyed Ones), among the most important of the ancestral groups of the Mongol clans. He soon was recognized as a superior warrior in a culture of warriors and, as such, was given increased power and responsibility, leading to his position at the head of the Mongol armies at a comparatively early age, which served to give him a long career at the head of one of the most impressive cavalry forces in the world. His military successes remained legendary long after his descendants lost the lands he had conquered.

As a tactician, he was one of the most innovative leaders of his time, an attribute that added to his near-mythic reputation; his abilities were so remarkable that his campaigns are studied and analyzed to this day. His strategic philosophy was of much the same school as Civil War General Nathan Bedford Forrest—get there first with the most men. When that was impossible or impracticable, then Jenghiz Khan made it a point to get there more quickly than most expected him to and to move his men at a pace much more rapid than his opponents generally could move their forces. Jenghiz Khan's campaigns are marked by swift movements of mostly mounted troops armed with bows, which meant high maneuverability in the field, making him a formidable foe. Add to that the strict discipline, impeccable organization, and intense loyalty of his troops, and it should be apparent that he had hit upon the formula for military success in medieval Asia and beyond. Early on in his expansion, he had trouble laying siege to various walled towns and fortresses—which is hardly surprising in a man from a nomadic culture where permanent fortifications were rare and most warfare was a matter of scattering or killing people and securing lands for grazing herds—but when he finally managed to break the back of the Chinese army, he had found out how to manage sieges with his cavalry and knew that isolating his enemy was crucial to his success, and made it part of his strategy whenever possible. For that reason, he also cut major trade routes, which, for the highly mercantile Chinese, was the last straw and led to their belated campaign against the Mongols, although by then Jenghiz Khan had a significant advantage, and having got it, he never let go as he drove his army from Beijing to the Middle East in one of the most spectacular campaigns of conquest ever undertaken.

The efforts of the Jagatai clan, even among the warlike Mongols, were impressive and had been for several generations before the expansion westward began. Jenghiz Khan's tenacity marked him from his youth as a force to be reckoned with, an assumption that proved accurate, for at the time of his death, Jenghiz Khan ruled territory that stretched from the Pacific Ocean in the east to the eastern shores of the Black Sea in the west and from what is now central Russia in the north to northern India in the south.

Born somewhere around 1165—when the Byzantine Emperor Manuel I Comnenus and Venice were making alliances against Frederick Barbarossa, and Salah-al-Din Yusef ibn-Ayyub was building the citadel that would become Cairo—the boy was named Temujin; this future conqueror had an austere early life, not atypical of Mongol children of the time but more demanding than many. His experiences of hardship and near-outcast status very likely fueled his determination not to be vanquished again. There are many stories about his youth, most of which are apocryphal, such as the tale of his forming his friends into tiny regiments and companies and staging pretend battles, which is said of almost every conqueror, but it is apparently true that he and his younger brother, Kasar, killed their half-brother Bekter for stealing a fish from their line and a bird from their trap. Although his mother reprimanded the two boys for this, she did not punish them as severely as custom allowed, suggesting that she was at least willing to accept what Temujin and Kasar had done and to some extent considered it justified.

Temujin was said to be tall for a Mongol, impervious to heat and cold, indifferent to pain, and able to sleep in the saddle, all virtues among his people and qualities to revere in a leader. He learned to be stoic, ruthless, and aggressive and to place a high value on loyalty. He worshipped the god of the blue sky, Tangri, yet, in the manner of his culture, was generally indifferent to the religions of others, caring more for conquest and land than any ideological conversion, an aspect of his character that both puzzled and infuriated the Islamic forces he met, who viewed all conflicts as having a religious component. By the time Temujin was in his mid-teens he was already an active war chief in his clan, and that led to his first major accomplishment: the unification of the highly competitive Mongol clans.

From the beginning of his empire building, Jenghiz (and it is correctly pronounced "jenges," the *J* as in "Jennifer," not the hard *G* in "Godfrey"; occasionally it is transliterated as Chingiz) Khan proved to be an excellent campaigner, moving his armies quickly and keeping relentless pressure on any and all of his foes. In terms of fighting another army in the open, he was unparalleled, having men who were used to warfare and willing to press on against any foe. But, as mentioned earlier, he was not always successful in sieges, which tended to keep him from using his cavalry—and nearly all his fighting men were essentially cavalry—to their most mobile advantages, since sieges, by definition, are limited to the locale of the siege. Speed and ruthlessness were on his side, and his ability to anticipate the movements of his opponents was dramatically successful over his long life.

The Mongol territories had a crucial advantage in paying for

war, for they straddled the Silk Road, the major caravan route between East and West; the Mongol clans had long employed banditry to reap some of the wealth of the Silk Road, but once
Jenghiz Khan took control of more than half of the Silk Road
early in his expansion, the nature of the exploitation changed to
more regularized predation. Taxes in livestock and merchandise
collected from travelers and merchants paid for a great deal of the
Mongol military supplies and matériel.

In 1219, when Jenghiz Khan, then in his mid-fifties and already
in control of northern China and all of Mongolia as well as most
of southern Siberia, including the region around Lake Baikal,
turned his armies westward and south and entered a bitter war
against the Persian Khwarazmshah Ala al Din Muhammed that
ended with the fall of several Transoxanian cities, including
Samarkand and Bukhara, and the death of Ala al Din Muhammed
on a small island in the Caspian Sea, where he had retreated, worn
out and in despair, his forces reduced by more than half and exhausted. The territory of Ala al Din Muhammed was in ruins, and
most of the people who survived were reduced to beggary. There
hardly seemed anything left to fight for, and that might have finished it but for Ala al Din Muhammed's son, Jalal al Din, who was
determined to continue the war, avenge his father, and reclaim his
territory and reestablish the presence of Islam.

With the remnants of his father's army around him, Jalal al Din
fled eastward, Mongols in persistent pursuit, often less than half a
day behind him. Their chase went on for many weeks, through the
increasing heat of the spring and into the summer. Half of his
followers deserted him, and no regional chieftain was willing to
take him in, for no one wanted to have to stand up to Jenghiz
Khan and his armies; the region had become thoroughly demoral-
ized by the Mongol successes. All looked dismal for Jalal al Din,
and the Mongols were confident of bringing him to heel in short

order and to that end chased him all the way to Afghanistan, where they were certain they could stop him.

But it didn't turn out that way. Afghanistan is a territory roughly the size of Texas that has geological characteristics similar to Death Valley—hot plains and steep, rugged mountains filled with defiles and canyons—with a population known for their skills as fighters and general enmity to strangers as well as a capacity for inter- and intratribal warfare; at that time its borders were not so definite as they are now and the country less a country than an inhospitable region filled with rival clans headed by bloodthirsty warlords with intense grudges and long memories who were prepared to fight anything and anyone who tried to conquer them. Afghanistan didn't become a defined country with borders until the comparatively late year of 1711 when the Ghilzai warlord Mir Vais defeated the Persian army sent to conquer the region. Tradition and exigencies made people inhospitable in a forbidding environment, which should have meant that Jalal al Din was out of luck, but, of course, there was one other factor in all this: because most of the Afghan tribes were Islamic, they were grudgingly willing to offer a safe haven to Jalal al Din, who quickly lost himself in the high, arid peaks and rocky defiles, forcing the Mongols to give up their pursuit.

With the Mongols no longer on his heels, Jalal al Din rallied support among the Transoxanians and Afghani and began to establish a resistance among his fellow Muslims, which was as unexpected as it was fierce. What was at stake was not only territory as such but two crucial trade routes, considerations that increased the determination of both sides to maintain control over the region. Jalal al Din and his men were able to inspire a sufficient number of people in the Afghan area to stand against the Mongols and, with that in mind, began looking for a place where they could start a campaign of revenge. Creating local alliances among various Islamic groups, Jalal al Din was soon able to form the nucleus of an effective army, which he hoped would be strong enough to defeat the Mongols when they finally attacked, as it was known they would. Jalal al Din had the presence of mind to anticipate a raid-and-trap strategy, hoping to turn the Mongols' greatest military advantage to a weakness.

The Mongols were acknowledged masters of cavalry warfare, evolved on the open plains of the Asian Steppes; their preferred weapon was the compound bow, a short wood-and-horn laminate that could draw up to ninety pounds; they were drilled in horsemanship as well as archery, and their units excelled at firing their bows while riding at full charge, none of which talents proved to be much use in steep, rocky terrain against an enemy who hid in the high ground and attacked with rocks as well as spears. The Mongols also had slightly curved cavalry swords for close work but did not rely heavily on them or on lances and spears, although they carried javelins and lances into battle, preferring the greater distance and impact possible with arrows. As Jenghiz Khan observed during one of his battles against the Chinese: if you do not strike and kill your enemy with a spear, you have given him a weapon.

It was not unusual for Jenghiz Khan to compel his opponents to move into the open in order for his troops to fight them in the most optimal conditions. The Mongols conducted highly mobile assaults that did not lend themselves to the successful use of throwing weapons but employed the bow more effectively than any other piece of thirteenth-century ordnance. They would charge in a body, then break into squads of nine riders—a tenth member of the squad remained at the rear, tending to the ponies for rapid remount. On open ground Jenghiz Khan's troops had few equals, but against entrenched positions, in prolonged sieges, or in the forbidding environment of rocky canyons they could sometimes be at a disadvantage, as the long Chinese campaigns ten years earlier had demonstrated, although as it turned out, the Chinese bureaucracy proved to be the staunchest supporter of the Mongol invaders: the governmental policies dictating that the movements of Chinese armies could only be undertaken with the specific written permission of the emperor in each and every action of the army kept the better-trained, better-armed Chinese from driving the Mongols out of China, for it guaranteed that an effective defense against a rapidly moving foe could not be mounted, in either the literal or the figurative sense, guaranteeing the Mongols a significant advantage in the field. This policy was designed to prevent Chinese nobles from raising their own armies and marching on the capital to overthrow the emperor, and it did that well enough, but with outside armies attacking, these limitations left the Chinese unable to respond quickly to the Mongols' highly mobile campaigns and ultimately contributed to the very thing it was supposed to prevent—the fall of the Manchurian Chin Dynasty.

The Mongols maintained a vast front for many years, with a number of separate armies in the field at many different locations at the same time, but all of which were coordinated under Jenghiz Khan's absolute authority. The generals were handpicked and staunchly loyal to Jenghiz Khan; about half of them were closely related to him by blood as well as culture and language. As practiced in the thirteenth century, Mongol warfare was fairly straightforward: they wanted land and they used their lightning attacks to take it; they were a grazing economy, and as such, saw land, and by extension, herds, as the primary rewards of conquest. Secondary considerations, such as urbanization, religion, and culture, had little or no impact on them, and many of the usual means of diverting assaults—bribes, superstition, trades—rarely worked with them, for they were not viable factors for the Mongols. Only defeat by superior force of arms or strategic execution bore any weight with them.

At the time of this particular campaign, they were actively fighting along an irregular line running from China to the Caspian desert when Jalal al Din began to shift his posture from defensive to offensive. By the spring of 1221 Jalal al Din had rallied approximately sixty thousand troops among followers of Muhammad, some Persian, some Afghan, some Turkish under the daring Amin Malik, some nomadic, and even a few Muslim Indians under Azam Malik; these he led to the head of the Panshir Valley, establishing a position there. At the town of Parwan, Jalal al Din and his cobbled-together army went on the attack against a portion of the Mongol army that was besieging the local fortress-castle located near an important bridge-head associated with access to the Khyber Pass, a route crucial to north–south trading, as well as the major land link to India in the south and eastern Russia in the north.

Because the attack was unexpected, it succeeded beyond Jalal al Din's expectations. His forces fell upon the Mongols, inflicting heavy casualties at the beginning and throwing the Mongols into disorder. Thousands of Mongols were slaughtered in the battle, and those fortunate enough to escape were forced to abandon their siege of the fortress and retreat across the river, literally burning the bridge behind them, a terrible loss for the Mongols. Taking advantage of the victory, Jalal al Din occupied the nearby town of Parwan, making it his regional headquarters and the gathering point for more supporters, and set about gathering new fighting men to his cause.

Jenghiz Khan was at that time campaigning in the Juzjan Mountains. When word of the rout of his force at Parwan was brought to him, he dispatched an army of thirty thousand men under his trusted general Shigi-Kutuku to reclaim the town and bring down Jalal al Din once and for all. Traveling at the trot from sunrise to sundown, Shigi-Kutuku and his men arrived at Parwan only eight days after Jalal al Din took over the town, roughly twice as quickly as Jalal al Din expected the Mongols to respond. It was this speed of response that had made it possible for Jenghiz Khan to conquer the vast amount of territory he had already added to his holdings. His skill in maneuvering his armies depended on the swiftness of his men and their unwavering dedication to him, which translated into unquestioned orders as well as total compliance. Without this unrelenting support, Jenghiz Khan could not have established, let alone maintained, the empire he left to his sons.

Still flushed with victory, Jalal al Din ordered his men out to take and hold a position approximately three miles outside Parwan. Jalal al Din commanded the center of this position, Amin Malik and his Turkish troops held the right, and Ighrac at the head of Turcoman nomads was on the left. At the first assault, Jalal al Din's men were ordered to dismount and face the Mongols on foot. It was a gamble, but Jalal al Din's army was no match for the Mongols in cavalry clashes, and he supposed they stood a better chance holding entrenched positions than riding against the Mongols. It was a very risky move, but it paid off.

When the Mongols attacked, they took on Amin Malik's men on the right, and the fury of that attack forced the Turks back, inflicting heavy casualties as well as causing disastrous demoralization. Jalal al Din sent in waves of reinforcements in order to keep the right from collapsing, resulting in high losses but, unexpectedly, a held position, which restored the confidence of Amin Malik's troops. Only the end of the day put a stop to the battle, when both sides withdrew to their respective camps, where the Mongols spent a good part of the night on a favorite ruse: stuffing straw into suits of armor and setting helmets atop them and then tying these life-sized dolls to spare horses to give the appearance of additional troops; these they lined up at the rear of their main lines,

fleshing out their formations and destroying the fragile morale of
the enemy.

By morning Jalal al Din's men seemed to be facing a swollen
host of Mongol warriors, which was demoralizing, as the Mongols intended. Local herders confirmed the report of increasing
numbers of the enemy, and that served to increase the stress to
Jalal al Din's forces, particularly since the reports they were provided hinted that there were many more Mongols coming. This
was a most discouraging development for Jalal al Din's army, and
in the face of intense sallies by the Mongols, for the first part of
the fighting, Jalal al Din's forces were in disarray, his men convinced that the apparently superior number of Mongols meant
their ultimate defeat. Only Jalal al Din's determination and inspired example restored purpose and discipline to his ranks and
made it possible for his army to stave off the second Mongol on-
slaught, this time on the left. The Mongols kept on the attack until mid-afternoon, when a series of lucky maneuvers on the part of
the Turcomans resulted in heavy losses for the Mongols and they
fell back, giving Jalal al Din the opportunity to rally his men, and
he soon managed to make the most of this opportunity. Jalal al
Din ordered his army to mount up and to pursue the Mongols and
kill all those whom they caught, turning the retreat to a debacle
for the Mongols, who compounded their defeat by mounting a
hasty counterattack that ended up in the Mongols riding into a
trap, which made it possible for Jalal al Din's army to inflict the final blows upon them.

Jenghiz Khan was already on his way to Parwan when word of
this defeat reached him, and it goaded him to increase the pace of
his travel, moving his augmented forces at an astonishing eighty-
five miles a day, a grueling pace even by the Mongols' standards.
His own troops were joined by large companies of soldiers under
his sons Jagatai, Tolui, and Ugotaei, creating a massive army that

swept over all opposition in the northern Afghan region, destroying all who stood against them and even those who didn't.

In the meantime, things were not going well for Jalal al Din. Amin Malik and Ighrac, who had fought the Mongols so well together, now quarreled with each other over loot, a dispute that ended in Ighrac ordering his Turcoman forces to depart and taking with him Azam Malik and his Islamic Indians, crucially reducing Jalal al Din's army just at the time more men were desperately needed. Without sufficient soldiers to hold Parwan, Jalal al Din shifted his position eastward, abandoning his stronghold at Parwan and heading toward the Indus River before Jenghiz Khan came and took the town from him, a prudent decision, for Jenghiz Khan arrived at Parwan less than three days after Jalal al Din left it. So rapid was Jalal al Din's retreat that he left behind some of his forces' food and other supplies, booty for Jenghiz Khan's men to seize. Aside from commenting on the tactics of both sides in the battle that had routed his troops, Jenghiz Khan wasted no time at Parwan but set off in pursuit of Jalal al Din at a ferocious pace.

The Mongols overtook the Islamic army as it was preparing to cross the Indus River; caught between the mountains, the river, and the armies of Jenghiz Khan, Jalal al Din was compelled to fight or capitulate, and for Jalal al Din capitulation was unthinkable. A last-ditch battle was fought on November 24, 1221, near what is now the Pakistani town of Kalabagh but what was then still heavily Afghan territory. It was an unfortunate location for Jalal al Din's army, for they had very little room to maneuver and almost no time to prepare for the assault, so that he had to make the best of a bad situation or give up entirely. It was also bitterly cold, and although the weather was clear, distant clouds heralded an approaching storm. The Mongols outnumbered their opponents by a considerable factor—accounts vary from two to one to an incredible nine to one—and they commanded more of the ground.

The position was not a good one for Jalal al Din, but he wasn't able to change that, nor could he hope for any reinforcements to help him. With the loyal Amin Malik and his Turks on his right with his men ranged along the riverbank and his left spread out to the rise of low hills, Jalal al Din made his stand.

Jenghiz Khan's battle standard was nine yak tails, and it marked his progress through the battle; judging from the various descriptions of the battle—which differ widely, but which do agree on this—he was unusually active in this assault, moving from one part of his armies to another, constantly in motion and demanding more than the usual immediate responses from his men. It was a dangerous tactic for him to employ, but Jenghiz Khan was an audacious leader of his troops, willing to trade protection at the rear for offering swift responses to the rapid changes of battle. Some of his foes have suggested that he ordered his standard to be carried about to make it appear he was constantly in motion, but that seems unnecessarily subtle for Jenghiz Khan, who was not usually inclined to such deceptions, so it is more likely that he was, as his standard indicated, uncharacteristically active in this battle. It is hardly surprising that some of Jalal al Din's men regarded Jenghiz Khan with superstitious awe, declaring that he was an evil djinn to move about so constantly. By contrast, Jalal al Din did not travel far from his center position until that position became untenable.

Amin Malik and his Turkish soldiers, on the Muslim right, seem to have been the first to move, although accounts of the events are somewhat confusing and sorting out the actual events as they, in fact, occurred, is nearly impossible. The Muslim right certainly had the most heavily armed soldiers, and it is likely that the Mongols pressed the attack on them initially. In any case, the Turks were able to force the Mongols back, and in order to take advantage of this, Jalal al Din ordered men from his left to reinforce the right, then led his own center in a daring charge against the Mongols, apparently with the intention of killing Jenghiz Khan himself. But this proved hard to do, for Jenghiz Khan did not remain at the center, as Jalal al Din supposed he would, but continued to move fluidly among his troops, making the most of all opportunities to break through Jalal al Din's right and thus blocking any possibility of a mass retreat across the river. This constant movement also proved a distraction to Jalal al Din, for he could not narrow his response to a direct attack on Jenghiz Khan himself but was forced to try to maintain a wide, uniform front against this swift-moving enemy. Jalal al Din continued to weaken his left to hold the riverbank on his right, depleting his troops almost recklessly in a forlorn attempt to strengthen the right, which was no longer on the attack but had been repulsed by the Mongols and was now struggling to hang on to the riverbank. Their position was compromised still further when Amin Malik was killed during an attempt to push his line in the direction of Peshawar, bringing confusion to the Turks and a faltering in Jalal al Din's defensive line, substantially weakening the position.

Things were already looking bleak to Jalal al Din's forces when another contingent of Mongol soldiers arrived and at once attacked on the Muslim left, driving against a much-reduced line in determined waves; they had been sent around behind the line of hills at the beginning of the battle by Jenghiz Khan. Whether in anticipation of just such a development or to hold men in reserve to reinforce his army is a matter of historical debate, but whatever it was, the Mongols were able to surround the Muslims on three sides, pinning them down in what proved to be a tactical turning point in the battle. It was a dangerous situation for Jalal al Din, yet he continued to rally his men in spite of the pounding his army was taking. He mounted a fresh horse and led a series of charges on the Mongol center, all of which proved useless. Finally, when no other course seemed possible, he, according to some accounts, shed his armor as a sign that he would fight no longer, before, according to all accounts, urging his horse off a cliff and into the Indus River in an attempt to escape the Mongols. He reached the far bank, but many others did not.

His men followed after him, Jenghiz Khan's troops immediately behind them, hacking them with their cavalry swords and shooting others with arrows until the Indus ran red with blood. The Mongols were not interested in prisoners but in wiping out the opposing army. Estimates are that between seven hundred and one thousand Muslims escaped, catastrophic losses for any military leader, and a decisive turning point in the battle.

According to accounts from the period, Jenghiz Khan remarked, "Happy the father who has such a son," when he learned that Jalal al Din had survived. Jenghiz Khan continued to be generous in his praise of Jalal al Din and insisted that his men show him respect. Such admiration did not keep him from capturing Jalal al Din's children, the oldest of whom was eight, and ordering them flung into the Indus to drown, to discourage any future uprisings as well as to terrorize Jalal al Din and his men. He also ordered three of Jalal al Din's wives killed, although the specifics of how the executions were to be carried out are not reliably recorded.

Jalal al Din lost any chance of reclaiming his father's lands that day but did not give up fighting for Islam, nor did he lose the hope that he might yet carve out a territory for himself. He emerged from the Indus River with his ambition intact. Despite catastrophic losses, Jalal al Din was determined to reclaim what he had lost and expand his territory, a commitment that compelled him to turn westward.

While Jenghiz Khan continued east by north to attack many Islamic strongholds in northern India, Pakistan, and Afghanistan and cross into Russia, Jalal al Din went into Persia, then on to what are now Georgia, Armenia, and Kurdish territories. Being a charismatic figure, Jalal al Din rallied many companies of soldiers to his cause and for the most part was able to hold his army together in spite of various hardships. He never again faced Jenghiz Khan's Mongols directly in battle. In time Jalal al Din's army dwindled, all but the most hardened soldiers leaving his ranks before 1228. Increasingly he made enemies among his fellow-Mohammedans, which served only to forge him into a more obdurate foe of most of those around him, a posture that eventually alienated all but the most extreme of his followers, who formed their own fighting unit that was almost as feared as the Mongols. After his murder in 1231, Jalal al Din's army continued westward to the Mediterranean Sea, conquering Jerusalem and driving the Crusaders out of that city for the last time in 1244, at last achieving the success that Jalal al Din had sought for so long. Jerusalem remained in Islamic hands until 1917.

This seemingly remote campaign out at the far edge of the Middle East ended up having great impact on the region for centuries. It dramatically changed the balance of power in Asia in a way that had lasting impact from China to Europe and established Mongol control not only of the Old Silk Road from Constantinople to Xian and Bei-jing but of the Khyber Pass, which connects northern India with Afghanistan and Russia; this control of trade routes had as enduring an impact on Central Asia as any aspect of the war. The vastness of Mongol conquest was a major military achievement, but it was only the beginning of the Mongol expansion that led to their eventual control of northern and central China, northern India, southeastern Russia and southern Siberia, northern Persia, eastern Turkey, and, of course, the vast plains of Mongolia, the Steppes of Central Asia. Unlike many conquest-built empires that were the product of the determination of a single leader, the khanates established by Jenghiz Khan didn't fall apart upon his death, although the territory he conquered was apportioned, creating discrete, governable regions. His sons and grandsons held his accomplishments and reputation in such high esteem that they generally found ways to negotiate disputes rather than squabble away their territories as happened in Europe upon the death of Charlemagne and to the sons of the last Mongol conqueror, Timur-i Lenkh (called Tamburlane in the West).

Securing the Afghani passes increased the mobility of the Mongol troops by putting them in position to take advantage of established roads to move troops, as well as instituting a foundation for wealth in taxing the various caravans that continued to use the old trade routes. Originally the Mongols taxed in the form of tribute—usually meat and milk, occasionally cloth and skins, very rarely animals and slaves—but over time this proved insufficient to the needs of the Mongol armies and money took the place of food, although not in Jenghiz Khan's lifetime: he continued to demand tribute in food and goods, in the ancient Mongol tradition, and to distrust money as useless and unreliable. It was his belief that if he could not put tribute to actual, immediate use, it was a hindrance, not an asset. His suspicions of money were not his only traditional Mongol trait: he was also almost superstitiously in awe of the written word and throughout his long campaigns made a point of destroying books and other written documents wherever he found them. For a nomad these attitudes made pragmatic sense, but for a conqueror they were severely limiting. Jenghiz Khan's son Tolui was the first to see the advantage of money and later, the usefulness of written records, and it was he who brought about the change in policies regarding taxation and record keeping, and it was his sons who became the most significant of the Mongol rulers, due in part to their respect for written communications.

Little though Jenghiz Khan trusted most of the trappings of what might be called civilization, he put great reliance on laws, and one of his most significant contributions to his conquered lands was the beginning of a uniform code of law and legal procedures that made maintaining his empire a manageable proposition and that his heirs respected enough to enlarge upon and use themselves. He was certain that uniform laws would hold his empire together more effectively than force of arms—an unusual understanding for a Mongol warlord and an indication of what was to come. This more cosmopolitan view eventually fitted into both Chinese and Islamic cultures, but with vastly different results.

Although the Mongol domination of the huge expanse of conquered territory was relatively brief—roughly 250 years—it made for a dramatic impact on all the conquered peoples and all groups near enough to have to deal with the Mongols, which eventually included people all the way from the Mediterranean to the Pacific. The Mongol legacy was long enduring and, in fact, exists to this day, not only in mythologies of Asia but in the ongoing Mongol culture and in the far-flung Mongol influence that touched so much of Asia and Europe.

The historically significant descendants of Jenghiz Khan include his grandson Kublai, who was founder of the Yuan Dynasty and Emperor of China; Kublai's brother Hulegu, who conquered Baghdad, Aleppo, and Damascus and expanded Mongol territory well into Turkey. Hulegu adapted many of the cultural assets of the Arabs, and his descendants converted to Islam, as did many of the Mongols in the western khanates. Known for cruelty as much as his brother Kublai was known for tolerance, Hulegu maintained an illustrious court in Baghdad that never achieved the social synthesis with his conquered people that Kublai accomplished in Beijing, and this was not entirely the result of the existing cultures of China and the Middle East: both men owed a great deal not only to their grandfather Jenghiz Khan but to their mother, a strong-willed woman named Sorkhaktani, a Nestorian Christian who, upon being widowed, refused the new marriage custom demanded and instead devoted herself to the advancement of her sons. It was she who shaped the temperaments of her sons for the worlds they would enter, and their behavior has as much to do with her understanding of their circumstances as it does with their personalities. It was said she was the only member of Jenghiz Khan's family who was able to stand up to him, for which he admired and respected her, but also disliked her.

By 1259 Mongol armies had penetrated as far west as Hungary and Poland and had made sallies into the eastern flank of the Holy Roman Empire, almost reaching Vienna. Soon the very thought of Mongols struck fear into the heart of the Balkans and eastern Europe. The legends of the Mongols were so overblown that in some regions just the suggestion that the Mongols might be coming was enough to cause the local populations to abandon their homes and land in order to avoid any confrontation with them. They had attacked Moscow and Novgorod in Russia, as well as Kiev. They had briefly held territory in what is now the Czech Republic. They had ravaged Serbia and northern Bulgaria and held territory in the Middle East as far as the Euphrates River. The Empire of the Great Khan included most of China and Tibet; the Jagatai Khanate held territory from the Atlai Mountains to Bukhara; the Il-Khan Empire took in most of the old Persian Empire, including Afghanistan, modern Iraq, Iran, and a large portion of Turkey; the Khanate of the Golden Horde stretched from Poland to the River Yenisei in Mongolia. It is significant to note that the Mongols were the only armies ever to invade Russia successfully in the winter. They struck in a brilliant campaign that assaulted Russia from three positions at once, a coordinated offense that was unprecedented at the time and unequaled since.

The last of the Mongol conquerors was, in fact, half-Turkish: Timur-i Lenkh, a devout Muslim who spent most of his career fighting other Muslims from India to Damascus. His territory included the regions of the Parwan and Indus Campaign. Descended from the Turkish Balas clan on his father's side, he was probably Jenghiz Khan's great-great-great-grandson on his mother's side, although the lineage is a little sketchy: he was most certainly half-Mongol. Timur himself declared he was a direct descendant of Jenghiz Khan, and no one during his lifetime disputed that claim. His military expansion was done in the great Mongol manner—a combination of Blitzkrieg and terrorist techniques—subjugating the old Persian Empire and the northwestern portion of the Delhi Sultanate; his reputation was equal to any of Jenghiz Khan's progeny, and Timur's success in battle was as impressive as his ancestor's. At the time of Timur's death in 1404, he was planning another assault on China with the intent of adding it to his dominion, convinced that as a descendant of Jenghiz Khan he was entitled to rule China, no matter what his Yuan Dynasty cousins might think. The pressure put on eastern Islam by the Mongol conquerors contributed to the Turkish Ottoman Empire focusing its expansion on the West, which had a long and significant impact on Europe as well as on western Islam, which was forced to turn westward for conquests instead of continuing an unending and fruitless campaign on its eastern flank. Timur's control of Central Asia would not have been possible had not his ancestor Jenghiz Khan prevailed at Parwan and the Indus, almost two centuries earlier.

The Mongols were a new kind of military force in the East, largely mounted instead of afoot, highly mobile, more interested in acquiring territory than loot—hardly surprising in a society of grazing-economy nomads—and culturally inclined to place high value on military excellence. The continuing success of the Mongol hordes depended on the compound bow and on the Mongol ponies. These were not the large, leggy, aristocratic horses of Europe but small, sturdy beasts, short necked, sure-footed, and hard hooved, shaggy in winter, sleek in summer, bred for stamina and endurance instead of speed, size, and looks. Mongol ponies can trot for hours, covering more than fifty miles a day over fairly rough ground. On campaign Jenghiz Khan was able to push this to more than eighty miles a day in summer, during good weather over moderate ground, compared to the speed of a European army of the same period, which rarely covered more than fifteen miles in a day. This speed was possible because Jenghiz Khan allocated four to six horses per soldier: on the move, each soldier would ride one horse and lead three, four, or five others. Riding from sunrise until sunset, the army kept up a steady trot for most of the day; in order not to exhaust their mounts, approximately every two hours the army would halt for a brief rest and an opportunity to water the horses, move tack and weapons to one of the led horses, put the most recently ridden pony at the end of the string, remount, and trot for another two hours, then repeat the switch. This enabled the horses to remain fairly fresh throughout the day, as well as providing remounts that could be immediately available during battle instead of waiting for the reserve horses to catch up with the van of the army.

Over hard ground Mongol ponies are the match for any equines but mules. The ponies are light keepers (they don't need a lot of high-quality food), and they can stand extremes of temperatures that many larger horses cannot. The Mongols used springy, lightweight saddles, not unlike the modern European military saddle, and preferred full-cheek broken-mouth snaffles for bits with single reins and modified standing martingales for increased control of the ponies' heads. Of necessity, the Mongols were superb horsemen, and they remain so to this day. By the time of the Parwan and Indus campaign, the Mongols provided sectioned scale armor for their ponies—that is, thin overlapping metal rectangles sewn onto leather in various buckled pieces designed to cover the head, neck, front, flanks, and rump of the pony—preferring maneuverability to protection, just as they, themselves, wore comparatively light armor in battle, also of sectioned scale. Earlier on in Jenghiz Khan's career, the armor for men and animals were considerably lighter for men and mounts than was the case later; protection of the Mongol ponies became increasingly important as his ambitions took his armies farther and farther afield, away from his herds in Mongolia, requiring a greater degree of care for these essential animals. The tactical contribution of these hardy ponies to Jenghiz Khan's successes cannot be overestimated.

Like the Legions of Imperial Rome, the Mongol armies were based on units of one hundred men; the Roman century (one-hundred-man unit) was most often an infantry unit composed of eighty fighting men and twenty support—armorers, cooks, farriers, physicians, wheelwrights, tent-makers, boot-makers, scouts, suppliers, and engineers. By contrast, the *jagun* (the officer in charge of one hundred men, and his troops) was entirely composed of fighting men, usually cavalry, no support included. Every man in the *jagun* was a fighting soldier and expected to be able to fend for himself in regard to assistance and supplies. Although not nearly so conscientious about matériel as the Romans were, Jenghiz Khan created a new position, *jerbi,* an officer in charge of supplies, inventing his version of the quartermaster corps, a strategic necessity for the scale of his military activities. Very early on he realized the danger of moving beyond the point of resupply and so did his best to make sure that never happened. He also established an elite unit, the aristocratic *kashik,* to be the heart of his army. In addition, he selected a thousand men to be his personal bodyguard to protect him against sudden attacks on his headquarters. His troops were fiercely loyal and strictly disciplined.

Speed and superior numbers made the Mongols the most successful military force of their time, capable of defeating almost any opponent by keeping up a highly flexible assault on all the armies that stood against them. Jenghiz Khan had a particular talent for reading land and using it to his fighting advantage and for lightning decisions during actual combat that resulted in many victories, often with the added satisfaction of being able to turn apparent defeats to triumphant advantage. His armies knew how to recover from momentary setbacks, how to keep discipline in the most harrowing circumstances, and how to isolate their enemies' forces, as was shown on the Indus. In sheer numbers, the Mongol forces proved to be noteworthy foes, but it was their skill in battle that made them victorious over so much of Asia. Jenghiz Khan's descendants never quite equaled his military prowess and endurance—although a few learned other kinds of warfare than his rapid massed cavalry assaults—but with all that he had done, they didn't have to.

The Mongol control of Central Asia remained the keystone of the khanates for two centuries and proved the most durable part of their conquests and the center point of their military expansion. It also provided a stronghold for Jenghiz Khan's descendants, one that allowed them to continue Mongol domination of Central Asia when positions in the west had been reclaimed by Islamic fighters and the eastern Mongols had been transformed into Chinese courtiers. Had Jenghiz Khan not conquered and held those crucial positions in Afghanistan and on the Indus, Mongol territory would have been far more vulnerable to invasion much sooner in the history of the khanates, and Tamerlane would have not been able to hold on to the territory he controlled. The general success of the Mongol expansion in Central Asia and into the Middle East made for a lasting influence in the regions that continued well into the nineteenth century, and to this day their exploits are remembered and studied, preserved by the very written word that Jenghiz Khan so particularly loathed; he might have appreciated the irony.

The Mongol Empire took over much of Asia and the Middle East, and although it was cut up into khanates, it still exerted a degree of control that lasted long after the Mongol presence diminished and the immediate danger of devastating warfare no longer threatened such ancient cities as Baghdad and Shiraz. The stress of long occupation told on many Middle Eastern societies, and that stress fueled long-standing hostilities that began to boil over as the iron hold of the Mongols gave way to the upsurge of regionalism and ethnic clashes.

The Rise of
the Ottoman Empire

*The Last Crusades, Mongols and Turks, the War of
the Black and White Sheep, the Fall of Constantinople*

T HE year 1210 brought a change
to Byzantine politics: at the Par-
liament of Ravennika the Greek lords gave official recognition
to Constantinople as having right and just rule over them, even
though it was currently in Latin hands and therefore following the
Roman, not the Greek, Church. While this submission brought in
much-needed taxes for Byzantium, it required military support
in hotly contested areas at the edges of the empire, as well as containment of regional uprisings against the Latin rulers, and while
none of these rebellions was large enough to erupt into open war,
each took a toll on Constantinople and the Byzantine economy. It
also put a greater dependence on Venetian economic and military
bolstering at Byzantine port cities.

As a result of this endorsement, Theodore Lascaris in what is
now northern Turkey defeated Alexius of Trebizond the following
year, 1211, flying in the face of the Byzantine suzerainty. He also
captured the Sultan of Rum, which was embarrassing to the Latin
Empire (the kingdoms established by the Crusaders for the supposed
purpose of protecting Christianity, and the European Crusaders in
charge of Constantinople) as well as to the Byzantine Greeks, but
no one seemed inclined to punish him for his undertaking. That

changed in 1212 when the Latin Emperor Henry I took his army to the southern coast of the Black Sea and challenged Theodore. Rather than face loss and defeat, Theodore surrendered part of Bithynia to the Latin emperor and withdrew from battle for the time being.

It was at about this time that the general sequestration of Islamic women became compulsory, not optional, as it had been for many parts of the Middle East. Among farming families, women were expected to work but were traditionally kept to areas controlled by their families, areas occasionally extending to the marketplace, but over time this access was curtailed, and women were expected to remain within walls and fences. In many Islamic cities, sequestration had been limited to married women and affianced girls, but there were other women, mostly in trade and crafts, who were allowed a degree of independence. Many pious women were self-sequestered, while others had too many realities impinging upon them to make sequestration practicable. But with Byzantines, Crusaders, and Turks about, women were considered too vulnerable to be permitted beyond the confines of the home and, within the home, to the women's quarters, so that within a century virtuous Islamic women would boast that they had never in their lives seen a man to whom they were not related by blood or marriage. On the rare occasions that certain women were permitted to go beyond their houses, they were swathed and hidden in what amounted to portable tents, a tradition that continues in parts of the Middle East to this day.

In 1212 one of the saddest events in the long and miserable history of Crusading took place: the Children's Crusade. Two boys from France, Stephen and Nicolas, in separate groups led vast numbers of children toward the Holy Land with the muddled notion that they could, with their innocence, accomplish what force of arms could not. Those who didn't die of exposure, hunger, exhaustion, or disease in Stephen's group were kidnapped and sold to Arab, Greek, and Turkish slavers. Nicolas' group became unraveled in Italy, and many of the children were captured and sent either as slaves or as prostitutes to Rome and Naples and to Spain. Estimates are that upward of fifty thousand children were the victims of this madness.

The Latins of Byzantium had their hands full trying to keep the Byzantines under control. Theodore Dukas Angelus took over Epirus and did his best to expand into Bulgaria and Byzantine positions on the Black Sea, believing, and not without cause, that he had a better claim to Byzantine rule than did anyone among the Latins (most of whom were German or French). He managed to take Corfu and Durazzo from Venetian control in 1214 and, confident of greater success, began to attract privateers to his cause, eventually assembling a small flotilla of ships bent on loot and intimidation. An unruly lot, the captains of this company often spent as much time fighting among themselves as pursuing Latin, Venetian, and Genoese ships. In granting the captains the right to keep all their profits from slaving, Theodore Dukas was able to maintain his control over them and to be confident of their cooperation for almost a decade.

1218 saw the Pope Innocent III preaching a Fifth Crusade, marking the succession of Sultan Malik-al-Adil by Malik-al-Kamil and the replacement of King of Jerusalem John of Brienne, a capable man long plagued by failing health and increasing paranoia, with the papal legate Pelagius as an indication of a need for action. Because Crusading was no longer the high-stakes activity it had been, the Pope also claimed to have had a vision of Roman Christianity triumphant in the Middle East, probably wishful thinking mixed with propaganda, but assertions of this sort no longer carried the weight they had a century ago, and the zealous support the Pope sought did not materialize. This Crusade was far less popular than the previous ones had been, and not just because of the outcome of the Fourth Crusade: Europe was preoccupied with internal strife that demanded military solutions, and therefore many European rulers were not inclined to spare armed men and knights for a campaign so far away. In addition, the lack of true conquest in the Holy Land was frustrating to many; the major lords of Europe were less willing to donate men and matériel to what was thought to be a failing venture, God's Will or not. The Pope might hold the key to salvation, but the European leaders had problems on their doorsteps that superseded their religious duties to Jerusalem. Thanks to continuing trade with Venice and Genoa, the Middle East was becoming more lucrative for Europeans without war than with it.

To modern eyes, the futility of the Crusades is obvious, given the singular lack of success of the first ones, but to the early medieval mind it was the duty of Christians to defend their faith as a means of demonstrating their piety. Failure to take the Cross could bring immediate suspicions of heresy upon the trained soldier who declined such an opportunity, especially if he were a younger son, and that, in turn, could be very bad for his family, for guilt by association was a common assumption in that time. This was more compelling than patriotic fervor; it redounded to the very heart of Roman Christianity: if the Crusades failed, it was a judgment on the Crusaders. Not a mistake in vision or simply poor preparation, it was a failure of faith. This assumption continued as the perceived benefit of Crusading long after true zeal had left the movement, for the Church had laid out this justification and to question it was tantamount to challenging papal authority. That meant that the Crusaders had to redouble their efforts in order to uphold the vision of victory or be damned for eternity for not doing God's Will as expressed by the Pope. It also excused any enormity practiced upon the opponents of their faith, no matter how bloody, and tended to encourage a degree of barbarity that appalled the Islamic faithful. Becoming a Crusader guaranteed the support of the Church for the volunteer's family, which could mean the difference between prosperity and beggary for many European nobles. So, confident of assembling another army, the Church trotted out its usual aphorisms and promised the spoils and pillage to the Crusaders, determined to get it right this time and, in doing so, perpetuated the errors of the past.

But this time, there was pressure from another direction: in 1218, on the other side of the Middle East, Jenghiz Khan's armies completed their conquest of Persia and began setting up their government of the region. The significance of this event was not fully appreciated in the West, where it was assumed that the Mongols had been sent by God to help in the fight against Islam, an assessment that seems more like whistling in the dark than a true appreciation of the situation. As a result, the Middle East found itself dealing with two kinds of threats, neither of which was acknowledged by the other. Precious opportunity to prepare for the coming Mongol onslaught was lost, and eventually the Middle East paid the price.

The Fifth Crusade set out for Egypt in 1219 and had an initial success at Damietta, which the Crusaders would not negotiate in trade for Jerusalem, confident that their original victory was an indication of things to come. The Crusaders attempted a march on Cairo, but a combination of harrying attacks by the sultan's men, insufficient food, and an outbreak of disease—possibly due to waterborne parasites—halted them before their goal was reached. In 1221 the sultan and the Crusaders made a truce that lasted for eight years, long enough for the Crusaders to withdraw from Egypt and to abandon Damietta and end the Fifth Crusade.

Toward the end of 1222 the Mongols invaded Russia in a

ferocious land grab that served to put the West on notice that the Middle East would not continue to be a buffer against their westward drive and that any hope of alliance with them was unrealistic. The relentlessness of the Mongol campaign terrified the Russians and delayed any effective resistance so that the time the Russians were able to mount an organized opposition the Mongols had penetrated well into Russian territory. In 1223 at the Battle of Kalka River, Subutai, the leader of the Mongol army, defeated the Russians, but having outrun his supply lines and destroyed crops in his advance, he was forced to withdraw or face starvation. His withdrawal provided the Russians a chance to prepare for the following year, but they made the dangerous assumption that the Mongols had retreated for good and made only minor improvements in their fortifications and roads, an oversight that cost them dearly.

The encroaching Mongols goaded the Turks into a determined defense of their annexed territory, and for a time the Turks made common cause with not only their conquered peoples but with the Syrians and the Armenians, with the intention of holding off any renewed Mongol assault. Upon the death of Jenghiz Khan in 1227, the allies of the beleaguered Turks breathed a sigh of relief, assuming that with Jenghiz Khan dead, his empire would unravel, as had happened so many times in the past, but this relief certainly didn't last. The sons of Jenghiz Khan were not only determined to hold on to the lands they had taken; they wanted to take more. In spite of the Turks' best efforts, they were driven farther westward as the Mongols continued to spread.

During this time Islam, which had been supporting all manner of intellectual exploration and had been the most intellectually forward-looking culture west of China, began to take a more rigid stance in matters long regarded as academic, not directly religious.

Increasingly religious men ran the schools and put primary emphasis on the teaching of religion. There was increased concern about the role of God and dogma in all branches of knowledge, and from that came a movement to purify Islamic thought to be in accord with religious precepts, even when the religious explanations flew in the face of known facts. That the Religious Right of the time should have got such a hold on nonreligious learning was not surprising, given the reality of the circumstances: Islam was beset from two sides, engaged in all manner of bloody conflict that left the land devastated and the population battered and decimated. The small, extremist military Orders such as the Hashasheen—begun as a kind of Islamic anti-Crusader ninja organization, an Islamic answer to the Templars and Hospitalers—enlarged and began to take on the Mongols as their attacks brought them into Arab-held land. The most warlike imams attracted the greatest support because they fed military and civic resistence to invasion. The emphasis on study and the expansion of thought and knowledge as a cornerstone of Islam took a backseat to a resurgence of clan-based nationalism. This stagnating of intellectual inquiry extended even to Spain, where the Christian rulers in the north were finally mounting an effective campaign to reclaim the land they regarded as theirs.

One of the great accomplishments of Islamic academic studies of the early thirteenth century was the *Dictionary of Geography*, completed in 1224, compiled by Yaqoot ibn Abdullah, an Islamic Greek who had spent his youth as a slave in Baghdad and had been sold to a merchant who paid for his education and for whom he served as a clerk and dispatcher for many years, acquiring the first information that led to his later work. Freed in 1199, he became a bookseller, traveling the Mediterranean Basin and the eastern trade routes until the Mongol invasions sent him back to Aleppo for safety. Works of this sort, originally encouraged by rulers and imams alike, after 1240 or so diminish sharply in response to the upsurge of strict religiosity. What had been a flowering intellectual society now adopted a religion-first approach to all learning, stultifying thought and restricting inquiry.

By 1227 a Sixth Crusade was readying to depart for the Holy Land under the Holy Roman Emperor Frederick II, but this was slowed by an outbreak of typhus among his soldiers. All through the winter he refused to set sail until most of his forces had recovered, and for this Pope Gregory IX excommunicated him, apparently to get him to embark, regardless of the unusually stormy weather and the condition of his army. Gregory said God would not tolerate such laggard defense of the Holy Land and that was Frederick's fault. In spite of the excommunication, Frederick continued his plans for the Crusade, absorbing the costs of wintering from his own fortune. It was not until the following spring that Frederick started on his voyage, his army reduced by a third thanks to disease and desertion. Unlike his predecessors, Frederick had taken the time to learn something about the Arabs, the Egyptians, the Turks, the Syrians, and Islam and so was able to deal with the heirs of Malik-al-Adil more through negotiation than through force of arms. Since Frederick was still excommunicated, the bargains he struck were not binding on the Pope, but they did require the adherence of subsequent Holy Roman Emperors, a kind of political sleight-of-hand that gave the Pope a tremendous amount of leeway in dealing with the Middle East that treaties had always imposed before. Despite Frederick's continuing to promote the Roman Church's cause in the Middle East, the Pope took advantage of Frederick's absence to send papal forces into Germany in a Crusade against Frederick because he was excommunicated. Papal forces took over almost a quarter of the Holy Roman Empire, claiming that Frederick had defaulted his claim to it.

Unaware of papal duplicity at home—in a fascinating combination of diplomacy and military good sense—he did not require his men to fight in traditional European heavy chain mail and padded actions but in Greek scale armor, which was lighter and cooler than their chain, and he usually planned his actions so they could take place well before noon or after the mid-day siesta—by the summer of 1229, Frederick held Jerusalem, Nazareth, Bethlehem, the corridor from Acre to Jerusalem, and a few of the most crucial Crusaders' fortresses. He had signed a formal treaty with the Sultan of Egypt, Salah-al-Din's nephew Malik-al-Kamil, a man who rarely mixed religious devotion with worldly practicality. The one group Frederick could not charm or battle was the Orthodox Church; it firmly opposed him and did not recognize his claim to Jerusalem through his late wife's father, John of Brienne, who had been King of Jerusalem. His Middle East Crusading goals completed, Frederick headed home to deal with the Pope. The following year, Gregory rescinded Frederick's excommunication and restored to him most of the lands the papal army had occupied but insisted that many of the fiefdoms be constituted as *vidamies*—those were estates owned by and for the Church but maintained the same way a county was, with a *vidame* instead of a count to run them—thereby ensuring regional political power for the Pope and the Church.

The general air of intellectual intransigence among the Europeans was typical of the period—Islam was not alone in stifling innovative thought. The pragmatism and empiricism of the Romans had given way to a view of the world as a flawed metaphor of Heaven, which was the perfected state of all creation. The world was circular, not spherical, and it was contained by rivers, one of which flowed from Paradise and contained the Water of Life. Jerusalem was at the center of the world, which functioned like a medieval fiefdom, with Jesus and God at the center of it in the New Jerusalem or the Celestial City where God ruled in perfect judgment. All men of all classes on earth were poor analogies to the angels, archangels, seraphim, cherubim, thrones, and dominions in Heaven, so that any religious contention not only damaged the soul of the living; it caused harm to the hosts of Heaven. This view reinforced the highly stratified social structure of the time, and its intellectual climate explains why the monks compiling the early medieval beastiaries (animal atlases) decided that camels represented humility because they knelt to be mounted and that tigers were the embodiment of vanity because they could be stopped in an attack by throwing glass balls at them that would transfix them with their reflection or their reflection would remind them of their cubs, admiration of which would keep them from continuing their attack. There is no record that this theory was ever put to the test.

The Greek Orthodox Church did not subscribe to the same general restrictions the Pope demanded of the Latins, for the Orthodox Church saw itself as less worldly—and therefore spiritually superior—than the Roman one and operated as a kind of parallel body to the complex political life of Byzantium, rather than as a political participant as the Roman Church did. With the ancient traditions of Athens, the Greek Orthodox Church did not oppose the study of philosophy but balked at supporting more practical fields of inquiry, such as engineering and metallurgy, which were relegated to military applications and given no place beyond the most minimal in the educational institutions that were under the control of the Orthodox Church and generally limited to those seeking a religious career. This included librarians and catalog makers. One academic discipline that overlapped the religious thought of both the Orthodox Church and Islam was the field of mathematics, the mysteries of which were regarded by both religions as much a mystical study as one of worldly application.

Within this increasingly hostile and divided society, the Latin Byzantines were soon beset by internal problems, not the least of which was a teetering economy and a high rate of desertion from the armies, especially those on the borders of the empire. The Turks were constantly nibbling away at Byzantine holdings in what today is Turkey, steadily increasing their areas of control and, since most had converted to Islam, gaining the support of the religious leaders throughout the region. There was another problem impinging on the Byzantines and Europeans at the time—an outbreak of leprosy that moved from the Middle East into Europe with the Crusading armies. Leprosy had been around and documented for nearly three millennia, but this outbreak was especially virulent. The Latins of Constantinople were particularly hard-hit by it in the 1220s, and over the next three decades the disease spread into Russia and Europe, where it remained until about 1300, when the disease diminished as mysteriously as it had worsened. The fear of the disease was profound, and at the height of this outbreak in Byzantium as many as 10 percent of the Latins were said to suffer from the disease, but medicine was so minimal that almost any skin condition, from psoriasis to porphyra, could result in a preemptive diagnosis and immediate isolation of the supposedly stricken individual. Since the most often prescribed remedy for leprosy at the time was a paste of mercury, cures were few and far between.

Thanks to the Turks and the Mongols, the style of warfare was changing again in the Middle East. The Europeans had been emphasizing siege warfare and attacks on specific sites—fortresses, cities, ports—with a surround-and-wait-it-out approach, marked by attempts to bring down walls by undermining them and putting holes in them with barrages of stones as well as rendering the besieged city/fortress dangerous with using the ballistae for lobbing scrap metal over the walls, along with less savory items, such as dead horses. The local region was raided for food and slaves, but the military attention was focused on specific installations and a well-defined surrender, with accompanying pillage and sacking. In Europe, fortified towns and castles were on the rise, armor was getting heavier, with chain mail slowly giving way to plate; massive troop movements in ordered ranks with war engines such as ballistae and trebuchets were standard military fare, as befitted the established castles and cities, the occupation of which were the goals of European campaigns. Static aggression was the standard of land warfare in Europe, and an approach they did not abandon in the Middle East for the stance had worked well for them in the past. But in the Middle East the development was toward opposite strategies: nomadic peoples gave less attention to towns and forts and favored rapid-deployment occupation instead of sieges. The mounted, mobile Turks and the lightning attacks of the Mongols moved the emphasis away from long encampments at a single location to the swift occupation of as much territory as possible and the control of roads and villages as the means to take over; from such strategies, the Mongols in particular soon routed opposition as they streamed into a region and shut it down, immobilizing opposition and gaining control of communications in the same dramatic attack. This general military control put the Europeans at a disadvantage, and even the Latin Byzantines suffered because of it. Instead of concerted charges of cavalry, the new reality of war required rapid, flexible skirmishes, more like hunting than warfare. The Arabs and Syrians adapted quickly to these tactics and the Egyptians embraced them soon after, but the Byzantines and the Europeans were in no position to change, and over the next century their inability to accommodate this new style of warfare cost them dearly.

The year 1224 marked a shift in the attempts of the Byzantines to be rid of the Latins in their empire. Ioannes Vatatzes, the most powerful military leader of the Nicean Empire—a kind of offshoot of the Byzantine Empire, dedicated to restoring Byzantium to Greek hands and regaining territory lost to the Syrians and Turks, centered in Asia Minor—made the most of his opportunities. Under Vatatzes, the Nicean army was able to defeat the largely Frankish Latin forces at Poimanenon, then went on to gain control over the important Greek Islands of Chios, Lemnos, Samos, and Rhodes, from where he could dispatch part of his army to make an effort to take Adrianople. Suddenly the Empire of Nicea, which was supposed to be an ally of Byzantium, was its most dangerous opponent. To make matters worse for the Latins, in the same year Theodore of Epirus not only defeated the Latins, he managed to keep the Niceans from taking Adrianople. All this while the Mongols were raging through Persia, headed west.

Not every part of the Middle East was in disarray at the time. At the eastern end of the region, the Delhi Sultanate was undergoing a vigorous expansion at this time: Atlamish's reign was marked by economic growth as well as military consolidation. Dedicated to the preservation of Delhi and Islam, Atlamish supported improved communications and a standard of justice unusual in that region at that time. By enlisting the Afghans in his cause, he was able to encourage Western trade at a time most merchants were beleaguered beyond their usual risks. He was one of the few who held off the assault of the Mongols under Jenghiz Khan, largely as a result of the Indus-Parwan Campaign, described previously in this book, which turned Mongol attention away from Delhi and toward the lands beyond the Caspian Sea. Upon his death in 1236, he was succeeded by his daughter, Razy'yat-ud-Din, whose successful four-year reign of unusually stable economic conditions marked the only time to that era in history that an Islamic woman ruled in India. She was killed by her Hindu subjects in 1240.

In 1237, the Mongols invaded Russia and for the next three years pressed on into Hungary and Poland in destructive waves that razed villages and decimated the population. This took some of the stress off the Latin Byzantines, but it didn't last. Batu, the Mongol general/warlord and grandson of Jenghiz Khan—as were his cousins, Kublai Khan, Emperor of China, and Hulegu, who reigned at Baghdad after 1258—reached well into what is now Germany and Austria, but a number of political complications arising in the khanates required him to draw back, which he did in a roundabout way, subduing Wallachia, Moldavia (in modern-day Romania), and Bulgaria before establishing himself and his Golden Horde in and around the lower Volga River on the north end of the Caspian Sea, with Sarai as his capital. By 1247 he was able to strike out at Georgia, Armenia, Mesopotamia, and Azerbaijan from this location. Like most khans of the Mongols, the Golden Horde pledged fealty to the Great Khan of Kara-Khorum, in Mongolia, but after 1300 this was more a formality than an actual acknowledgment of authority.

1244 brought Jerusalem once more under the control of Islamic mercenaries led by the Egyptian Pasha Khwarahzmi. This in turn created a knee-jerk response from the Roman Church, and the call went out for a Seventh Crusade. Since the Pope and the Holy Roman Emperor were still at odds—Frederick had been re-excommunicated—Louis IX of France was given the task of leading the Crusade, which he agreed to do, although his mother and his treasurer advised against it, an unpopular move that later gained him sainthood. Louis' designs in undertaking the Crusade were somewhat less exalted: he was hoping the Pope would grant him some of Frederick's lands in exchange for leading the Crusade. In 1245 Louis and about forty thousand men headed for the Holy Land. This time, the Genoese did much of the transport, since the

Venetians had become suspect for their long dealings with Middle Eastern ports and their suspiciously cordial treaties with Islamic governments. Wanting to make the most of this opportunity, the Genoese began their own campaign to gain control of important Greek islands and in 1248 they occupied Rhodes.

In the spring of 1249, the Seventh Crusade reached Egypt and took Damietta almost unopposed, thanks to the judicious use of siege towers, fairly new in the Middle East but well developed in Europe and therefore difficult for Egyptians to defend against. The Crusaders used Damietta as a base from which to march on Cairo. That march was delayed because shortly after securing Damietta the Crusaders suffered from an outbreak of typhoid fever and scurvy and many of their horses—all of which had been shipped from Europe, the Arab and Barb horses being too small and light to carry a knight in armor and a bard as well— had come down with thrush (a hoof infection) and were not sound for riding. The Crusaders stopped at Mansûra and attempted to get themselves in better condition to fight. For more than eight months the Crusade languished while the new Egyptian Sultan Turanshah hastened from victories in Syria to deal with the Crusaders. His attack was ruthless. After killing almost a quarter of the Crusaders, Turanshah captured Louis of France and used him as a bargaining chip to force the Crusaders to withdraw from Damietta and then to pay a ransom of around 750,000 gold pieces, about two-thirds of which was actually paid, to the outrage of the Pope.

Ironically, Turanshah's great skill in battle made the emirs, who had advanced him to his position, wary of him, for they feared he was gaining too much power over the populace; the army was deeply loyal to him and would protect him. The emirs settled the matter by overthrowing him by treachery within the court and, before the army could react, advancing a new dynasty, the Mameluke dynasty, one of the most enduring Egyptian dynasties since the Pharaohs and one that held up into the nineteenth century. The Mamelukes had been slaves brought from Georgia and trained as soldiers for the sultan and were able to depend on the army for support. While internal skulduggery didn't cease with the new dynasty, it was on a solid enough footing that challenges to its authority could be met and ended without displacement. Even the Mongols, in 1260, were unable to wrest Egypt from the Mamelukes. Having preserved the Islamic Egyptian culture from Mongol domination, the Mamelukes then invited the heirs of the Abbasid dynasty to Cairo as resident rulers-in-exile.

Because of Egyptian governmental stability, trade increased, and Egypt prospered in markets all over the Mediterranean Basin, the Red Sea, and the Arabian Sea. Egyptian cotton, Chinese silk, and spices from all over Asia and the Middle East reached European markets through Egypt, while skilled European artisans, beginning at Egyptian-controlled ports, found work as far away as Kara-Khorum in Mongolia, where in 1249 the French goldsmith Guillaume Boucher built a silver fountain for Mongu Khan that dispensed wine, mead, saki, and kvass (fermented mare's milk, a Mongol favorite). A group of iron-workers was employed by the Il-Khans in Persia to improve their pikes, arrows, and military tools during the Mongol attacks. While the weapons were improved, it was too little too late and the Mongols crushed the Persians. The fate of the iron-workers, like that of so many others, was unknown. Three Benedictine monks found employment as herbalists in Tabriz, maintaining gardens where they cultivated European herbs as well as local plants. Cousin furriers from Udine in Italy in 1261 were engaged to make elaborate fur cloaks for Balban, the new sultan in Delhi.

This former slave Balban, who had served the sultan as chamberlain, married the daughter of the late sultan Mahmus and commenced his rule at Delhi in 1266. Thanks to his years in government service, he had a good idea of what needed fixing, and he instituted land reforms, made a push to stop the banditry that was rife throughout the western trade routes, and established fortresses to protect merchants on the road. He regularized Delhi's position with other Indian rulers and made an attempt to achieve some kind of treaties with the most active of the Afghan warlords. In his twenty-year reign, he held on to the eastern end of the Middle East against Mongols and bandits alike and survived three known attempts to oust him from power.

The Mongols continued their westward expansion, and in 1243, at the Battle of Kosedagh, they conquered the Seljuk Turks, who had controlled the region since 1052, and drove them back south and west, where the Turks had to regroup to make for an effective opposition to the Mongols. In 1258, after Hulegu had taken Baghdad, which had been in Seljuk hands since 1055, his men had sacked it, and the Caliph Musta'seem had been executed, the city became the capital from which Hulegu could continue his westward assaults. Established as a Mongol court but modeled on the Islamic one, it combined luxury and austerity in an uneasy mix that could only be sustained while active warfare was continuing, and Hulegu pursued a policy of unrelenting military action as much to sustain his improvised societal adaptation as for any immediate aggressive advantage: he knew he had to keep his warlords occupied or they would turn on one another and on him. With that in mind, he cast about for new lands to conquer and found no lack of possibilities. Later that year, Hulegu invaded Syria and occupied Aleppo, garrisoning the city with his most experienced troops. Known for his cruelty and his taste for excess, Hulegu ordered most of the Syrian captives killed outright, their bodies to be left in piles for vultures to pick clean. Those who were not killed were made slaves and those capable of hard labor were put to work improving Baghdad's defenses as Hulegu made plans to subdue the rest of the Middle East.

On the Arabian Peninsula, there was an increase in the incidents of fighting between various religious factions, made more severe by the threat of the Mongols that put most of the population on edge as stories about the harshness of Hulegu spread, improving as they went. The Mameluke Empire, marginally the protector of the peninsula, had not expended much in the way of military presence to keep the region secure. Some of this was because of ongoing religious conflict between the Shiites and the Sunni, as well as various clan disputes that the imams seemed unwilling or unable to stop; some of it was reluctance to get dragged into conflicts from which they could not extricate themselves. Due to the need to preserve the sacred cities of Mecca and Medina for pilgrims and the honor of their religion, the Mamelukes imposed a certain order on Red Sea ports and attempted to keep the internal conflicts localized away from the main pilgrimage roads, with varying degrees of success, but by and large spent forty years trying to stay out of the quarrels on the Arabian Peninsula. With the marked exception of a well-organized distribution of food to prevent widespread famine in 1262 after a drought, the Mamelukes kept apart from their Arab neighbors, as much to discourage religious fighting as to avoid interfering with trade, for the Mamelukes were keenly aware of how important trade was to the economy of their empire.

At the Empire of Nicea, after giving up a good portion of what is now eastern and central Turkey to the Turks and the Mongols, the position of the Greeks was growing precarious and would not likely be maintained without some kind of détente with Constantinople, which was considered impossible while the Latins still ruled there. In 1259 Michael VIII Paleologus, a determined, ruthless, and intelligent general who had ended his co-emperorship with the child Ioannes IV Lascaris by having the young boy imprisoned and blinded, undertook to reclaim Byzantium for the Byzantines and commenced a campaign to drive the Latins out. One of Michael VIII's first encounters was with the combined forces of Michael of Epirus, the King of Sicily, and the Prince of Achaea at the Battle of Pelagonia. His success there convinced Michael VIII that he was on the right track. He made treaties with the Bulgarians and the Genoese, promising the latter all the favorable trade terms heretofore enjoyed only by Venice. Waiting until summer in 1261 when the Venetian fleet had departed from Constantinople, the clever general Alexius Stragopulos led Michael VIII's army across the Bosporus, drove out the Latins, and once again claimed the city and the empire for Greeks. Although the Byzantine Empire was much reduced from its earlier size, reunited with the Empire of Nicea, the Byzantine presence was once again a power to reckon with in the region. Economically there were real problems, for as dependent as the Byzantines were on trade, the Mongols had cut three major Asian trade routes, and this rippled through the Middle East in collapsing markets and compromised agreements with several important ports.

A severe earthquake in Silicia in 1268 caused widespread damage and killed an estimated sixty-five thousand people. It disrupted a minor siege at Tarsus and caused disturbances in at least a dozen ports in the region. The earthquakes bothered the Latin Byzantines for religious as well as pragmatic reasons, for they were terrified of God's Wrath, which the earthquake clearly revealed to them. They had not yet brought the Middle East under Roman Christian rule, and the dogma of the period warned that failure to do so could bring about the end of the world. Willing to take advantage of the Latin Byzantines' qualms, the Turks in the region claimed several crucial ports and prepared to hold them against Mongol advancement.

One outpost of the Byzantine Empire at Trebizond on the southeastern end of the Black Sea enjoyed an upsurge in trade after 1270. The Trebizond Empire managed to maintain a balance between Turks and Mongols that made it possible for Trebizond to become the safest and most prosperous of the eastern Black Sea ports, attracting merchants from Armenia, India, Persia, Mongolia, and China. Because of its strong commercial position, the Trebizond Empire was able to establish powerful trade agreements with both Venice and Genoa, securing the whole Mediterranean Basin for its business range. Using a largely mercenary army of Huns, Bulgars, and Turks, the Greeks of Trebizond kept their independence in spite of incursions from armies, pirates, and bandits alike. Their determination was often marked by sharp bargaining as much as good generalship in battle. After 1280 one of the most valued of Trebizond's services was their paid escort companies that were contracted out to traveling merchants to protect their goods, a business that continued virtually unabated for two centuries after the collapse of Byzantium, although the Greek rule of the empire ended in 1461. But this kind of high-stress cultural brinksmanship comes at a price, and Trebizond wasn't exempt from it. Corruption was widespread throughout the empire, and the degeneracy of a number of emperors was reflected in the behavior of the court and the military. Occasionally a charismatic leader checked the debauchery and venality, but those were the exception, not the rule. Trebizond exemplified the virtues and vices of Byzantine society against a background of constant conflict as well as unresolvable ethnic and religious hostility. Under such circumstances, it is a testament to Trebizond's durability that it lasted as long as it did, particularly as the Ottoman Empire established itself more or less on the doorstep of the Trebizond Empire.

Harried by Mongols and determined not to surrender more land to them, in 1290 the King of Bithynia, Osman al-Ghazi, a Seljuk Turk, founded an empire at Osmanli—from which came the word "Ottoman"—with the intention of taking back the land around him from the Mongols and anyone else who stood in his way. He was energetic, intelligent, and determined, and he had gained the support of his generals, most of whom were part of his own clan. Because he was reputed to be blue-eyed, he was considered favored by his fellow Turks, who were willing to make alliances with him as a move to reclaim what today is Turkey. Over his thirty-eight-year reign, Osman maintained an expansionist policy that not only enlarged his fledgling empire, it brought the Ottomans to their first prominence in Middle Eastern affairs. At the beginning of Osman's reign, Seljuk Turks controlled parts of the Black Sea and Aegean Sea coasts of Anatolia; by the end of his life, that territory had almost doubled in size, an example of the expansionist policies that were to mark the next four centuries for the Ottoman Turks.

As these major shifts were taking place, the Kurds were once again being squeezed out of the region where they had made their homes for four centuries. Divided by faith—about two-thirds of the population was Islamic, but the remaining third maintained the practice of their ancient pantheism mixed with Manichean elements—the Kurds nonetheless formed resistance bands dedicated to holding off the assaults of Turks and Mongols alike. The Kurdish groups, never large or controlling major fortresses, tended to attack by ambush and stealth. They managed to hold their people together until around 1311, when epidemic disease reduced their numbers and drove them into isolated locations where they would remain for about fifty years.

In 1271 Michael II of Epirus died just as Charles of Anjou, King of the Two Sicilies, made his assault on Epiran territory in

preparation for a campaign in Thessalonika and leading to the reconquest of Constantinople for the Latins. In 1271 Ioannes Angelus
was forced to relinquish Epirus to Charles, who shortly thereafter
proclaimed himself King of Albania and began a tricky alliance
with the Serbs, who also had imperial ambitions in the region. In
a desperate response to this two-pronged threat, Michael VIII Paleologus made a treaty with the Pope, temporarily reuniting the
Orthodox and Roman Churches as a way to constrain Charles of
Anjou. Over the next decade, the Byzantine Greeks not only held
their own against the Europeans; they also regained ground they
had lost a century earlier. The Byzantine victory at the Battle of
Berat in 1281 forced Charles to enter into a complicated alliance
with Venice and the papacy. The ascendency of Andronicus II, the
pious and learned but politically naive son of Michael VIII, added
to the problems, for as a devout Orthodox Christian, Andronicus
could not continue in an agreement that was clearly a conflict of
interest for the Pope, who could not uphold both Greek and European political intentions in the Mediterranean Basin and therefore
could not honorably execute the terms to which he had agreed. Andronicus ended the reunification of the Greek and Roman Churches,
much to the relief of both Churches, for they had become locked
in debate over doctrinal inconsistencies and neither had any inclination to capitulate to the other.

As Osman al-Ghazi was beginning his reign in Bithynia, in
Delhi Firuz Shah Jalal-ud-Din rose against Balban's dynasty to establish one of his own, changing the character of the Delhi Sultanate for the next fifty years. As much bandit as military leader,
Firuz had lived the first half of his life in Afghanistan among the
Islamic people there, and he had learned early to defend his territory and his faith. His Khalji dynasty, which he hoped to endure
for centuries, lasted until 1320 but colored the resistance to the

dynasty so much that the next dynasty worked tirelessly to disassociate themselves from Firuz's Khalji dynasty, without having to give up anything Firuz had done or acquired that was to their advantage. Firuz himself became mentally impaired and in 1296 was murdered by his nephew Alah-ud-Din, who then assumed the throne and instituted a campaign of consolidation during which he made several attempts to bring the Afghans under his command, without any lasting success.

In 1291 the Egyptian Mamelukes took Acre from the Crusaders, crushing the last military stronghold of European military power in the Middle East and gaining a strategically important site for Islamic forces. The Knights of Saint John of Jerusalem, who had been the principal defenders of Acre, resettled on Cyprus with the promise of Venetian support enabling them to be assured of some degree of security. Since the Venetians had begun to build their large galleys for long-distance voyages, having a military presence in their trading theater was distinctly to their advantage. These big merchant ships could carry significantly more cargo than could their previous versions of the craft. In addition, they were more maneuverable, which made them harder for the pirates to catch. The Venetians were also developing a new war galley not only for naval engagements but for merchant-fleet escort duties, a development viewed with some alarm throughout the eastern Venetian trading theater. With improvements in cannon-casting, these armed war-galleys had the capacity to become floating fortresses when facing opponents. Many saw this improved double-purpose fleet as more of a threat than an opportunity but were too tied into Venetian trade to endanger the very lucrative markets that existed between the West and the Middle East, and Venice, more than any other European trading city, had linked its fortunes to working between the Middle East and Europe. Venetians traded as far as Calais,

Bruges, and Southampton, where they dealt with traders of the
Baltic Hanseatic League, an affiliation of ports from Russia and Germany to Scandinavia centered in the German city of Lübeck. From
Europe the Venetians brought hides, furs, finished leather, vellum,
brass, pewter, iron, lead, tin, all manner of domestic implements
from scissors to scythes, Cambrai, Leon, and Ypres cloth, tapestries,
serge of all sorts, including Nimes serge, the ancestor of denim,
sailcloth, and salted and smoked meats to markets in the Middle
East where they traded for spices, sugar, dates, raisins, currants, Syrian wine, paper, cotton, Antioch and Chinese silks, Damascus cloth,
Calicut cloth, Egyptian linen, dyes, books, rare woods, perfume, and
lightweight armor. From Venice itself the Venetians traded their
magnificent glass everywhere.

In 1294 Michael IX became co-emperor with his father, the impractical, unworldly Andronicus II, and was given the job of holding the Serbs at bay as well as containing Ottoman ambitions, all
without causing any political embarrassment to Andronicus II.
Michael IX was a canny campaigner, but he had not enough men
or strong enough alliances to stem the Serbian tide into Macedonia and Albania, and it was finally realized that the Byzantines had
not sufficient men to implement the strategies Michael IX was attempting; between injuries, desertion, and illness, the Byzantine
army was reduced by a third in the course of a year.

With a depleted army and a need for European backing, in 1302
Andronicus II appealed to Roger de Flor and his Catalan Company
of six thousand mercenaries to come help the Byzantines rout the
Italians from the territory that Byzantium wanted to control and
from Constantinople itself. The Catalans wreaked havoc on Constantinople, taking credit for killing more than three thousand
Italians living in the Byzantine city. The Catalan Company then
went to reinforce exposed Byzantine cities. In 1304 they stopped a
Turkish attack on Philadelphia, then decided to establish themselves

as a power in Byzantine territory. Although they could not take Constantinople, they seized the duchy of Athens after spending five years rampaging through the region, looting, killing, enslaving, and raiding as they went. It is hardly surprising that in 1305 Roger de Flor was murdered. Some accounts say his own men did it; some say it was the Byzantines; still others say it was the Serbs. Whoever killed Roger de Flor didn't get rid of the Catalan Company, which now had grown to close to eight thousand in number, sufficient to hold Athens against Byzantine counterattacks. Often beset with internal strife, the Catalan occupation of the duchy of Athens was bloody, treacherous, and relatively brief.

Beginning about 1306 and lasting for over three years, a blight struck trees throughout Persia and into Mesopotamia in the southwest and Afghanistan in the southeast. Forests that had been shrinking as the climate became drier all but disappeared; vineyards and orchards perished, leaving famine and poverty as their legacy. Those able to nurse their trees through this period were able to regain some of what they had lost, but many were permanently forced to rely on herds instead of trees for their existence. For the next decade as Persia recovered from this mysterious arboreal plague, seedlings of trees brought to Europe from the Middle East a century before were now traveling the other way along the trade routes to restore the orchards that had been lost and to replant as much of the forests as could be managed. Just as the trees began to flourish again, a climate shift, possibly linked to a massive volcanic eruption in Indonesia, cooled the climate and slowed down the reforestation in Persia. It also created severe winters and famine in northern Europe, Mongolia, and Russia, conditions that persisted for decades and contributed to the continued withdrawal of European troops from the Middle East as famine spread and food riots erupted at home, requiring military policing as well as defense of what productive regions remained. Although the Middle

East did not suffer the same heavy impact of climate change that Europe and Russia did, there was a sharp increase in demand for grains and wines from the region as more northern fields fell victim to the cold; economically at least, the colder weather proved profitable for many parts of the Middle East, as well as containing the Golden Horde at Sarai, who suddenly had to contend with a sharp increase in raiders from the north and so spent less time harrying Persia, Armenia, and Georgia.

In western India, a new Islamic dynasty was founded in 1320 by Shah Ghiyas-ud-Din Tughluk. This middle-aged Turk had been fighting Mongols for twenty years when he was able to overthrow the Khalji dynasty and set himself up as Gharzi Khan, establishing a new capital for his rule to the east of Delhi, calling it Tughlakabad. He made plans to make the city better armed and more defensible than Delhi. From this new city Gharzi Khan set out to annex more of India into his empire as well as regain control of eastern Afghanistan. Gharzi Khan held the throne for five years, and then his son, Mohammed, killed him and assumed his throne, which he held for twenty-six years. It was Mohammed Tughluk who, in 1334, welcomed the Moorish traveler and author Ibn Batuta, in the hope that he could provide information that would aid Mohammed in his plans of conquest.

The Byzantines from 1321 to 1328 were beset by civil war: with Michael IX out of the picture, Andronicus II was locked in conflict with his grandson, Andronicus III. As their supporters tore the empire apart, the Turks eagerly occupied more of the borderlands and put pressure on the remnants of Byzantine interests still active in Anatolia. In 1325 Andronicus II was compelled to accept his grandson as his co-emperor, but this came too late to save Bursa from the Turks, which had been besieged since 1317 in one of the first Turkish attempts at European-style encampment sieges, a tactic that proved so successful that the Turks began to factor in sieges as part of their campaign of conquest. Despite help from Venice and Genoa, the Byzantines were no longer able to keep their empire safe from incursions. After the Siege of Bursa, in 1326 Orkhan I declared himself Sultan of the Ghazis and ordered the first Ottoman coins struck, making it clear that he and the Turks were there to stay. Under his command, the Ottoman Empire reached from what is now Ankara in modern-day Turkey to Thrace in Greece, driving the Byzantines out of long-entrenched positions and putting pressure on Constantinople itself; the Byzantines were forced to enlarge their army and navy at a time when such expenditure was a drain on an already-depleted treasury. The Turks kept up their assaults, gradually gaining territory that the Byzantines could not afford to lose. It was an impressive beginning to what proved to be a durable and wealthy empire.

In June of 1329, the Byzantines suffered a crippling defeat at Pelekanon and Andronicus III was routed, some claiming that he had been unprepared for the rigor of battle, others that his generals had advised him badly. His retreat was made more difficult by ongoing Turkish attacks on his scattered army, so that by the time Andronicus III reached safe territory he had nothing left with which to mount a counterattack, although the Byzantines did manage to reclaim Chios from the Genoese. The next year, the Serbs defeated the Bulgars and began to raid Byzantine territory, creating trouble on two fronts, splitting the depleted Byzantine army still further. In spite of all his efforts—and for the next three years, they were vigorous, if somewhat erratic—the Turkish advancement continued, although the Serbs were checked for a while, their leader, Stephen Dushan, having his plans set for the long term. All this weighed on Andronicus III, who was unable to deal with the demands of his office; judging from contemporary reports, Andronicus III gradually

fell into a severe depression and alternated between spiteful out-
bursts and sullen lethargy, neither of which helped the Byzantines.
Matters improved a bit when the Byzantines retook Thessaly and a
good portion of Epirus by the end of 1335. By the end of the following year, they had once again regained control of Lesbos. This
served in part to off-set the losses to Stephen Dushan's Serbs, who
occupied much of the Albanian coast as well as Janina in the interior, which they took in 1340.

Trade along the Silk Road was slacking off in 1333 and 1334
due to an outbreak of bubonic plague in northern and central
China. Merchants and guides alike were wary about undertaking
the long journey with the disease spreading. Even bandits hesitated to attack caravans coming from China, for fear of contract-
ing the terrible disease. In spite of reduced travel, the Black Plague
continued to spread slowly westward, reaching Persia in 1339 and
the Black Sea in 1342. With Europe already weakened by the
climate-shift famine, the population was more than usually vulnerable to epidemic disease, which arrived on Genoese and Venetian
ships from Black Sea ports in 1346 and began its twenty-five-year
ravages in three separate epidemics that left a third of the European population dead and medieval society in a shambles.

By 1341 Andronicus III was dead and his son, Ioannes V Paleologus, became a child-king under the regency of his mother, Anna
of Savoy. Almost at once Ioannes Cantacuzene, who had important
ties to a good portion of the Byzantine aristocracy, proclaimed
himself emperor in Ioannes V's place and began a civil war in 1341
that would last until 1347. The war was complicated by a rift in the
Orthodox Church that divided along politico-military lines, zealots
versus rationalists. The zealots (Hesychasts) sided with Ioannes
Cantacuzene and participated in his victory but lost influence with
the Church in Thessalonika, where the populace refused to support Ioannes Cantacuzene's claims. While Byzantium was so

distracted internally, the Venetians occupied Smyrna in 1343 while
Stephen Dushan declared himself King of all the Serbs and Ruler
of Greece, Bulgaria, and Albania, established a court along Byzantine lines at Skoplye, and in 1346 headed for Constantinople, which
had been weakened by a summer epidemic of Black Plague. It was
Stephen Dushan's intention of beating Ioannes Cantacuzene to it
and thereby gaining the Byzantine Empire for himself. But Dushan
reckoned without Cantacuzene's duplicity and craftiness, for in 1347,
before Dushan could prepare for an all-out attack, Cantacuzene
was able to take the city by treachery and hold off the Serbian advance, making himself Ioannes VI Cantacuzene and co-emperor
and guardian of Ioannes V Paleologos, who disappeared within
the year so that Ioannes VI Cantacuzene could advance his own
son, Manuel, to the position of despot of Morea, where he could
check the advances of the Serbs, who held Macedeonia.

In 1345 the Ottoman Turks crossed from Anatolia into Europe for
the first time, invited by the Byzantine Emperor Ioannes VI Cantacuzene to back him up in his dispute with the Empress-Regent
Anna, an effort that proved successful. To cement this useful support, Cantacuzene married his daughter Theodora to Orkhan I, the
Sultan of the Ghazis, assuming this would provide for continuing
Byzantine influence among the Ottomans. Cantacuzene was apparently unaware or unconcerned that the children of Theodora and
Orkhan would have a claim on the Byzantine throne.

Thanks to this marriage, Cantacuzene called upon the Ottomans
again in 1352—most Europeans were struggling with the bubonic
plague and were unable to come to Byzantine assistance—to help
in holding off the latest assaults from Stephen Dushan and his
Serbs. In exchange for the Ottoman assistance, Cantacuzene offered the Turks a grant of land on which to settle on Gallipoli, the
narrow peninsula at the Hellespont, the channel between the Thra-
cian Sea and the Sea of Marmora, intending to keep the Ottomans

close to hand in case he should need them again. The Ottomans seized all of Gallipoli in March of 1354, brought in more of their soldiers to hold the place, and, using it as a base, moved into Thrace, gaining power as well as territory by the move and making the Byzantine emperor dependent upon their support. The Ottomans were expanding their hold in what is now Turkey as well; in 1359 they took Angora (modern Ankara) and began to fan out from there, bringing in more of Anatolia to their empire.

In Constantinople, in 1354, Ioannes V Paleologus, now an adult, raised an army and took Constantinople, forcing Ioannes VI Cantacuzene to abdicate in his favor and to retire to a monastery rather than be executed. Barely had Ioannes V got a toe-hold on the Byzantine Empire when Stephen Dushan brought his Serbs up, preparing to take Constantinople. Only Dushan's sudden death in 1355 stopped the Serbs in their tracks and spared Constantinople another major battle. Without Dushan to command them, the Serbian Empire fell into regional bickering and fell apart, sparing the Byzantines from having to fight on two fronts but also leaving a wide swath for the Turks to occupy with only minimal opposition, and the Ottomans made the most of their opportunity—in 1365 they occupied Thrace.

In 1359 the Ottoman sultan Orkhan died after a twenty-four-year reign marked by steady expansion, increasing wealth, and relative calm. Orkhan's successor, Murad I, made the most of the Turkish expansion, establishing the Ottomans as the greatest military presence in Anatolia and the Balkans. Sometime fairly early in his reign, he made the Janissaries an official corps of the Ottoman army, manned by youths taken in levies of Christian boys under their Islamic regime. It had existed unofficially for about twenty years, during which Christian boys from all over Ottoman territory were seized and put in the army, not only swelling the ranks for the Turks but diminishing the potential opponents among the Christian communities. While conversion was not required of these soldiers, absolute loyalty to the sultan was, and promotion came much more readily once the Janissary converted. Although technically slaves, the Janissaries could and often did make fortunes while serving the sultan and reached high positions in the sultan's court.

Murad, sensitive to the commercial realities of the time, made a number of trade agreements with the Genoese, who, unlike the Venetians, had few ties to the Byzantines. He took advantage of the continuing rivalry between the two mercantile republics, opening ports to the Genoese and also the Pisans, in an attempt to gain the lucrative markets in France and western Italy. He added European quarters to several of his cities, offering preferential housing to the Genoese. This not only outraged the Venetians; it worried the Byzantines, who were still allied with them and saw Murad's policies as damaging to both Venice and Byzantium. For the next ten years, matters remained in an uneasy stalemate, until, in 1381, Venice prevailed over Genoa after the War of Chioggia.

Far to the east, the khanates were undergoing another power-shift: in 1369 the Turko-Mongolian Timur-i Lenhk (called Tamburlane in the West) became the lord (Khan) of Samarkand. Descending from the Turkish Balas clan and the Mongol Jagatai clan, he had claim to vast territories, all of which he pursued with determined ruthlessness for more than thirty years. His initial successes put pressure on Persia and the Golden Horde and promised more to come once he had subdued his own cousins within his clans. It took him almost a decade to go from skirmish raiding to full-blown military campaigns, but at last he was ready: from 1380 to 1381, Timur-i launched his first concerted attacks, beginning with Persia. In fourteen months, he occupied what are now Jurjan, Mazandaran, Khorasan, Sijistan, Fars, Afghanistan, Azerbaijan, and Kurdistan. With the Mongols defeated at the gates of Moscow,

Timur-i turned his sights on Russia and prepared to invade the following year.

In 1366 the Turks suffered a set-back: the Crusade of Amadeus of Savoy—a strictly military venture with little or no pretense to religiosity—managed to reclaim Gallipoli, which it would hold for almost seven years while the Turks directed their efforts at the Balkans, going around the Crusaders and reaching the region north of them, effectively imprisoning them on the peninsula. Lala Shahin led a well-mounted and well-armed force into former Serbian holdings while Evrenuz-Beg did the same in Macedonia, forcing the warring Serbian princes into a fragile alliance that lasted until the autumn of 1371, when the Ottoman Turks decisively routed the Serbs at Chernomen in Macedonia. After that, Bulgaria, Macedonia, and the western Byzantine Empire recognized the suzerainty of the Ottoman Empire. With their northern flank relatively secure, the Ottomans put pressure on points of resistance in Anatolia, and in 1377 they began a campaign against the city of Koniah, a venture that lasted nearly a decade. Another campaign against the Albanians ended in defeat for them in 1385, with the fall of Sophia and the Battle of Voissa. In 1386 Serbia officially became a vassal of the Ottomans, and the following year Thessalonika fell to the Turks and they began to raid in Greece and Morea.

During this vigorous expansion, the Venetians took advantage of Turkish attention being directed away from the Greek Islands. In 1386 they reoccupied Corfu, and two years later, in a much more typical deal, they purchased Argos and Nauplia, assuring themselves ports fully under their control as well as a source of food for Venice, since all three locations had grain to sell. For the first time, Venice had a viable system of bases from which to deal with pirates; squadrons of war-galleys and scouting ships were assigned to those islands, and the losses to piracy diminished while Venice continued to expand its trading empire.

The kingdom of Armenia, always a flash point for trouble, in 1375 finally capitulated to the Islamic governor of Aleppo and his Mameluke army. Most of the Armenians were given the choice of converting or dying, so the conversion rate was fairly high, and although officially tolerated, the Armenian Orthodox Church shrank in size and importance. The capital city of Sis was pillaged and the defeated King Levon was carried off to Cairo, where he languished for seven years until he was ransomed by his royal cousins of Aragon and Castile, after which he lived in France, housed and pensioned by Charles VI.

Even though they had officially surrendered, the Serbian princes were restive. They made a covert pact with the Bosnians and the western Bulgarian warlords and in 1388 staged an uprising that drove the Turks out of Bosnia. That winter, the Ottoman general Ali Pasha turned his attention to Bulgaria and Bosnia, and in June 1389 the Turks defeated the Serbs and Bosnians at the Battle of Kossovo, but at the cost of the life of Murad I, who was killed by Serbs. Bayazid I was proclaimed sultan upon the death of Murad I at Kossevo; his first act was to have his brother Yakub strangled as a guard against palace coups, a not uncommon precaution of the time. With Murad I dead, much of the newly conquered land broke out in spontaneous rebellion while more serious insurrections loomed in Anatolia, challenging Bayazid's right to rule. Under pressure in Greece and at home, when they needed it most, the Ottomans lost their hold on the important port of Saloniki. Not one to waste resources in minor skirmishes, Bayazid made a deal with the Serbs and headed back to Anatolia to quell the uprisings there, actions that would demand men and matériel that it turned out he could ill afford to lose.

In an astonishing westward thrust, Timur-i came out of Persia and cut through Mesopotamia to Baghdad, conquering the city in 1393. Although technically Islamic himself, Timur-i did not let that

stop him from ordering the slaughter of almost half the population
of the city, either by execution or starvation in improvised prisons.
Heads of important victims were set up in piles at the gates of the
city as a warning to the people. The rest of Mesopotamia was simi-
larly subdued by 1394, while the Mamelukes were in strategic retreat
and the Ottoman sultan Bayazid put his sights on conquering Bulgaria, away from Timur-i's depredations.

There was trouble from Europe as well: a new Crusade, the
Crusade of Nicopolis, set out in 1396 under King Sigismund of
Hungary, who had the support of both the Pope of Rome and the
Pope at Avignon in France, the papacy having split in 1378. The
Crusaders, a company made up of German, French, and English
knights as well as Balkan princes, advanced down the Danube
causing havoc wherever they went, raiding and burning Christian
towns, apparently as practice for what they proposed to do to the
Turks. Twenty thousand strong, the Crusaders reached Nicopolis,
where, toward the end of September, they faced a similar number
of Turks. In a battle of brutality remarkable even in this brutal
time, the Turks defeated the Crusaders, taking many of the survivors prisoners, and either held them for ransom or enslaved
them. According to the records of the time, fewer than three thousand Crusaders actually returned to Europe.

Encouraged by his success, in 1397 Bayazid attempted a siege
of Constantinople. The city, defended by Jean Bouciquaut, the
Marshal of France, proved harder to defeat than Sigismund's
Crusaders, and Bayazid was preparing for a long encampment-
and-blockade to starve Constantinople into submission but had
to break this off as Timur-i continued to ravage Mesopotamia
and eastern Anatolia until the next year, when he turned eastward
to northern India, sacking Delhi in December and slaughtering
an estimated one hundred thousand Hindus. January saw him at
Meerut, which he took by storm, but at the cost of cutting off his

avenue of retreat: he was forced to fight his way back to the Indus, leaving all of Delhi in his wake destroyed. By 1400 he had
taken Syria from the Egyptian Mamelukes, and in 1402 he was
back in Anatolia, where his forces, resupplied and replenished,
took Angora (Ankara) and captured Bayazid, whose men had deserted him. Timur-i continued his advance virtually unchecked by
Ottoman opposition, since Bayazid's sons were at war with one
another over the succession of rule; none of them had sufficient
support to command the army. By the end of the year Timur-i had
added Bursa and Smyrna to his conquests. With Bayazid's death in
1403, still a captive of Timur-i, the hostility among Bayazid's sons
turned into civil war, with Isa in Bursa under the tolerance of
Timur-i, Suleiman at Edirne, and Mehmed in Amasia, supported
by his brother Musa, a conflict that shifted balance when in 1404
Timur-i withdrew to Atrar to plan an attack on China. But his
plans didn't materialize. There were rumors of an illness, all ve-
hemently denied, but in February 1405 he was dead and his empire passed to his son Shah Rukh. Soon after, it began to fall
apart.

That unraveling wasn't happening in the Ottoman Empire. In
1404 Mehmed defeated Isa at Bursa. In response, Suleiman advanced into Anatolia, confronted Mehmed, and drove him out of
Bursa and into the mountains, reclaiming suzerainty over the
emirs who had been made independent of the Ottomans by
Timur-i. Sporadic fighting continued in the region until in 1409
Mehmed sent his brother Musa into Wallachia in what is now
Romania in order to put pressure on the Greek territories held by
the Ottomans under Suleiman. In 1410 he went to defend those
positions. As soon as Suleiman and his troops had departed,
Mehmed once again occupied Bursa. In June 1411, Musa and a
loose confederation of Serbs attacked Suleiman and defeated him
at Edirne, where Suleiman was killed. The alliance disintegrated

almost at once, blame being laid on Musa. Undaunted, Musa enlisted more of the Serbs who endorsed Mehmed's claim on the Ottoman throne and, with their assistance, moved on Constantinople in 1413, with the excuse of rescuing Mustapha, Suleiman and Musa's brother who had been held for ransom. The campaign was only partially successful, for before any real contest could begin, Musa was killed and the Ottomans united under Mehmed, who became Mehmed I, a canny emperor who began by negotiating a peace between the Serbs and the Byzantine emperor. Then, with the assurance of relative calm from the Byzantines, Mehmed regained control over all Ottoman territory in Anatolia. In 1415 Mustapha attempted to overthrow Mehmed during a religious uprising under the leadership of Sheik Bedred-Din. It took a year for Mehmed to quell the rebellion, and as soon as that was over, a war erupted with Venice, in which Venice prevailed under their admiral Giovanni Loredan, who went on to become Doge of Venice. In 1417, peace concluded with Venice, Mehmed took his army into Wallachia to assert his personal authority over the populace.

These were not the only upheavals on the western edge of the Middle East—there were ongoing struggles throughout the region, not all of which were associated with the Ottoman civil war. In 1409, through a combination of force of arms, bribery, and outright purchase, Venice reclaimed its territories along the Dalmatian Coast, once again broadening its commercial base and using this to leverage more and better trade agreements with both Byzantine and Ottoman ports. It added the city of Thessalonika in 1423 by purchase and began to reinforce the fortifications of the port cities as well as to protect the harbors it had gained and regained. Venice held on to them in spite of Byzantine victories in Morea in 1428, losing Thessalonika to the Ottomans in 1430 after a successful Ottoman blockade of the port.

In the first quarter of the 1400s, there were shifts all through the Middle East: in the Golden Horde, Faulahd Khan was deposed in 1407 and Timur-i was installed at the head of the empire, a reign that lasted until 1410, when the situation was reversed, until two years later when Timur-i was replaced by Jalal-ud-Din. Also, in 1412 the Mameluke Nasirudin Faraj died and was succeeded by Al Moayad. In 1413 the Golden Horde had another leader— Kareem Bardo was installed and Jalal-ud-Din was removed—and the next year Kareem Bardo was gone and Kubakh Khan took his place, ruling for two years, until 1416, when first Jahar Balrawi and then Chaigh-ray were advanced as rulers. In 1419 Chaigh-ray was overthrown and, after a short internal war based on clan blood-feuds, Ulugh Muhamad emerged from the chaos to rule, exerting his control through executions and banishment for those who had opposed him and rewards for his supporters, not unlike any other regional martinet of the time.

In Europe, the separation of the Roman Church into two, mutually antagonistic institutions came to an end in 1417, at the Council of Constance. They elected Cardinal Oddone Colonna Pope Martin V after having thrown out Benedict XIII, John XXIII, and Gregory XII and declared them to be anti-popes and guilty of every sin the council could think of. Within a year, the Roman Church began to make overtures to the Orthodox Churches, and it is rumored they also sent a delegation to the Coptic Christians in Egypt in the hope of once again mounting an effort to push back Islam from what they saw as traditionally Christian territory. But the Orthodox Churches were disinclined to come to the aid of Rome or to put themselves under Roman authority and withdrew from the dialogue with the Roman Church. There was no official response from the Copts that was released to the Roman faithful. The Renaissance was starting to take hold in Italy, creating a more secular culture than had existed for a millennium before. Soon after, the

Roman Church began to worry about outside influences within the faith and heresy.

In Turkoman territories there were a few, fairly small empires, the most cohesive of which was the Black Sheep Empire—named for the predominant color of sheep in the flocks the people of the region raised. In 1420 their ruler Qarah Yusef was succeeded by his son. Qarah Iskandar (Alexander), who had more ambitions than his father, set about expanding the holdings of the Black Sheep Empire, supported by most of the warlords of his clan. Although his army was not nearly as large or as well disciplined as the armies of Timur-i had been, Alexander made a degree of headway that was sufficient to alarm his neighbors. Whatever Ottoman opposition might have been mounted to quell the Black Sheep was cut short in 1421 by the death of Mehmed I; his son Murad II inherited the throne, not without difficulties attached. The Mamelukes also lost a leader in that year: Al Moayad died and Muzaffahr Ammad succeeded him briefly, only to be replaced by Amir Sayf-ud-Din Tata, who died shortly after becoming sultan and was succeeded by his son Muhammed, who reigned briefly, until Emir Bars-Bey took over.

With Murad II made sultan, in 1421 the release of his brother Mustapha was arranged. As soon as he was out of Constantinople, Adrianopole's people proclaimed him sultan and prepared to support any action he might take against Murad. In 1422 Mustapha tried to take Bursa, but his effort failed, Mustapha was captured and executed, and Murad reasserted his rights as sultan. One of his first acts was to mount another siege of Constantinople, but he was forced to abandon it when another potential uprising began in Anatolia. After arranging a peace with the Byzantines, Murad set about enlarging his empire and ensuring stability for his people.

1424 proved to be another tumultuous one: Daulat Bairawi, who had wrested control from Ulugh Muhamad almost two years before, died. Berq took his place and reigned for not quite three years when Ulguh Muhamad was able to seize power once more, following a spate of particularly vicious internal warfare. Two years (1425–1427) of bad weather in Central Asia and the Middle East imposed a halt to hostilities during these hard times that began with an unusually wet winter followed by a late, cool spring and a stormy summer. Autumn turned cold early, blighting crops before they could be harvested. This hit the Golden Horde particularly hard, and for the rest of the autumn of 1426 they raided their neighbors for as much grain and livestock as they could in the hope of surviving a bad winter. By the end of 1426, Persia had outbreaks of what they called Bone Fever, and that quickly spread into the Khanate of the Golden Horde, Afghanistan, and Mesopotamia even as a hard winter hit that was followed by another wet spring. Silk Road trade dropped off, and those cities relying on traders suffered accordingly. The conflict between the Turkoman Black Sheep Empire and the White Sheep Empire intensified as scarcity struck the two groups with equal severity. In the Ottoman Empire, these difficult years were marked by storms and diminished food supplies, and while this did not entirely check their annexing of territories, it did slow down their adventurism. It also curtailed trade with Europe—not only did they have less to offer due to lessened trade with Asia, but the storms kept many ships in port also. The one advantage of this restricted travel was that Bone Fever didn't spread as it would have in better years and both Ottomans and Byzantines were spared another epidemic. At the end of this bad weather, in 1427, Berq was finally overthrown by Ulugh Muhamad, who once again seized control of the Golden Horde and began the painstaking business of restoring the region to agricultural prosperity.

The Byzantine Empire, now shrunk to Constantinople, the adjacent territory, and a few Greek ports, lost its emperor Manuel II

Paleologus. He had overseen the monetary collapse of his country and the paying of tribute to Murad II and done his best to shore up the remaining bits of empire remaining to Constantinople. His son, Ioannes VII Paleologus, succeeded him and was confronted with the same problems and a similar lack of chances to restore Byzantium to its former glory. Despite his efforts and tricks, the empire continued to erode from without and within.

Among the Turkomans of the Black Sheep Empire, 1434 was a difficult year: Qarah Iskandar was deposed and his brother Jahan Shah took his place, while in the White Sheep Empire their leader Qarah Othman died and was succeeded by his son Ali Beg, an unhappy confluence of political changes that rachetted up the hostilities between these two empires that had been brewing for decades, and in terms of clan rivalries, for centuries. Raids and skirmishes between various Black and White Sheep warlords increased and began to interfere with trade. By 1438 Ali Beg was overthrown and his brother Hamzah took his place. He ruled for two years and was, in turn, deposed by Jahangir, the son of Ali Beg.

For the Mamelukes matters were hardly less turbulent. Bars-Bey died in 1438; his young son Jamal-ud-Din Yusuf was raised to fill his father's position, but his reign lasted only a few months. The Vizier Saif-ud-Din Gamuk then became sultan. One of his first moves was to get rid of four potential claimants to the throne and then to gain the support of the emirs. His long experience as the equivalent of prime minister had made it possible for Saif-ud-Din to draw on the relationships he had cultivated for years. During his reign, the power of the sultanate increased internally.

The Ottomans, continuing their expansion in 1439, took over Serbia and drove George Brankovich into exile in Hungary. Murad then besieged Belgrade in 1440, but inconclusively, while the two armies he sent into Transylvania in 1441–1442 were defeated by the smaller but more desperate forces of János Hunyadi, the most effective Christian leader facing the Ottomans at the time. The Hungarians, Poles, Serbs, and Transylvanians united long enough, under Vladislav, King of Hungary and Poland, with Hunyadi and the exiled Brankovich to mount a counterassault on the Ottomans. In 1443 they took Nish and Sofia but were halted at the Battle of Zlatica, a pass in the Balkans, where Murad was able to ambush them. All through Europe there were calls for another Crusade, but the Pope was not at first inclined to support one. In 1444 the Hungarians, Serbs, Poles, and Transylvanians signed a truce with Murad that restored Brankovich to his despotate, but as a client of the Ottomans.

Soon after the truce took effect, the Hungarians broke it and, with the support of the Wallachians, began the Varna Crusade for the express purpose of forcing the Turks to withdraw entirely from Europe. This was nothing like the Crusades of two and three centuries ago—this was another strictly military adventure aimed at a military, not a religious, solution. That the Pope finally endorsed it was more to take advantage of European fears of Ottoman might than to gain spiritual currency. Murad, who had retired earlier in the year in favor of his son Mehmed, once again took command of the Ottoman army. When Murad's men tried to cross the Dardanelles, they were hampered by the Venetian fleet. Murad then moved his forces so that they could cross at the Bosporus and come in on the Crusaders' flank. This proved so successful that not only was Vladislav killed, but a great many knights and nobles were captured. By the end of 1444, the Varna Crusade had failed.

In Timur-i's old empire, 1446 marked a change in leadership: Shah Rukh died and was succeeded by Ulugh Beg. By this time, the empire was falling apart, most cohesion was gone, and the various warlords no longer supported Samarkand without the assurance of reward and favor for providing it. The Timurids stuttered on for a while, but all hopes of renewing their former conquests had ended. Ulugh Beg, the scientifically minded ruler of Turkestan, died in 1449, in what was rumored to be an assssination, and Abdul Latif took power. His reign lasted a year until he was murdered by agents of the new leader, Abu Sayed.

In 1446 Murad II resumed control of the Ottoman Empire. The Turks fought the second Battle of Kossovo in 1448, that year, and this time they triumphed over the army of János Hunyadi, annexing Serbia and Bosnia as vassal states and installing Ottoman officials to deal with the people. Made confident by their success, the Ottomans in 1449 turned on Albania and its warlord, George Castriota, called Scanderbeg, whom the Ottomans had fought a few years before. Scanderbeg was a wily commander who made the most of his limited forces, depending on guerrilla tactics long before there was a word for them. The Ottomans kept up their assault for the greater part of a year but were unable to achieve the kind of victory against Scanderbeg that they had against Hunyadi. In 1451 Murad II died and Mehmed II resumed power, earning himself the sobriquet of the Conqueror, bringing all aspects of the empire under his autocratic control and centralizing the government in a sweeping series of reforms reminiscent of what Augustus had done for the Roman Empire almost fifteen centuries before. Mehmed II established territorial centers to facilitate the administration of government, ending local dynastic control, and pushed back the Hungarians, then drove the Venetians out of many of their holdings in Greece and along the Dalmatian Coast. That done, Mehmed felt prepared to take on Constantinople and the last of the Byzantine Empire.

In 1448 a young Wallachian princeling of the Dragon clan escaped from his Ottoman captors who had held him for leverage against János Hunyadi and the Romanian warlords, among whom the princeling's father had been a distinguished leader until his murder the year before. Young Vlad IV only held the throne for half a year before, afraid that he, too, would be murdered, he fled to Transylvania and Moldavia for the purpose of leading the anti-Ottoman forces there. He became known for his preferred method of execution—impaling. A national hero among the Romanians for his successful defense of their country, Vlad Tepes continued to oppose the Turks all his life, adding to the high regard in which the Dracula clan was held.

By the time the Turks broke down the walls of Constantinople at the end of May 1453, the city was in serious decline; its government was unable to deal with the crisis, and the military lacked men and matériel to prevent the Ottoman siege from fatally crippling the city. Not only had the Ottoman forces brought the Byzantine Empire to an end; they had exhausted the defendants, who, under the rule of a series of weak and/or despotic emperors, had been floundering internally for almost a century. Lack of Western support had been the final straw for the Byzantines, who had become increasingly dependent on Europe for the means to hold the Turks at bay, which support the Europeans had become far from eager to provide. Perhaps if the Pope had made common cause with the Patriarch of Constantinople, things might have been different, but relations between the two major branches of Christianity were too much strained to make shared defense possible. Only the Most Serene Republic of Venice had regular and on-going dealings with Constantinople and provided some support against the Ottoman attack. But that support was subject to trouble over time, for the Venetians also did business with the Turks and most of the other populations of the Middle East and therefore had serious commercial considerations to weigh against their dealings with the Byzantines. In spite of the Venetians' recent war with the Ottomans, the Byzantines were well aware that both the

Venetians and the Ottomans needed each other to continue their commercial success, which inclined the Byzantines to distrust the Venetians. The major Turkish weapon used against Constantinople was cannon fire provided in part by six impressively large bombards made by an Islamic Hungarian. Toward the end of the siege, the Ottomans brought about seventy small ships overland as a means of getting around the massive chain blocking the Golden Horn. They concentrated their firepower on the city's gates and broke through the Romanos Gate on May 29. The last Byzantine emperor, ironically named Constantine XI, was killed in the attack while those Constantinopolitans who could fled on Genoese and Venetian ships.

After three days of pillage, Mehmed settled down to the job of taking care of administering this crown jewel of a conquest. He began by attempting to repopulate the city entirely with Turks, but found this not only difficult but impractical and so allowed in Greeks and Serbs, many of them Christians, for the task of rebuilding the city. In order to limit religious and ethnic conflicts, he allowed Orthodox Patriarch Gennadios a fair amount of religious and civil authority over the Orthodox Christians remaining in Constantinople, as well as the Orthodox Christians in the European portion of the Ottoman Empire, and ordered that the patriarch was to be respected by his court and his administrators. He established similar executive positions for the Jewish and the Armenian Orthodox communities, with similar privileges. Knowing the strategic advantages of Constantinople's location, Mehmed decided to make it his capital and began his establishment by ordering the transformation of almost all the churches within the city walls into mosques. He also ordered civic buildings restored and enlarged and new palaces constructed for him and his court. When appropriate, he adapted Byzantine ceremonies to his own purposes, and he set about adding

Turkish and Islamic celebrations to Constantinopolitan life even as he campaigned to bring all the Balkans under Ottoman control.

The Mamelukes lost their sultan Saif-ud-Din Gamuk, who was succeeded by his son Farkhr-ud-Din Othman, who was overthrown later in 1453 by the great Mameluke general Saif-ud-Din Inal, and a period of turmoil resulted from the coup that continued through the death of Saif-ud-Din Inal, the succession, the succession of his son Shahab-ud-Din Ahmad in 1461, and his overthrow by yet another Mameluke general, Saif-ud-Din Khushqahdam. The Mamelukes were not the only ones to lose rulers in 1453: the Turkomans of the White Sheep Empire also lost their ruler, Jahangir. His son Uzun Hassan replaced him and managed to hang on to his power for many years in spite of almost constant warfare with the Black Sheep Empire that culminated in 1467 with the attack by Jahan Shah of the Black Sheep Empire in a desperate campaign against the White Sheep Empire, a truly catastrophic move, for the Black Sheep Turkomans were decisively defeated by the White Sheep Empire and all their lands annexed to the White Sheep. In what was becoming routine among the Mamelukes, in 1467 Saif-ud-Din Khushqahdam died and his son Saif-un-Din Iel Bey replaced him, only to be deposed by the Mameluke general Temur Bugha, who was overthrown in 1468 by a rival general, Qait Bay. The White Sheep Empire became a major power in the Middle East in 1468 when Uzun Hassan broke the last of Timur-i's empire at the Battle of Qarahbagh and took over Persia and Khurasn, shifting the military demands of the Ottomans toward the east once again even while they continued to fight in the Balkans.

With Byzantium lost to the Ottomans, Europe began to feel the pressure of the Turks in new and unpleasant ways. Piracy increased throughout the eastern Mediterranean Basin, and the costs of imported Asian goods rose accordingly. Despite belated efforts from Austrian, Italian, and German leaders, there were insufficient numbers of soldiers available to halt the Turkish invasion, and those few direct conflicts went so badly that Europeans began to fear that the Ottoman Empire could not be stopped, and over the century to come, those fears increased.

THE OTTOMAN CENTURY
AND BEYOND

*The Fall of Athens, the Fall of Trebizond, European Retreat,
the Moghul Empire, the Decline of the Ottoman Empire*

O NCE Constantinople was secured, Mehmed II resumed his
campaign of conquests, and for a time it seemed he could not be
beaten by any force sent against him. A man of tireless energy and
visionary ambitions, he realized that he could use the European
failure of morale to press farther into their territories, dishearten-
ing the Europeans still further, a plan he put into effect almost at
once. The fall of Athens in 1456 to the Ottomans was a shocking
blow for Europeans and Christians, for it had been assumed that
Athens would hold out against any and all attack as a bastion of
Western thought and moral superiority. Its surrender had a dramatic impact on Western trade as well as morale, in spite of János
Hunyadi's attack on the Ottoman navy that destroyed half the ships
in July of 1456; many Europeans feared that the Ottoman conquest was coming and they would be helpless against it. For Europeans, eastern Europeans in particular, the outlook was dispiriting.
1458–1561 brought the Ottomans another series of victories that
boded well for their future; their army occupied Morea and the remaining bits of Serbia they had not yet taken. Although their attempt on Belgrade did not end in victory, that failure was minor
compared to the many successes Mehmed II achieved, successes that

permeated throughout the Middle East, shifting the dynamics of the entire region to an Ottoman-centric one.

Not all the Turks were happy about the establishment of a capital, particularly Constantinople. Turkish society had long been semi-nomadic, and the necessary shift to a centralized seat of government and military authority troubled many of the clans, especially those clans who had dealt enough with the Europeans to know how symbolically important Constantinople was in the West. Those Turkish clans who had remained at the fringes of Ottoman expansion now attempted to withdraw from the Ottoman ranks, but this was met with stern resistance on the part of the sultan, who feared that disruptions just at the time of their greatest success could develop into something that would endanger all that had been accomplished within the empire. Mehmed II was keenly aware that any sign of fragmentation among the Turkish ranks would be seen as a sign of fatal weakness and would bring the enemies of the Ottomans down upon them at a time when he was striving for unity. A number of judicious imprisonments and executions stilled the rancor, at least on the surface, although a few minor clan leaders hurried off toward Afghanistan and another handful retreated into the Tarsus Mountains. Most who left the empire ended up as mercenaries for the Persians and the Afghan warlords.

Also at the other end of the Middle East from Constantinople, in Delhi, Mahmud I was enjoying a period of expansion, and again, as in Mehmed's case, it appeared that Mahmud was unbeatable. In 1458 his armies took Girnar and Champanir, accomplishments he marked with the construction of mosques and palaces, in particular, the palace at Sarkhej. Construction and conquest went hand in hand in Islamic India for a decade, and the prosperity they brought improved the region in many ways, from commercial infrastructure to safer markets for farmers. Aside from occasional

Afghan incursions, the Delhi Sultanate remained fairly stable for not quite two decades, during which time agriculture flourished, the arts gained sponsorship, learning expanded, civic enterprises increased, and a posture of tolerance toward non-Islamics was encouraged by governmental and religious leaders alike.

While the Ottomans continued their efforts in Europe, they also turned eastward, and in 1461 they conquered the Trebizond Empire, the last offshoot of the Byzantine Empire at the southeastern end of the Black Sea. In the next two years the Ottomans gained control of all the southern coast of the Black Sea, and once these ports were garrisoned, in 1463–1478 the Ottomans waged war on the Venetians, who, with the support of Pope Pius II, mounted a kind of secular Crusade with the Hungarians. The Crusaders assembled at Ancona on the Dalmatian Coast in a force inadequate to the task and paid the price for their shortsightedness. In 1470 a large fleet of Ottoman galleys took Negroponte, expelling the Venetians remaining there. In retaliation, a combined force of Venetian and papal galleys attacked Adalia and Smyrna in 1472, burning both cities as part of their attempt to reach their ally, Uzun Hassan, a campaign doomed to failure: Mehmed met Uzun Hassan in the Battle of Otluk-Bely and defeated the last major rival to Ottoman control in Anatolia and Mesopotamia. As an added advantage, the vanquishing of Uzun Hassan removed Venice's strongest ally in the region, leaving the Ottomans the unquestioned masters of the region. Flush with success, in 1473, the Ottomans, still fighting the Venetians, went to war with Persia, and in less than a year Persia was taken by the Ottomans as the war with Venice dragged on. In spite of the Venetian war, Mehmed was able to annex the Crimea in 1475 and secured crucial ports for Russian trade. By 1477 the war with Venice was reaching a crisis. Ottomans raided to the outskirts of Venice itself. The following year, Mehmed's navy took Koria, Drivasto, and Alessio, crucial Albanian trade centers. Finally, in 1479, a peace was concluded that not only turned more Venetian holdings over to the Ottomans but added an annual payment of ten thousand ducats to the Ottomans in order to preserve Venetian trading privileges with Ottoman ports. From 1450 to 1550 the Ottomans were the most formidable fighting force in the Middle East and had the richest trading empire.

In 1488–1489 an outbreak of typhus on Cyprus quickly spread to Venice, Genoa, and Spain as the various soldiers and sailors who had been defending Cyprus and other Venetian holdings headed for home at the end of the conflict. The disease hit Europe hard, and for the next three years it continued to ravage northern Italy, southern France, and Spain, exhausting the people and disrupting commerce as well as devastating the countryside. In those regions hardest hit, death from the disease was estimated at approximately 12 percent of the population. More than the fatalities, those who contracted the disease and survived were often unable to recover full health, impacting the families and workforces for decades.

Although the White Sheep Empire had lost almost all of Persia to the Ottomans, the Turkomans were not yet entirely out of the picture, nor were they wholly subdued no matter how many misfortunes they suffered. Uzun Hassan died in 1478 and his son Khalil succeeded him, reigning for not quite a year before being ousted by his uncle Yakub, who ruled the much-shrunken region until 1493, during which time there was an outbreak of Sweating Sickness, which had a fatality rate of close to 20 percent among the White Sheep Turkomans over two years and led to a minor famine in 1495. It was a calamity for the White Sheep Empire and caused as much damage as any war could have done. Recovery was slow, and trade diminished, throwing the already fragile economy into collapse and making it all but impossible for the White Sheep Empire to continue to fight against the Ottomans.

Continuing their expansion, the Ottomans occupied Otranto on Italy's southern coast in August 1480 but were unable to do the same to the Greek island of Rhodes, where the Knights of St. John defended the island tenaciously. With the death of Mehmed II in 1481 some of the zeal for conquest faded, as the Janissaries elevated Mehmed's scholarly, cautious son Bayazid II to sultan, an elevation that was challenged almost at once by Bayazid's brother Djem, who was proclaimed sultan at Bursa, and he proposed to Bayazid that they divide the empire between them, a suggestion that even the circumspect Bayazid found unacceptable. The two brothers' forces met in battle, and much to his surprise, Djem lost and was forced to leave Ottoman territory, seeking refuge in Egypt, then on Rhodes, from where the Knights of St. John escorted him to France, then managed to negotiate a peace treaty between the brothers. After a number of European leaders attempted to become Djem's host or jailers, many for less than honorable reasons, he ended up under the Pope's protection, and during the invasion of Italy by Charles VIII of France, Djem died at Naples in 1495, possibly the victim of murder.

During this time, the style of battle was changing again, for now heavy artillery had entered the picture, and lightning strikes of archer horsemen were unable to stand against such weapons. Cannons were a necessary part of any campaign, awkward though they were to transport, and the balls they required needed to be carried in wagons rather than on horseback. Armor of all sorts thickened and became more heavily padded as protection against all manner of projectiles. Decks of galleys were reinforced to carry more and heavier ordnance, and gunnerymen were rapidly becoming an essential part of any serious fighting force. The Turks still continued to use cavalry as the predominant part of their army, but they also had cannons because most of their opponents had cannons. Handguns and early long guns, such as muskets and arquebuses, were not as reliable as cannons, and most took time to load and prime, making them less efficient than arrows, but they were steadily improving, so that over the next fifty years reliance on guns of all sorts became essential to all armies and navies of the period. Cavalry remained important in land campaigns, but increasingly such units were used in massed attacks, not skirmishes, and for that, greater discipline of horse and rider was needed, a lesson the Ottomans took almost a century to learn.

In 1495 the Ottomans took on Egypt and their empire, but the Mamelukes were ready for them and over six years managed to fight to a stalemate. Some in Bayazid's court and military criticized the sultan for not making more aggressive war on the Mamelukes and cited the Venetian control of Cyprus—it was bequeathed to the Venetians by Cyprus' Christian ruler in 1489 but had been under de facto Venetian control since 1473—as proof that Bayazid was unable to do his job properly. There was also growing concern about the Balkans and the possible interference of the Holy Roman Emperor in Ottoman affairs. Discontent among Bayazid's advisors and the army subverted most of the military ventures that the sultan undertook, and interior squabbles made any effective expansion even more unlikely.

In 1493 the faltering White Sheep Empire entered a last, difficult stage. Yakub died; his son Bayangir succeeded him, only to be removed two years later by his cousin Rustam, who in 1497 was overthrown by Ahmad, an act that proved to be the final straw. After many years of internal struggles for the control of less and less, the clan warfare reasserted itself, and the cohesion that had been ever more tenuous failed at last. What little remained of the White Sheep Empire disintegrated, leaving the last of the populace exposed and vulnerable to attack on several fronts. Many clan groups headed for the Golden Horde that had moved east of Sarai toward the Aral Sea and north into Russian territory, bringing their sheep and goats with them. A few hired out as mercenaries in Delhi and Afghanistan, and some became outlaw bandits, preying on the trade caravans along the Silk Road and the Amber Trail.

The peace between the Ottomans and the Venetians unraveled in 1499, when the Turkish fleet went on the offensive under the capable admiral Kamal Re-is, who may have been an Islamic Greek and who was completely familiar with Aegean, Ionian, and Adriatic waters. Under Re-is, the Ottomans took Koron and Modon and drove the Venetians out of the Gulf of Corinth, also known as the Gulf of Patmas, and seized the Venetian port and fortress of Lepanto, an action that, although fairly minor in the confrontations of this period, would resonate among both the Turks and the Venetians seventy-two years later at the second Battle of Lepanto—the one that really counted for both sides. While the Ottoman navy was taking over important sea-lanes and harbors, the Ottoman cavalry ravaged as far as Vicenza before a peace could be concluded, in which the Venetians gave up more of their empire to the Ottomans but kept their trading rights—at a higher price and with major concessions to Ottoman taxation demands, all the while facing stepped-up pirate activity on their trade-routes, for the sultan had not agreed to curtail the pirates' activities as part of the peace. As a result, the Venetians arranged for more war-galleys to escort the merchant ships and led to better-armed pirates, a cycle of increasing hostility that lasted for nearly three-quarters of a century. Had not the Venetians and the Ottomans been so commercially dependent on one another, this escalation would have ruptured their trade treaties in two or three decades, but since both the Venetians and the Turks gained their prosperity from continuing trade, the impasse was allowed to continue.

In 1501 Ismail I, the charismatic founder of the Safavid dynasty in Persia, made Shiism the official state religion and began a long campaign to keep control of the non-Shiite portion of the population. He began with forced conversions, and when that didn't work he started with public executions. Ten years later, he had to contend with a rebellion among non-Ottoman Turks living in the Tarsus Mountains and practicing their own form of Islam as well as opposing the shah's authority in general, neither of which was acceptable to Ismail. Although Ismail prevailed, the incident left behind a rancor that had not often surfaced in Persia and would continue to haunt the country for the next century. The Persians began a limited expansion and by 1508 had gained full control of the crumbled remnants of the White Sheep Empire. By 1514 Ismail was caught up in the war of Ottoman succession, siding with Ahmed. Since Persia was Shiite, it supported the Ottoman Shiite prince, unwisely, as it turned out.

At last Ottoman support for Bayazid II waned and his son Selim I, in 1511, forced his father to abdicate in his favor. A civil war had broken out among Bayazid's sons, with Ahmed, Qorqoud, and Selim vying for top position, a conflict that Bayazid II was unable or unwilling to stop. Once Selim gained control, in 1512 he set about ending his brothers' rebellions, defeating Ahmed in 1513 and having him executed at once to stop any renewal of hostilities, or so he claimed. Selim, devoutly Sunni, ordered over forty thousand Shiites killed before he attacked Persia as a means of preventing sympathetic uprisings at home and to destroy the last vestiges of internal support for Ahmed. That it made Sunnis more powerful was only a side benefit, according to Selim.

In August 1514 Selim triumphed decisively over the Persians at Chaldiran; then he took Tabriz and ordered the city looted and burned but advanced no farther, since the Janissaries objected to the savagery of Selim's campaign. It was about this time that Selim earned the sobriquet the Harsh or Grim. The following year, Selim annexed Kurdistan and established dominance over the eastern end of Anatolia. Determined to conquer Persia, Selim made a second attempt in 1516, only to be halted by the Mamelukes under Sultan Kansou-al-Gauri. The Egyptian had made common cause with the Persians and moved to halt Selim's advance near Aleppo. Having superior artillery, Selim routed the Egyptian army and killed Kansou at the Battle of Marjdabiq, then offered peace to the new sultan, Touman Bey, if he would accept Turkish suzerainty and state Sunni-ism. Touman Bey, aware of the risks such a treaty would entail, refused the conditions and, through his refusal, turned Turkish at-tention toward Egypt instead of Persia. In January 1517 the Ot-tomans took Cairo, plundered, pillaged, and destroyed a quarter of the city, and began to push into the Arabian cities held by the Mamelukes. Mecca surrendered without a fight on the assurance that the holy city of Islam would not be sacked. The caliph, Mutawaqil, was taken captive and sent to Constantinople, where he remained un-til Selim's death. The Mameluke ruler, Touman Bey, was executed, but Selim, in a rare moment of diplomacy, left the Mameluke beys in key positions under an Ottoman governor, as a means of gaining Egyptian support against Persia. It was claimed that Selim cut the Egyptian trade routes, but records have shown that the Portuguese were responsible for the decrease in trade, for they occupied ports at the entrance to the Red Sea, effectively blocking Egyptian and Arabian ports.

Trade was changing in any case, and not for the better in the Middle East. With the Europeans now capable of reaching India and China on their own, to say nothing of the burgeoning trade with the New World, the Silk Road and the Spice Roads lost some, but not all, of their importance in the European markets. The Portuguese and the Dutch were in the first stages of develop-ing what would be a colonial presence in India and Batavia (modern

Indonesia) and over the next century would exercise a profound influence in Asia. By 1525 a good portion of the European China trade had moved from the long land crossing to travel by ships, although the Middle Eastern markets remained, particularly those serving land-locked cities and populations, as well as those traders whose business was protected by treaty and charter. By the 1540s the Spanish and Portuguese made the most of the Asian trade route across oceans and through their New World holdings, carrying goods from Spain and slaves from Africa to Central America in ships, transferring the goods to wagons, crossing southern Mexico or Central America by oxcart to their emerging ports on the Pacific, then loading the European goods, along with trade items from the Americas, aboard ships bound for Asia. It was through these new routes that New World plants such as potatoes, yams, maize, pineapple, vanilla, chocolate, tomatoes, and peppers spread to Asia and Europe. Spanish and Portuguese ships then returned across the Pacific with silks, rare woods, spices, precious stones, and metals, picked up gold, silver, foodstuffs, and slaves in the New World, and returned across the Atlantic. It was a long and arduous journey, but it significantly diminished European dependence on Middle Eastern markets, and it provided a vast array of new products that for about thirty years only Spanish and Portuguese traders could provide. Although the ramifications of this mercantile shift were not appreciated for more than a century, the diminished tribute payments and customs fees eventually caught up with the Ottoman Empire and the trading centers from China to Mesopotamia to the Black Sea and Syria.

In September 1520 Selim I died and was succeeded by his only surviving son, Suleiman I, called the Splendid or Magnificent. Cultivated and intelligent, Suleiman was also arrogant, ambitious, and fond of grandiosity, and he left a great portion to the actual affairs of government to his viziers, although he began with a major triumph in the capture in 1521 of Belgrade, from which base the Ottomans could advance into Europe. As sultan, Suleiman quickly became known for his charm and cultured manners with foreigners as well as his subjects and for his devoted advisors and staff. Suleiman's first, very capable vizier was Ibrahim Pasha, an Islamic Greek, who was the main force behind the throne from 1523 to 1536. Loyal to the Ottoman Empire but cagey, Ibrahim Pasha had dealt with the Egyptian Ottoman governor's attempt in 1524 to establish Egypt as an independent sultanate by reorganizing the bureaucracy. Ibrahim Pasha possessed a gift not only for administration but he knew how to handle Suleiman, catering to the sultan's vanity as well as being content to remain in the background so that Suleiman could take the credit for all Ibrahim Pasha had done.

The Ottoman occupation of Rhodes in 1522 routed the pirates that preyed not only on European merchant ships but on Ottoman ships plying the waters between Constantinople and Egypt. It also forced the Knights of St. John—who defended their fortresses with great determination—to withdraw from the island, which left the Order without a central base until 1530, when the Holy Roman Emperor Charles V stationed them at Malta. The Ottomans continued their advance into eastern Europe. In 1526 they defeated the King of Hungary at the Battle of Mohacs. King Louis was killed and his ill-prepared army of roughly twenty thousand fell apart as the Turks advanced to Ofen. At this worst possible time, there was a dispute about the Hungarian succession: in Pressburg, a Hapsburg, Ferdinand, claimed the throne; in Transylvania, Janos Zapolya advanced his claim. It took two years of civil war before Janos Zapolya was defeated and Ferdinand became king. In an imprudent move, the displaced Zapolya in 1528 asked

Suleiman to intercede on his behalf, prompting the second Hungarian campaign. With Zapolya to keep the Turks protected on their northeastern flank, the Turks made it all the way to Vienna, where they besieged the city and made a number of assaults but were unable to break the defenses. The weather turned cold and wet and the Ottomans could not bring up the heavy artillery they had hoped to use to end Viennese resistance. Ferdinand made offers of peace with tribute to be paid to the Ottomans, somewhat similar to the arrangement in existence with Venice, but Suleiman, already committed to Zapolya's claims, refused any such treaty. As a result, the Ottomans were forced to withdraw from Vienna and in 1529 to take Buda in Hungary instead. One of the factors in European divisions at this time—divisions that kept Europeans from prosecuting a more aggressive war with the Ottoman Empire—was that Europe was in the first throes of the Reformation, and religious conflict was on the rise throughout Europe, keeping many of the countries from being able to respond to exterior threats.

Far away from the Ottoman downturn and the European turmoil, in eastern Afghanistan and northern India, the Moghul Empire was established in 1526 by Babar, who had begun as a robber and warlord but upon taking over the Delhi Sultanate promoted himself and his country to imperial status. As a descendant of Timur-i, Babar had had a rough beginning to leadership, having succeeded his father as warlord at age twelve. By age twenty-one, Babar was on the run from his relatives and enemies, taking refuge in Kabul, where he was asked by a group of clan leaders to help them resolve their ongoing warfare. Babar did so by making himself the ruler of Lahore and cemented his position by emerging the victor from the Battle of Panipat. By defeating Ibrahim shah Lodi, Babar became ruler of Delhi and Agra, all of which provided the foundation for the Moghul Empire and the conquest of much of India.

By 1533 Ferdinand and Suleiman made peace, allowing Ferdinand to keep the portion of Hungary he still occupied and giving the rest to Janos Zapolya. Both Ferdinand and Zapolya had annual tribute they had to pay to the Ottomans. The Holy Roman Emperor Charles V did not participate in this treaty, turning the major Ottoman–European conflict into a naval one, complicated by the Ottoman efforts to evacuate thousands of Moors from Spain (a Hapsburg country), from which they had been expelled. With his western front marginally stabilized, Suleiman took on one of Charles V's few allies in the Middle East, Shah Tahmasp of Persia. The Turks marched on Tabriz in 1534, then took Baghdad, from where they were able to gain all of Mesopotamia for the Ottoman Empire. To cap off these victories, Suleiman entered into a formal alliance with Francis I of France in March 1536, an agreement that bolstered both the Ottomans and the French against further Hapsburg intrusions, as well as opening needed markets for both countries. Not content with challenging the Holy Roman Empire, in 1537 the Ottoman Empire once again went to war with the Most Serene Republic of Venice. Suleiman began with a threat to blockade the mouth of the Adriatic—essentially cutting off all Venetian markets but two—and for part of 1537–1538 blockaded the island of Corfu but ended up having to abandon this action due to bad weather and an outbreak of disease among the oarsmen on the Turkish galleys. The Holy League, a cobbled-together alliance of the Holy Roman Empire, Venice, and the Papal States, joined the battle in 1538, stepping up the hostilities. After a hard defeat for the Venetians at the Battle of Préveza, the Venetians in 1540 gave up the last of their ports on Morea and paid the sultan a sizable indemnity. Continuing its naval expansion, the Ottoman navy on the Red Sea set out in 1538 for northwestern India and, in the course of the expedition, took over Aden and Yemen for the Ottoman Empire.

Janos Zapolya died in 1540 and was succeeded by his son, Janos Sigismund Zapolya, who was only a child. In spite of Suleiman's recognition of the boy as legitimate King of Hungary, or perhaps because of it, Ferdinand invaded Hungary to exercise his right to rule there, prompting Suleiman to counter Ferdinand's invasion with one of his own; in 1546 he took over Moldavia; next Ottoman forces occupied Buda and set up Ottoman administration, in theory to protect Janos Sigismund but in actuality to take over most of the country without open warfare. Then, to make certain the Ottoman occupation was not challenged, Suleiman and Frederick entered into a five-year truce in 1547 that allowed Frederick to retain a small portion of Hungary, for an annual tribute. The Hapsburgs dealt with, Suleiman was able to focus his attention on the eroded situation in Persia. In 1548 Ottoman troops once again took Tabriz and tried to set up a stronger presence in the region, but in 1551 war with Ferdinand once again resumed, and an eleven-year campaign of sieges did little to change the terms of the earlier truce, although it destroyed cities, trade, and lives in the process. While Suleiman was dealing with eastern Europe, in 1551 the Turks occupied Tripoli in northern Africa after a failed attempt at conquering Malta, home of European pirates and the Knights of St. John. In 1552 the Persians were able to form an effective resistance against the Ottomans, capturing Ezerum and preparing to expand their efforts. Once again Suleiman was obliged to break off his European campaigns to return to Persia and Mesopotamia, where, in 1555, after a number of minor but cumulatively significant victories, he made a truce with the Persians, one that restored most of Persian territory to the Ottoman Empire.

All this waging of wars was expensive, and in a matter of a decade the Turkish treasury was beginning to feel the pinch. In spite of taxes and tribute pouring in, the military budget was expanding at a rate twice that of the rest of administrative expenditures.

This meant that such projects as road improvements and bridge building had to be balanced with military utility, so that increasingly the public works activities became linked with military usage to the detriment of general public benefits, particularly those associated with trade. At first this made very little impact, but its cumulative effect created situations that brought about increasing policy-making accommodation to military agendas instead of the administration of the empire.

In November 1556 the Battle of Panipat returned the Hindustan empire to the Moghul Empire. The Moghul emperor, an impulsive but determined fourteen-year-old, Jalal-un-Din Mohammed, called Akbar, returned from exile and went on the next year to defeat the Afghans as well and for six years waged constant war from northern India, to Afghanistan, to Turkestan before reaching a level of conquest that made his borders secure enough to allow him to begin to reestablish the Moghul Empire in its former glory. Jalal-ud-Din Mohammed was fortunate in having a long reign—forty-nine years—during which time the Moghul Empire was relatively free of internal squabbles, allowing for the development of schools and arts as well as repairing and improving public buildings and annexing more territory. The Moghul Empire was even able to take in a few thousand refugees from a catastrophic earthquake in Shansi Province in China in 1556 that killed over 825,000 people. Survivors fled as far as Indonesia, Korea, Mongolia, and Persia and may have contributed to the smallpox epidemic that hit Mongolia in 1557 and spread west for the next four years, turning up in Russia with terrible results in 1562.

Malta became an issue for the Ottoman navy again in 1565; they besieged the island, only to be driven off in September when reluctantly dispatched Spanish forces arrived to break the blockade and end the siege. Approximately thirty-two thousand Turkish soldiers and naval men-at-arms were driven off the island, and

then the Ottoman fleet was forced out to sea, a costly and humili-
ating defeat at a time when Ottoman prestige was so high that this
sorry development could only be seen as an aberration. Turkish
losses were unusually high in this series of battles, which the Ottomans blamed on the hostility of the Spanish as well as the
bloodthirsty Knights of St. John. The following year, the Ottomans
suffered another terrible loss: Suleiman the Magnificent/Splendid
died at age seventy. His reign, Splendid though it was—and although it was not obvious for more than a century—marked the beginning of Ottoman decline. In 1553 Suleiman had had his oldest
son, Mustafa, strangled for supposed treason. Immediately after
Mustafa's death, Selim and Bayazid, Suleiman's remaining sons by his
wife Roxelanna, began a dispute that lasted until 1559. Suleiman's
son Selim II, who succeeded him, did not help to slow the waning
of Ottoman might. Calling himself the Grim or Stern in homage to
his imposing grandfather and with the hope of reawakening the
spirit of Ottoman resolve, Selim II was intelligent but depressed and
given to drink. The sobriquet he was given (as differentiated from
the one he gave himself) was the Sot, a particularly insulting nick-
name for a follower of Islam, for Muslims were and are forbidden to
drink intoxicating beverages. One of Selim II's first acts was to make
a truce with Maximillian II, the new Holy Roman Emperor, agreeing
that each of them would retain the lands they already held and
honor the other's holdings. Depending on his grand vizier, Mehmed
Sokolli, to take care of running the empire, Selim devoted himself to
luxury and alcohol for a good portion of his reign.

Another man who had a great deal of influence on Selim II for
a while was the Sephardic Jew Don Joseph Nasi, who had wanted
to make Cyprus a refuge for European Jews, especially those who
had been forced out of Spain and had ended up in north Africa,
where they established small communities in port cities and a

larger one in Alexandria. Don Joseph urged Selim to go to war with Venice in order to conquer Cyprus. Threats didn't work well with the Venetians, so in 1570 the Turks declared war on Venice and, after an unexpectedly long siege at Famagusta on Cyprus, took the island, although Selim did not hand it over to Jewish refugees as Don Joseph had hoped. The Venetians became enthusiastic supporters of the Holy League, a renewed papal treaty that enlisted the Papal States, almost all European territories controlled by the Hapsburgs—Spanish and Austrian—and Venice in a naval alliance against the Ottomans.

After a shaky beginning, the Holy League caught up with the larger Ottoman fleet in the Gulf of Patmas at the fortress of Lepanto in October 1571 and, against all odds, delivered a crushing defeat to the Ottomans from which their navy never truly recovered, although Selim ordered a full rebuilding of ships the following year, an effort that turned out less successfully than any of the naval commanders liked, for unlike the Venetians, the Ottomans had no single shipbuilding center and had to press harbors, dry docks, and even gardens into the effort of naval rebuilding and had to rely on ill-trained shipwrights to do the job. There were constant rumors among the Europeans that the Ottoman navy was double its former size and might, at any moment, take to the seas, a belief that kept the Holy League from pressing their advantage— had they had funds enough to provision such a campaign, funds that Spain, the wealthiest empire in the Holy League, promised but would not provide. In 1573 the Holy League broke under the stress of politics; Cyprus was abandoned to the Turks. The Venetians continued to trade with the Ottoman Empire and to pay their annual fee for the privilege, plus an indemnity for the Lepanto victory of three hundred thousand ducats, for fear of provoking another confrontation. But the Ottomans were understandably reluctant to take on the better-designed Venetian war galleys after Lepanto, and did so only after the Spanish took Tunis in northern Africa in 1573. The Turks took it back in 1574 and might have pressed the advantage to begin a campaign against Sicily and Malta but for the death of Selim II in December.

The succession of Murad III to the Ottoman throne marked another stage of Ottoman decline. Murad III was not well prepared for his role as sultan, no matter how much he believed he was. He spent a good deal of time playing court politics and advancing his favorites instead of the men who had been trained for high governmental posts. Those whose advice displeased him he banished or had executed. Murad changed the Janissaries' policy of admission to include Turks, not just forcefully drafted Christians from client countries, and that in turn led to the Janissaries being politicized, with drastic results for the next century as loot and rewards became increasingly crucial to military loyalty as clan divisions more and more impacted Ottoman life. The Janissaries still swore unswerving loyalty to the sultan but demanded that loyalty give them greater authority and more political influence, as well as regular financial recompense. Over the next century, the Janissaries would become, as the Praetorian Guard had been in Imperial Rome, fourteen hundred years earlier, the makers and unmakers of rulers. Murad's court was filled with groups relentlessly promoting their own interests to the exclusion of the interests of others. Not that everything Murad III did was ill considered; in 1585 he made peace with Spain, keeping the might of the Spanish Empire out of the European efforts against the Ottomans, a move that bought the Ottomans a century in which to continue to attack European targets without concerted European opposition.

But that wasn't going as well as it once had. Ottoman conquests were no longer as easily secured as they had been, on both the eastern and western fronts. Penetrating more deeply into Europe, the Ottomans found themselves dealing with the better-armed and better-trained Austrian Hapsburg armies, and what had once been assured victories now were chancier and more costly. As Lepanto had proven to be the breaking point for Ottoman power on the seas, so the assault on Austria and Austro-Hungary cumulatively proved to have the same impact on land. To the east, the Moghul Empire was making forays in the direction of Persia and encouraging a greater degree of banditry on the Chinese trade routes than had been tolerated for the last fifty years, predation that the Ottomans were not in a good position to counter.

Taxation throughout Ottoman territory was rising, and customs charges increased as well, but the Ottoman treasury in Constantinople, generally but not officially known now by the truncated version of the name, Istanbul, continued its slow but steady losses. The high cost of the court and the ever-increasing payoffs to the army and Janissaries took a toll that grew greater as the borders of the empire grew weaker. War itself was increasingly costly, cannons and other ordnance becoming a major expense and one that could not be compromised. Soldiers needed to have more training with these dangerous weapons, and that meant at least a year of preparation before being useful in the field. Ships, too, had gunnery problems, and new developments in shipbuilding required a more systematic education for the sailors before they were ready to man the ships efficiently. Throughout the sixteenth and seventeenth centuries, the Ottomans lost income on almost all fronts: agricultural, commercial, military, and diplomatic. These losses—unthinkable a century ago—became a worrisome fact of life, requiring a number of concessions within the empire, not only financial ones but political ones as well. As the court became a more and more expensive establishment to maintain, rancor between the military, the regional governors, the treasury administrators, and the sultan grew to disruptive proportions.

After almost fifteen years of war with Persia, the Ottoman Empire made peace with Persia in 1590, by which the Turks gained Azerbaijan, Georgia, and Shirwan, outwardly a favorable development, for the treaty restored lost territory and additional holdings to the Turkish Empire, but it also meant more and farther borders to protect and greater costs to do so. With military personnel and resources already stretched thin, this reacquisition of territory strained the army to the limit. The Ottomans could not afford to hire more than a supplementary force of mercenaries, paying them with small land grants in order to hold on to as much ready money as possible and to give the mercenaries something of their own to defend. When, in 1593, war erupted with Austria, with the Prince of Transylvania, Sigismund Bathory, siding with the Hapsburgs, the Ottomans had to divert many needed soldiers from the new Persian frontiers to the Balkans, stretching their resources to the limit. The Turkish victory at the Battle of Keresztes in northern Hungary gave a momentary burst of optimism to the Turks, but for the most part, the fighting was indecisive. The Austrians, having an agenda beyond defeating the Ottomans, took advantage of this war to occupy Transylvania and Moldavia, which the Ottomans countered by throwing their support to Stephan Bocskay in 1605 and pushing the Austrians out of Transylvania and most of Moldavia. This might have provided the Ottomans a chance to continue to press the Austrians, but another war with Persia had begun, and the Ottoman Empire was no longer able to fight two wars at the same time without compromise to one war or another.

Another development shook the Christian population of the Middle East, perhaps reflecting the shifts in religion in Europe: in 1589 the Russian Orthodox Church became wholly separate from the Greek Orthodox Church. Moscow created its own patriarchate and undertook to reform the liturgy to meet Russian needs. This was a severe shock to the Greek Orthodox Christians, who feared this separation might lead to the end of the Orthodox Church in the Ottoman Empire; they had seen the distress the Reformation was causing in Europe and feared that something of the same nature would now erupt in the Orthodox Church. The Pope in Rome said little officially, but he apparently unofficially authorized missionaries to go into Orthodox regions for the purpose of converting the remaining Orthodox Christians to Catholicism, in theory to protect them from the dangers of Islam. Some of these unofficial missionaries went as far as Armenia and Georgia, where Ottoman conflicts with Persia were growing heated and the common people would be in need of salvation.

Hard winters in 1591 and 1592 brought near famine to Hungary and Transylvania along with the rest of Europe; this meant that imported foods from the Middle East would be needed, especially grain and dried fruits. But unlike past weather-caused famines, this time the Europeans had a second source of food— the Americas. Spain in particular stepped up imports of all manner of foodstuffs, not just for the commercial market but also for its own starving population. Imports took time arriving, and the crossing was hard on perishables, so the captains carried the hardiest foods from the Americas, with heavy emphasis on maize, yams, and potatoes. Initial European resistance to these crops was fading in almost all European countries except France, and so the famine was not the commercial or the diplomatic windfall that the Ottomans expected. Trade did increase but not in the dramatic way it had in the past.

In northern India, Akbar, the Moghul emperor, expanded the land he controlled by his conquest of Sind in 1592 and began to receive delegates from European merchant houses with an eye to making Delhi and northern India a commercial center for all European merchant-travelers; the worldwide explorations of the Europeans was continuing to reduce European dependence on the Middle East for Asian goods. Akbar was astute enough to realize that he could gain monetary advantage for his empire by encouraging European traders, although he distrusted all Europeans and occasionally imprisoned a few of them and seized all their money and possessions as a guard against European ambitions in the region.

After a reign marked by excesses, debauchery, treachery, profligacy, and continued financial erosion, Murad III died in 1595. His successor, his preferred son, Mehmed III, aware of the dangers inherent in the Ottoman court, began his reign by having nineteen of his brothers put to death to prevent any dynastic infighting. He justified this by declaring that dynastic wars would be devastating to the Ottoman Empire and had to be avoided at any cost. In spite of this precaution, his reign—not as dissolute as his father's but still quite decadent—lasted only eight years; upon his death in 1603, his fourteen-year-old son took the throne as Ahmed I. The Ottoman Empire was changing.

Persia was also changing. Under Abbas, the shah known as the Great who succeeded his father, Shah Mohammed Khudabanda, in 1587, the Persians were not the same kind of military presence that they had been when the Ottomans took them on again in 1602. Already established at his new capital, Isfahan, Abbas had begun his reign by ordering the construction of grand buildings, mosques, gardens, schools, roads, and caravansaries, all aimed at showing the world that the Ottoman Empire wasn't the only important power in the Middle East. Continued dealings with the West had brought the reorganization skills of Sir Robert and Sir Anthony Shirley to assist the Persians in modernizing their armies and the manner in which their armies fought—this in exchange for favorable trade agreements with western powers along with provisions for a permanent English commercial mission in Persia. 1603 proved to be a significant year for the Persians: Abbas reoccupied Tabriz, then reclaimed Erivan, Shirwan, and finally Kars. With the

Ottomans flummoxed and short on supplies, the Persians made a strategic push to gain more territory, conquering Baghdad, Mosul, and a number of smaller cities in Mesopotamia. Worn out, the Ottomans agreed to a peace treaty in 1612, one that held for four years.

The Ottomans finally signed a treaty with the Austrians—the first one for which they had gone outside Constantinople for the ceremonial signing, since they occupied the city. The Treaty of Zsitva-Torok (1606) provided for an independent Transylvania and stopped Austrian tribute to the sultan; Turks and Austrians agreed to be diplomatic equals and to prevent any outbreaks of war with each other that might happen as part of regional rebellions. Middle Eastern and European spheres of influence were undergoing an important change, and that made this peace not only prudent but maintainable in ways previous ones had not been.

Another major change dividing Europe from the Middle East was the development of the galleon. Atlantic-based ports had had sailed ships for five centuries and had not been dependent on oarsmen since shortly after the Vikings were at their most obstreperous; Atlantic storms were too frequent and the ocean too cold for oarsmen to handle. With the New World offering land and riches, ship design in those countries making Atlantic and Pacific crossings were forced to change. Taking a galley, with its complement of oarsmen, on a prolonged sea voyage was not a workable venture: the galley had too little room for large cargoes and too many mouths to feed. Galleons were more maneuverable, carried a much smaller crew, and had double the cargo capacity of a galley, and by 1600 were in the forefront of shipbuilding in most of Europe. Only those European powers, such as Venice, operating in the Adriatic, the Aegean, and the Black Seas had any use for galleys, which over time made these nations fall behind in matters of naval innovation. The French, who had galleons, also retained a small fleet of galleys to operate between France and their holdings in northern Africa. Almost all of these ships were manned by convicted criminals, serving both as prison and transport. The Ottomans continued to use galleys and smaller, faster galliots as their principal ships well into the eighteenth century. The range and cargo capacity of galleys continued to shrink. For Ottoman ships in the Red Sea, the Arabian Sea, and the Persian Gulf, a modified galliot based on Indian design was the preferred model until nearly 1820. They also developed a merchantman ship in the mid-1600s that had both Indian and Portuguese elements in its design, variations of which served them for more than two centuries.

The British East India Company initiated trade with Persia in 1616 through their Indian commercial center at Surat, eliminating the Middle East from their Asian trading hegemony. It was not a major change at first, but it was a harbinger of the reduction of trade through the Middle East and in a matter of a century meant a significant loss to Ottoman merchants and tax collectors, as the British relied increasingly on the East India Company for Asian trade and expanded their colonial presence in the subcontinent.

In 1617 the Ottoman sultan Ahmed I died, less than thirty years old, worn out by court intrigue and his own decadent habits. His incompetent cousin Mustapha I succeeded him, lasted slightly less than a year, and was deposed in favor of his brother, the fourteen-year-old Osman II. One of Osman's first acts was instituting a necessary peace with Abbas the Great of Persia, relinquishing control of Georgia and Azerbaijan as part of the terms of the treaty. Persia continued to press the Ottoman Empire for its eastern territories. Despite his efforts to stem the vicious infighting at the Ottoman court, Osman proved unable to handle the clan-affiliated struggles or to control the Janissaries, now all but ruling the country through their threat of military action against those governors and administrators they disliked. In a desperate ploy, Osman in 1622 planned to make a pilgrimage to Mecca, where he intended to raise an army faithful to him as sultan, and march back to Constantinople to confront the Janissaries and wrest power from them. The Janissaries learned of the plot before Osman could leave Constantinople, and they denounced him, humiliated him publicly, killed him, and returned the mentally compromised Mustafa I to the throne, confident that he would be an acceptable puppet. Again Mustafa's reign was brief: in 1623 he abdicated in favor of his fourteen-year-old nephew, Murad IV, with Murad's mother serving as his regent for five years. Murad was challenged almost as soon as he was advanced to the throne, for in that same year Abbas the Great of Persia occupied Baghdad. Murad attempted to retake Baghdad in 1625 but was subverted as much by uprisings within his empire as by the resistance mounted against him by Abbas. Confronted by massive insubordination from the Janissaries and regional administrators, Murad responded with fierce suppression, and for a while his ruthlessness helped him to regain control of the military and to curtail treachery, which terrified the court into following him and allowed the Ottomans to conquer Hamadan in 1630, driving the Persians back and culminating in the reoccupation of Baghdad in 1638, then cementing the occupation with a treaty that gave the Persians Erivan and the Ottomans Baghdad in perpetuity.

While returning from Kashmir in 1627, the Moghul Emperor Jahangir died. He had been a despot for most of his reign, bloodthirsty and uncompromising, so much so that his oldest son, Jahan, had rebelled against him in 1617 and then had taken eight years to reconcile with his difficult father. Upon succeeding to the rulership of the Moghul Empire, Shah Jahan began by having most of the possible male claimants to the throne murdered to forestall any more conflict. Less consistently bellicose than his father, Jahan undertook a program of building and aggrandizement that made Delhi and Agra splendid in a way they had not been since Timur-i sacked them more than two centuries ago. Among the spectacular buildings Jahan commissioned was the Taj Mahal, a mosque and mausoleum built in honor of his favorite wife and completed in 1648. He also undertook monetary reform that not only stabilized the coinage but managed to gain wealth for him and for the city of Delhi. By 1638 Delhi was flourishing and gaining influence throughout Afghanistan and the eastern Middle East.

In that year, Murad ordered the drafting of Christian youths into the Ottoman military stopped, believing that he needed an Islamic army to fight against the Christian forces of Europe. He did not trust the forcefully drafted young men not to shift their alliances to their Christian brethren, as he would expect Ottoman youths to do, were their situations reversed. He also reorganized the military, regularized military privileges, reduced and purged the Janissaries, and was embarked on establishing a new administrative policy for the empire when he died in 1640 and was succeeded by his half brother, Ibrahim I, the lone survivor of Murad's elimination of rivals. By accounts of the period, Ibrahim was prone to odd behavior, which some said was his way of avoiding the wrath of Murad, but since it continued after Murad was dead, it may be that Ibrahim was a bit odd; he was inclined to take advice from his storyteller, Sheqer-Pahre, and his mother and to distrust all court officials, including viziers and emirs. Ibrahim was slow to respond to a new threat from the Venetians as war broke out over Crete, and so, after eight years as sultan, he was deposed and killed in 1648 by the Janissaries, who then put ten-year-old Mehmed IV on the Ottoman throne. Because of the new sultan's youth, another six years of rebellions ensued, during which time Venice was able to take back a number of ports from the Ottomans and to stage a blockade at the Dardanelles in 1656. Even though the war dragged on until 1687, Ottoman losses continued to eat away at their borders. With ineffective leadership, opposition to these challenges was sporadic and minor.

Not that Venice was in such good shape, either. More than any other European trading empire, Venice had put nearly all its eggs in the Asian trade basket, never expecting to have any serious external competition for their control of the goods they carried to Middle Eastern and European ports. New World trade was taking a toll on their once sacrosanct domination of eastern trade, and between that shift and Ottoman pressure to control all the Aegean and eastern Adriatic ports, Venice was hard-pressed to deal with either threat in any lastingly effective way. With those two sources of wealth dwindling, all that Venice had going for it was the range of its trading ports and the goodwill created with long-established merchant houses and trading treaties from England to Georgia. Venetian galleys were unable to compete with the transatlantic fleet of Spanish galleons and so had to make do with serving as a distribution service in the Mediterranean, Adriatic, Aegean, and Black Seas, not nearly as profitable as the role of primary distributor for the goods of Asia had been, and one that for the first time had Venice beholden to other Italian regional governments. The most intrusive of all of these was the Papal States, which applied political pressure to the last remnants of the Venetian Empire, increasingly imposing conditions on trade not only in foreign ports but in Roman ones as well.

On the Arabian Peninsula, religious conflicts between Sunni and Shiite factions continued to make resistance to the Ottomans fairly ineffective; watched carefully by the Mamelukes of Egypt, who were technically still administrators for the Ottoman Empire, the religious differences in Arabia provided a balance to the potential for continuing control. In 1649 there was a hint of possible revolt in Arabian territories, but an inspiring Arab cleric, variously reported as Sullah-ibn-Mohammed and Salah-al-Mohammed, a devout Shiite, would not allow Sunnis to join his cause, which resulted in the Sunnis attacking the Shiites, and the uprising against the Mamelukes—and by extension the Ottomans—came to nothing.

Financial woes continued to plague the Ottoman army, and plans to annex Ukrainian territory had to be curtailed and then postponed because of the money shortages. Cossacks were raiding Ottoman ports of the Crimea, and that once again stretched the Ottoman resources and resulted in a diminution of Ottoman-held territory in the Crimea. To complicate the situation, in 1654 there was an outbreak of Bubonic Plague that spread from the Crimea to eastern Europe in Ottoman ships, forcing the Turks to refrain from reinforcing their remaining holdings until the epidemic had run its course, by which time the disease had arrived at Constantinople. While this epidemic was not as devastating as earlier ones had been, it still served to halt many Ottoman ventures for four months into 1655. In 1656 Mehmed Kiuprili was made Grand Vizier, and to all intents and purposes, he took the reins of power from the boy-sultan, Mehmed IV, and with the support of the Janissaries, whom he had brought to heel, did his utmost to shore up the empire. Albanian by birth, Kiuprili was sensitive to issues at the edges of the empire, and he tackled the problems he saw in a direct and pragmatic way, unwilling to risk troops or money on marginal causes such as building up the Crimean ports again while the war with Venice ate away at the empire. As if to make up for this reduction in eastern activity and to press for a resolution in the Venetian war, in 1657 the Ottomans retook the island ports of Lemnos and Tenedos, strategically and commercially important to the empire.

The year 1658 was significant in the east as well: the Moghul

Shah Jahan was deposed in favor of his son Aurahngzeb and then imprisoned. Aurahngzeb proved to be a despotic ruler, greedy and bigoted and unable to deal with the non-Islamic people of his empire. In his almost fifty-year reign, he brought about a change in social policies that weighed heavily on Hindu, Zoroastrian, and Jewish portions of the population, some of whom rebelled against him in 1669 and continued to do so sporadically for fourteen years. He was so preoccupied with the state of his political and religious issues, he neglected the world at large, a posture that damaged his government badly and caused the Moghul Empire to lose a number of important trade agreements with the Portuguese and the British; with the forsaken treaties, the monies anticipated were lost, to the financial detriment of the empire.

In 1661 Ahmed Kiuprili succeeded his father as Grand Vizier. A less formidable man than his father but undoubtedly more clever, Ahmed indulged the sultan and handled his enemies with wit and deftness that allowed him to remain in power for seventeen years, during which time his one significant failure was his inability to reach a compromise peace with Venice, although in 1669 the Turks succeeded at last in taking Crete from the Venetians. But the Venetian war wasn't the only one demanding Ottoman responses: after the Peace of Westphalia in 1648, Austria was once again in a position to deal with Ottoman encroachment beyond the Balkans, and so for almost two years (1663–1664) the Turks fought the Austrians, suffering a defeat in early August of 1664, at the conclusion of which Transylvania was established as a kind of buffer zone between Austro-Hungary and the Ottoman Empire. The Ottomans were luckier in their war with Poland over possessions in the Ukraine (1672–1676), in which they managed to gain a good portion of what had been Polish territory, but had the unhappy result of drawing them into conflict with Russia, during which war the Ottomans lost most of the land they had gained in their war with Poland and had to agree to granting Black Sea trading privileges to the Cossacks.

Persia's Abbas II died in 1667, leaving the empire to his son Shah Sulyman. Abbas II had had a steady, if fairly pedestrian, reign of twenty-five years during which time Persia lost territory and standing in the Middle East, as much because the empire had been governed in a nonresilient way as because internal corruption was taking a toll on the economy. Shah Sulyman was a disappointing successor to a lackluster father, for Sulyman was dissolute and petty, a bad combination at the best of times but particularly damaging during this transitional time for Persia, causing religious as well as economic distress throughout the empire. Even a few European merchants hedged their bets when dealing with Persia, unable to believe that so ruinous a regime could last long, although Sulyman remained in power until 1694 and persisted in his ruinous policies through almost all of his long reign.

In 1683 the Turks under Kara Mustafa besieged Vienna; his attacks were belligerent and he used a number of techniques, including undermining walls, as a means of forcing a surrender. The Austrians under Rudiger von Stahremberg defended the city valiantly, and the populace kept up their morale by consuming a new roll shaped like the Turkish emblem—the crescent roll may be the one good thing to come out of the siege. Polish and German troops relieved the siege on September 12, and the Ottomans were forced to withdraw as Venice joined with Poland and Austria under the sponsorship of the Pope in a new Holy League. In 1684 the Austrians took Buda-Pest, the Venetians reclaimed a good portion of Morea in Greece, and, to add to these Ottoman problems, Russia took advantage of the war in eastern Europe to mount a siege at Azov.

The result of these prolonged conflicts was a significant decrease in trade throughout the Middle East, and for once, there was little effort on the part of most European nations to renew their commercial treaties once the wars calmed down. Only Venice made any serious effort to continue its commercial ventures with the Middle East, and did so on a reduced scale, stepping up its efforts to carry New World goods from Atlantic ports into the Mediterranean, Aegean, and Adriatic Seas. The Venetians did still number a few Black Sea ports as ports-of-call, but they could not and did not depend on Middle Eastern trade to be their main commercial thrust as they had for so long. With the New World filled with colonies, and the various European trade missions in Asia, the Middle East was no longer a risk that Europeans had to take for trade, and the long interdependency entered its long twilight that lasted until the First World War. Sultans still continued to rule from Constantinople/Istanbul for another two-and-a-half centuries, as shahs did in Persia well into the twentieth century, but the wealth now moved from East to West, and the practical, gadget-happy, egalitarian, left-brain West began to lose touch with the mystical, austere, traditional, hierarchical, right-brain Middle East. Not even Napoléon's romantic invasion of Egypt in 1798 was based on any real appreciation of the nature of the region—it was an iconographic gesture intended to set Napoléon in glorious historical context, not to open a working cultural dialogue, a mind-set that still dominates mutually shared misconceptions between the peoples of the West and those of the Middle East. Over time this misunderstanding has increased and become entrenched.

If there were no oil, no mineral wealth, in that vast region, it is unlikely that the West would have much interest in the societies throughout the region, with the possible exception of the only successfully secular Islamic society in Turkey and the grand monuments of Egypt. At least those two attractions can make a good place to start. If history shows nothing else, it reveals the high cost of military solutions to cultural problems. The New World provided the impetus for the separation of the West and Middle East; it may also provide, through the diversity inherent in its societies, the means to bridge the gap of misunderstanding that has been thriving on internal and external aggression and xenophobia for millennia—without resorting to the futility of war or embracing bigotry.

INDEX